Relativism and Human Rights

Claudio Corradetti

Relativism and Human Rights

A Theory of Pluralistic Universalism

 Springer

Dr. Claudio Corradetti
Researcher in Political Philosophy and Bioethics
at the European Academy, Bozen
Temporary lecturer in Political Philosophy
University of Rome II "Tor Vergata"
Claudio.Corradetti@uniroma2.it

ISBN 978-1-4020-9985-4   e-ISBN 978-1-4020-9986-1

DOI 10.1007/978-1-4020-9986-1

Library of Congress Control Number: 2009920942

Printed on acid-free paper

9 8 7 6 5 4 3 2 1

springer.com

This book is dedicated to M. Teresa, Cristina and Caterina who are all fighting in different ways for their rights.

Contents

Part I

1 Cognitive Relativism and Experiential Rationality 3
   1.1 Beyond Cognitive and Linguistic Relativism 5
   1.2 Epistemic Relativism Refuted 12
   1.3 The Experiential Validity of the Cognitive System 19
       1.3.1 Judgement and Truth 28

2 Beyond Moral Relativism and Objectivism 35
   2.1 Forms of Moral Relativism 36
   2.2 The Two Horns of the Dilemma: Relativism versus Objectivism 47
       2.2.1 Harman's Inner-Judgments Relativism 49
       2.2.2 The Limits of Nagel's Objectivism in Morality 53
   2.3 Wong's Mixed Position: the Idea of Pluralistic Relativism 59
   2.4 Discursive Dialectic of Recognition: for a Post-Metaphysical
       Justification of the Domain of the Ethical Life 62

Part II

3 Human Rights and Pluralisitc Universalism 73
   3.1 From Purposive Action to Communicative Action 75
   3.2 The Priority of Recognition and the Formal System of Basic Liberties 90
   3.3 The Exemplar Validity of Human Rights 99
   3.4 Deliberative Constraints and Pluralistic Universalism 106

4 The Legal Dimensions of Human Rights 111
   4.1 The Source and the Content Validity of Law 112
   4.2 The Structure and Function of Human Rights 130
   4.3 Transplantability and Legal Commensurability 137
   4.4 What is Wrong in the Democratic Peace Theory? A Defence of
       International Legal Pluralism 143

Bibliography 153

Author Index 165

Subject Index 167

Introduction

When he finished writing, he raised his eyes and looked at me. From that day I have thought about Doktor Pannwitz many times and in many ways. I have asked myself how he really functioned as a man; how he filled his time, outside of the Polymerization and the Indo-Germanic conscience; above all when I was once more a free man, I wanted to meet him again, not from a spirit of revenge, but merely from a personal curiosity about the human soul. Because that look was not one between two men; and if I had known how completely to explain the nature of that look, which came as if across the glass window of an aquarium between two beings who live in different worlds, I would also have explained the essence of the great insanity of the third Germany.

> PRIMO LEVI [*If this is a man*, pp. 111–112,
> in, *If this is a man and The truce*,
> trans. S. Woolf, Abacus, London, 1987]

If all propositions, even the contingent ones, are resolved into identical propositions, are they not all necessary? My answer is: certainly not. For even if it is certain that what is more perfect is what will exist, the less perfect is nevertheless still possible. In propositions of fact, existence is involved.

> LEIBNIZ [*Sämtliche schriften und briefe*
> *vol VI pt 4* Deutsche Akademie
> der Wissenschaften, 1449A VI 4]

We live in a rule-constrained world. Even our most insignificant practices are somehow dependent upon a socially agreed standard regulating their structures, procedures, and general goals. We can, for instance, appreciate our neighbour's ability to keep her garden tidy and in good shape, but we can also observe the unusual combination of ingredients in the preparation of an exotic dish, or be impressed by the refined style of Chinese pots. We can discuss and disagree about whether our moral judgments are sufficiently argued and produce well-founded contrasting arguments. What happens in all cases is that our diverging opinions are defended on the basis of compliance with a rule, a standard which we consider as deserving priority over alternative considerations. If, in contrast to the experiential pervasiveness of norms, their appreciation were restricted to certain domains of human action, there would be little resistance to the idea of a social construction of reality. My argument, instead, is that the entire domain of human understanding is sensitive to rule-governed practices based upon what I will term as "experientialism". To claim that understanding and meaning are strictly embedded within social practices does not amount to say that world's objects do not exist independently from our cognitive activities. Indeed, too often ontological issues, as those concerning the very existence of an external word, have been confused with the epistemological ones. While ontology is existentially independent from our knowledge, this latter always projects classificatory standards to ontological independent objects both institutional and non institutional.

Standards, as well as values, arise on the basis of social practice. To say that something is a value is to implicitly affirm that there is or that there has been a social practice supporting that something. And yet, while admitting this general background condition, some have advanced the hypothesis that there is still room for at least some "enabling and facilitating values" not subject to any sort of sustaining practice. But even in these cases, one must come to see that "enabling and facilitating values" can *at least partially and indirectly be considered as dependent* upon a social practice, and that their aim is to "[...] enable the pursuit and realization of others [values], and, to the extent that the others are socially dependent, so are they, at least in their point and purpose" (Raz, 2005, 34–35). This introduces an important notion defended in this work, which takes the form of both the idea of *cognitive structures as emerging from experience*, but not of a direct categorization of the experience itself in its cognitive version, and the form of *experiential normative* conditions of validity, as far as its moral-political side is concerned. Throughout the work, I will show also how these conditions bear relevant connections to the notion of contingency and context dependence, as well as how they are connected with the notion exemplar universality.

Overall, the naïve opposition of objectivist and idealistic understandings of physical and social phenomena is here seen through the lens of the notion of "experience" as an interpretive concept capable of conjoining the two above-mentioned adversarial positions. Intuitively, when one speaks of her own experience, she is immediately readdressed to an idea of privacy which in principle implies incommunicability. This is not how I define the notion of experience and language in general in this work. Wittgenstein offered extensive proof of the inadequacy of the idea of a private language in his *Philosophical Investigations* (1953) and I take his arguments in favour of the idea that experience depends on public use of language – as well as on publicly-agreed practices – and what I try to do is to indicate how certain domains of cognitive categorization are primarily sensitive to the specific characteristics of our bodily interaction with the environment, so that cultural variability and different conceptual schemes remain within the constraints of inter-linguistic partial commensurability and epistemic accessibility. In short, I will speak of the embodiment of our minds.

If this element facilitates the task of producing convincing arguments against a strong form of cognitive, linguistic and epistemic relativism, the reliance on partially commensurable conceptual scheme variations looks much more vague when applied to possible moral inter-cultural comparisons. I will argue, therefore, that one can show that neither an absolute incommensurability nor an absolute commensurability between competing moral systems can be proved to be at all convincing. Indeed, if persistent moral conflicts upon the goods can be paired with a selective form of reasonable pluralism, then the refusal to surrender to moral relativism is possible only once certain conditions oriented to mutual understanding are satisfied. Such conditions for purposive agency in general, and for communicative agency in particular, are what I will term as human rights.

Understanding the conceptual implications of a notion of human rights appears as one of the most promising research fields for contemporary political theory. Recent literature on the subject has been largely devoted to the impact that any theory of human rights has for the notion of a global theory of justice, development, overpopulation, famine, war. Yet, even if the extension of applied studies in human rights has acquired great relevance – and certainly urgency – nowadays, proportionate attention to the assessment and justification of the conceptual status of fundamental rights has been lacking.

One of the main tenets of this study is that the two spheres of analysis cannot be easily separated and that the extent of application of any normative model is to be seen as strictly dependent upon its modality and degree of justification. This work is an attempt to analyse these two aspects and to construct a normative theory of human rights as dependent both on a model grounding our cognitive and linguistic possibilities and on a model validating our moral principles and claims. Indeed, both cognitive and moral elements play a role in human rights judgments, therefore implying, moreover, the necessity of their functional differentiation and asymmetry. This differentiation is certainly an ambitious task, which would ideally require a separate monograph expanding and more fully justifying each chapter. As it stands, however, this work has the advantage of providing several relevant background notions and arguments for a theory of validity of human rights.

The first chapter is oriented precisely to the characterization of the universal validity of truth-claims through the challenges posed by the notion of relativism in accordance to its different dimensions: semantic, epistemic, ontological.

As far as the cognitive-linguistic dimension is concerned, it is possible to find a justificatory route for inter-linguistic translatability and epistemic partial commensurability on the basis of conceptual bridgeheads, as in the case of colour and spatial categories. The first chapter, indeed, addresses the issue of cognitive-linguistic relativism, in particular through the Davidsonian considerations concerning partial incommensurability. On the basis of an extensive use of the discoveries coming from cognitive linguistics a thesis of the embodiment of concepts and of the image schemas is proposed. This allows the defence of partial inter-linguistic commensurability which, unlike the "anti-schematism" of Davidson, can rely on the idea of conceptual schemes as "bridgeheads" universally sheared.

In particular, then, the topic of the metaphoric status of thought and of the processes of categorization is addressed. This cognitive aspect is useful for the criticism of philosophical objectivism, and in particular for the criticism to all those linguistic and philosophical theories that have seen in the idea of correspondence of names to external objects a valid model for the explanation of the cognition and of the propositional truth. The central idea is that notwithstanding that conceptual schemes do emerge directly from experience and do remain dependent upon bodily structures in their environmental interaction, they are organized in cultural and contextual terms.

The epistemic use of the reflective judgment, then, relaunches an inter-subjective-dialogical notion, on the basis of *experientially constituted* conditions, for the construction of meanings and propositional truths. In contrast with previous models, the peculiarity of the present proposal is that cognitions dialogically tested are connected to inter-subjective constructions of propositional validity at an intermediate level, one of which is in between the subject and the object: the experiential interactional processes of categorization. In this case, as it will be for the practical sphere, the notion of truth, far from being considered in terms of its *criteriological* role, is adopted according to its *regulative* function. If the *criteriological* perspective considers truth as based upon a correspondence with the world, the second makes use of a model where the validation of subjective claims is to be measured "as if" it had to be valid for the entire community of fellow human beings.

The second chapter, then, discusses the notions of moral relativism and of objectivism. The initial section offers a general structural picture which distinguishes between descriptive, normative and metaethical relativism. The three spheres can be combined in various ways and, for instance, when integrated by universalist methodological elements it is possible to formulate a theory which is normatively relativist but remains universalist at the metaethical level. Thus, a general perspective is offered on the different possible articulations within different moralities, which integrate universalist and relativist elements. Some specific positions are then presented and criticized both on the side of ethical relativism and on that of the universalism.

Considering Harman's position, it is claimed, among various objections, that he misses to consider both the relevance of the principle of recognition and the normative/factual distinction towards the "ought-can" implication. In the case of Nagel's universalism, the impossibility is observed of constructing an objectively valid paradigm which can rely on a supposed "view from nowhere". But the abandoning of a form of classical universalism does not necessarily commit us to a defence of a revised form of relativism as the one recently defended by Wong. This allows to elicit some options and to prepare the ground for the form of validity of human rights which will be presented in the third chapter: the idea of an exemplary validity contextually situated and constrained by the experiential presuppositions of communicative action. The result is that of a reformulation of the initial conditions of deliberation as presented by Rawls in terms of primary goods within an original position under the "veil of ignorance", in terms of avoidable "enabling conditions" of communicative action: the right to an equal system of freedoms. The third chapter, in particular, provides a critical evaluation of the Habermasian idea of human rights as presuppositions of the communicative model. Notwithstanding the many advantages of the discursive model resulting from an extremely proceduralized framework for the validity of the ethical-political argumentation, Habermas does not consider that, within the pragmatic-discursive dimension, the always criticisable contextual pre-suppositions of communicative action do not provide a sufficient ground for reach-ing his principal objective of subordinating perlocutory functions to illocutionary ones. Such a point connects, within the cognitive aspect, to what is said in the first chapter regarding to the truth-validity of speech-acts as in terms of the experiential basis of the semantics.

The central dependence of purposive action to action aimed at achieving social coordination (communicative action) is also addressed on the basis Gewirth's ar-gument on human rights as the universal conditions of purposive agency. From the difficulties emerging from both Gewirth's and Habermas's arguments, I reformulate the normative conditions expressed in the Habermasian model for communicative action and propose a model of justification taking into account the idea that illocu-tionary speech-act validity is dependent upon both a procedural standard of recog-nition among agents, leading to a formal system of equal liberties, and upon the satisfaction of the conditions of exemplar validity articulated along both epistemic and ethical dimensions.

Indeed, by moving from a system of liberties as a non-avoidable system of purpo-sive presuppositions, I propose a model of judgement capable of mediating between the abstract universality of a system of freedoms and the multiple and partially in-commensurable conceptions of the good spread along the multiplicity of conflicting comprehensive views. In this sense the purported project attempts at considering "the necessary disjunction as well as the necessary mediation between the moral and the ethical, the moral and the political" as well as answering the question: "How can one mediate moral universalism with ethical particularism? How can one mediate legal and political norms with moral ones?" (Benhabib, 2004, 119).

Just to simplify, whereas liberals, on the one hand, have favoured liberty rights as individual rights claimed against the state, and communitarians, on the other hand, have favoured community rights against individual reason, the relation between liberty and participatory rights is here understood in terms of a deep interconnec-tion and mutual interrelation between private and public freedoms. Drawing on the Habermasian theory of communicative action, the notion of communicative agency adds not only a substantive constraint to pure proceduralism. It also conceives, on the one hand, the liberties of the private sphere as themselves justifiable on the basis of an ideal community of agents and, on the other hand, the deliberative out-comes of participatory liberties as delimited by respect for the rights to life, security, and freedom of expression. The liberties of the moderns cannot be taken, then, as defining in an autonomous way a private sphere without of a shareable public notion of justification, nor can public deliberation overrule the basic constraints of the purposive agency. More specific considerations of the characteristics for a theory of human rights are then advanced by connecting the deontological element of human rights with a consideration of the maximization of rights in the case of internal or external conflict among rights. Such a point is strictly connected to the principle of the "finality of rights" previously posed at the normative justificatory level.

It is precisely when individuals can freely reach a form of self-understanding based upon a universalizable frame that human rights can ground a community of right-holders. This is not to deny that variations and specificities can be maintained across self-determined communities and groups. Human rights as principles are, indeed, abstractions which, even if universally justifiable, point to specific interpretive applications taking into account both the political context of implementation as well as the specificities of the cases to which they are applied. If a general and an independent model of human rights can be provided, its validity claims must also be tested by the strategies of application it brings forth. Therefore, a view must not only recognize some rights as fundamental but also combine a deontological perspective with a form of goal-oriented maximization. In so doing, variability can be admitted only in so far as different equilibria for the maximization of core rights can be achieved through the balancing and eventual restriction of respectively attached duties, introducing, in so doing, an element of contextualism within a universalist paradigm.

By considering that even within a political community conflict on human rights is unavoidable, I have then turned to the construction of the conditions of deliberation in the public sphere that would better favour agreement in pluralistic societies. The imaginative interpretation of the constraints of freedoms by the constructive activity of the reflective judgment pluralizes the forms of acceptable public reasons within a system of equal cooperation. The result is therefore a pluralization of the public sphere which calls for possible redefinitions of exemplarily agreed forms of civic coexistence. This process of continuous tension and revision of publicly valid plural judgments refers to what I have termed as second-order exemplar judgments. Since the formal system of liberty-rights grants a plurality of publicly valid exemplar judgments, each system needs the possibility of redetermining the conditions of mutual understanding in accordance to the reflective use of judgment. This new form of exemplar universality, by taking into account all the reasonable and yet conflicting views confronting each other at the public level, is then recognized by the competing parties as representing a new construction of the political identity of the socially interacting subjects themselves. Second-order reflective judgments do create new political identities by reframing, exemplarily, those same conflicting views satisfying the conditions of reasonableness.

Finally, in the fourth chapter, I consider the legal dimensions that human rights bear both in the domestic and in the international domain. In order to elucidate this issue, I consider the relation between law and morality and propose a distinction into four according to the following criteria: internal/conventional, external/conventional, internal/normative, external/normative. The subsequent section, then, reconsiders the issue of variability of the juridical codifications on human rights from the perspective of a common moral justification of fundamental principles as deduced in the previous sections. It is once again underscored, that, even if the concepts of the good can remain partially incommensurable, from the perspective of the juridical interpretation and articulation of the fundamental conditions of agency, it is possible to advance an idea of *partial commensurability on balance* which, even if contextually sensible to the socio/cultural environment of reference, does not impede a possible horizontal revision (interstate relation), of the juridical codifications.

To claim that a form of partial commensurability on balance can be advanced without infringing the political autonomy to self determination of community of citizens, does not amount certainly to provide rationale for "forced processes of democratization" as advanced by individual states in the name of a liberal *ethos*.

For this reason, while defending the conceptual possibility of mutual cooperation among states in matters of legal reforms, in section 4.4 the wide-spread idea that international peace and stability can be granted simply by increasing the number of democratic states and coalitions is rejected. Democracies have been capable of exhibiting external behaviours that are as aggressive as non-democracies, even in situations of no threat to their national security. Also, war and democracy are very complex terms to define, and certainly the so-called democratic peace theorists have not done much for their clarification. While democratic institutional configurations are necessary conditions for the achievement of international peace, they are not sufficient elements. What is required is the development of conditions of regional coordination *within the medium of law* which can bind – internationally – both democratic and non-democratic states. But such external mechanisms of political rationalisation, in order to avoid a form of legal imperialism, would have to rationalize democratic external behaviours under the condition that the maintenance of a multi-level constitutional dialogue is granted. Constitutional confrontation and functional differentiation remain the core point for granting pluralistic self-determination at the local regional and international level.

This book collects and organizes all my recent enquiries into human rights and cultural diversity of the last five years. While initial seeds were contained in some of my previous works, here I offer a systematic philosophical framing for a post-metaphysical conception of human rights.

As so happens in the arts and in scientific discoveries, intellectual improvement is sensitive to the influence of several occasions of exchange, both formal and informal, such as public readings, presentations, and private conversations. Even if the solitary dimension of research scholarship is unavoidable, it is only through critical debate that ideas flourish and improve. For this reason, first of all, I'd like to thank the directors and the academic committee of the annual conference "Philosophy and the Social Sciences" at the Czech Academy of Sciences of Prague where in the last few years I had the chance to present two papers that are now part of this work: in particular I would like to thank M. Hrubec, N. Fraser, W. Scheuerman, D. Rasmussen and M.P. Lara. The questions and the criticisms received in such occasions allowed me to improve some of the crucial points defended in the book. Additionally, a challenging international exposure to contemporary philosophical theories of human rights came from speakers at the Colloquium "Philosophy & Society" at the American Academy in Rome. I'd like to thank the advisory panel for the offering of such excellent opportunities of discussion, and in particular V. Marzocchi, S. L. Cedroni, S. Semplici, S. Petrucciani, M. Rosati, D. Archibugi. Further, thanks to a fellowship granted by Istituto Pareyson Turin, I had the possibility to follow and intensive training seminar with J. Searle and to discuss with him some of my central theses. I would like to thank U. Perone for this splendid initiative. Finally, as a visiting fellow in Law at the European University Institute in Florence, I had the chance to complete some of my earlier drafts on the legal dimensions of human rights and to present part of this work in the advanced seminar in Philosophy of Law. I wish to thank G. Sartor and W. Sadurski for their seminars in Legal Theory and Political Philosophy as well as A. Pizzorno, M. Rosenfeld and G. Postema for their comments. This writing, though, would have not existed without the profound inspirations of the works of A. Ferrara. I am grateful to him both as a scholar and as a person for his encouragement and for the innovation he has inspired in my research. Finally, a thanks goes to K. Fischer for the proofreading and to the anonymous referees of Springer. Both have not only provided me with the chance of improving substantially many parts of the manuscript, but also with the possibility to make myself more understandable to potential readers.

Part I

Chapter 1
Cognitive Relativism and Experiential Rationality

In the attempt to defend a notion of pluralistic universal validity of human rights, the first, perhaps unintuitive step consists in the rejection of possible relativist claims regarding the cognitive-epistemic possibilities of our faculties. The relevance of this starting point lies in two reciprocally interconnected reasons which compel any research into the philosophical justification of human rights to consider the challenge of cognitive-epistemic relativism. The first reason is related to the Habermasian difference between "mutual understanding" (*Verständingen*), as a form of understanding the subjective reasoning of an interlocutor which is valid only for her, and "agreement" as a mutual acceptance of a validity claim (*Einverständnis*). Any form of agreement must presuppose a pattern of mutual understanding which can either proceed to justification, or to a suspension of a process leading to agreement. In practical discourses, the possibility of rejecting contrasting beliefs depends upon the satisfaction of a preliminary condition oriented to the construction and definition of the cognitive context which validates judgments, and in order to achieve a commonly shared definitional context, agents must be capable at least to clarify and exchange, mutually, the very semantic frames that are adopted for the justification of their opposing beliefs. This implies that the option of an absolute form of cognitive incommensurability be ruled out, and that with the overcoming of such theoretical distance, the requirements of understanding presuppositions are satisfied.

The second reason concerns the same possibility of epistemic certainty that becomes particularly crucial in the assessment of the reasons pertaining to opposing moral standards of evaluation and in particular the balancing of the different principles of human rights when implied in the judgmental activity. Let's take for instance the case of the recent debate in bioethics in genetic research, in environmental law as well as that concerning the health risks presented by certain cultural practices such as genital mutilation or, for some, the forbiddance of blood transfusions. The relevance of the interconnection between our epistemic and moral dimension, together with the presumption that certain standards must be satisfied, constitute the general theoretical presuppositions for the grounding of a non-relativist account of human rights judgments. These cases do not exhaust the spectrum of possibilities which should be assessed and epistemically *agreed upon* before any *reasonable* political

C. Corradetti, *Relativism and Human Rights*, DOI 10.1007/978-1-4020-9986-1_1,

debate can take place in the public sphere. Another interesting research laboratory in which historical truth acts as a precondition for the reconstruction of democratic and peace processes is that which is today known as transitional justice. Transitional justice encompasses all those institutional and non institutional changes which are required for the democratization of a non-democratic state or for the internal conflict resolution of purely procedural democracies. Within these contexts, there is no chance to rebuild the democratic functions of a country characterized by conflicting groups without a prior assessment of past violations through trials, truth-telling processes, historical reconstructions and collective recognition of individual and group responsibilities.

As is evident from such cases, it seems that in order to move from a situation where collective decision making has collapsed into a stage where it is rehabilitated, a long process of collective truth consolidation is required before the boundaries of legitimate public discourses within the new born public sphere can be re-established. In other words, the use of public reason, contrary to some sceptical implications of the Rawlsian notion of the "burden of judgment" later discussed, requires a *minimum amount of shared cognitive truths* for the production of *reasonable public disagreement* on moral and political issues. On the basis of which criteria and constraints are such truths consolidations possible? Is truth simply a matter of correspondence to facts or does it follow a socially constructed procedure? I will defend this latter option and claim that coherence of moral and political views with scientific models entails neither a form of naturalistic reductionism nor pure cultural hermeneutics. Nor does it imply a form of subordination of the practical domain to the epistemic one. Both epistemic and ethical spheres remain separate even if publicly argued views of ethical validity must be seen as internally connected with – or "coherent with" – one or more models of epistemic validity and vice versa. With this, it is not my intention to claim that the validity of ethical theories depends on empirical facts – such a relation of corresponding fact with ethical principles does not exist. What I claim, instead, is that the practical activity of judging something to be the (morally relevant) case is sensitive upon the (pre-) understanding of its truth conditions.

Accordingly, in the first section, I will attempt at refuting several versions of relativism advanced within the cognitive-epistemic sphere in order to reach the broader objective of constructing an articulation of morally valid deliberations combining the validity of the epistemic certainty, drawn from the epistemic use of judgements with the validity of moral principles of human rights. As far as the notion of understandability is concerned, my argument relies principally on the development of some of the Davidsonian insights against the principle of "total incommensurability" while maintaining at the same time a universalist understanding of the idea of "conceptual scheme". Such schemes are part of our bodily interactions with the environment and do ground, from the cognitivist-epistemic perspective, our understanding of physical and social phenomena. It is important to clarify that this level of experiential interaction is somehow fictional, constructed by analysis without any pretence of reflecting the structure of our existing languages and cognitive frameworks. Rather, it intersects a "pre-cultural" approach to reality on the basis of the notion of the "embodiment" of our faculties. Diversification of our linguistic systems occurs at a second stage, that is, when forms of social and environmental adaptations organize and reformulate this first level of bodily interaction. Partial commensurability of our cognitive faculties is thus the result of such common pre-cognitive grounding, so that the meta-condition of mutual "understandability" is defended.

As already mentioned, the second central idea defended in this chapter is that of "epistemic truth" as part of a broader framework of public reason. Relativism in truth can broadly amount either to the so called "standard-related" hypothesis or, to the "no neutrality" hypothesis. Here, the argumentative strategy which I have defended has been oriented, on the one hand, to the rejection of possible forms of solipsism as attached to the idea of an internal standard of validity conceived of as in principle private, and then to propose that the "no neutrality" hypothesis does not necessarily commit us to relativism. This point is defended through the critical discussion of several authors, such as MacIntyre, Rorty, Putnam. The conclusion is that while a contextualist approach can coexist with a non-relativist account of our faculties, the defence of a criterion of truth can be defended without an objectivist paradigm of explanation. The concluding remark points indeed to the idea that the standard-related hypothesis must to be understood in relation to a notion of truth based on the principle of subjective universalism and exemplarity. These two elements maintain the "situated character" with the form of an inter-perspective criticism considered in terms of adequacy to a subjectively universalizable standard of validity.

1.1 Beyond Cognitive and Linguistic Relativism

There is a version of the notion of relativism that must be considered in order to understand the epistemological difficulties involved in the notion of cognitive and linguistic relativism. Some of its most renowned representatives are Lyotard, Malinowski, Wittgenstein, Kuhn, Whorf, Herskovits and generally all those who have been interpreted, rightly or wrongly,[1] as proposing a notion of meaning, or an epistemic category, as strictly determined by the non-universalizable conditions attached to the contextual practice of a community.[2] According to this

---

[1] For example, it is not clear at all that Kuhn can be read as proposing a strong form of relativism: Kuhn nowhere shows that meaning shifts are necessitated by paradigm shifts. His historical examples support only the weaker thesis that limited meaning shifts have occurred as paradigms have been replaced or transformed" Harré and Krausz (1996, 80). Later in this chapter I will provide a non relativistic/solipsistic reading of Wittgenstein.

[2] In the Italian debate over the issue, Zolo represents one of the most tenacious defendants of the incommensurability of values, when he writes: "Within differentiated societies, social complexity appears as a process of increasing semantic discontinuity among languages, knowledge, and values that are practiced within any social subsystem. The meaning of an experience lived in a specific

version of relativism, cultural diversity implies that diversity of images of the world is such that it leads to a complete incommensurability of epistemic categories. Such a form of relativism conceives of each epistemic category as referring to different conceptual schemes which, in their turn, are taken as totally untranslatable.

The relativist argument that will be considered here underscores, first, the dimension of cross-cultural variation in the notion of "conceptual schemes", and secondly, the idea according to which "different schemes" imply seeing the world through different eyes. All this bears as a consequence the view that there are different and incommensurable systems of life and thought and that no mutual understanding nor agreement can bridge such epistemic gulfs. What is philosophically interesting in this argument is that, by asserting cultural diversity, this version of relativism also declares a mutual conceptual inaccessibility among cultures.

In order to provide an answer to the difficulties encountered by such a position, in the following sections I will first proceed by reconstructing the Davidsonian theory against total incommensurability (1984), which indeed addresses the general problem of the "dualism between scheme and content", that is, the dichotomy between a non-conceptualized datum and a conceptual scheme organizing the empirical datum. This will provide the starting point for subsequently analysing, autonomously, the issue of cognitive relativism through a new frame provided by cognitive linguistics, in order to rehabilitate, *contra* Davidson, both the notions of conceptual scheme and of partial commensurability.

Davidson's argument proceeds as follows:

(1) The notion of conceptual scheme and empirical content must be reciprocally interdependent.
(2) A conceptual scheme is possible only if it results possible a plurality of conceptual schemes incommensurably alternative.
(3) Conceptual schemes are necessarily associated with languages.
(4) If conceptual schemes are incommensurable, then their related languages are untranslatable.
(5) But since total failures of inter-translatability are not the case, then conceptual schemes are not totally incommensurable.

From this, it follows that the problem of linguistic incommensurability may assume two different versions, that of total incommensurability (I) and that of partial incommensurability (II), which may, respectively, be addressed as follows.

Argument (I):

(1) Total failures of inter-translatability are the necessary and sufficient conditions of radical divergence of conceptual schemes.
(2) Total failures of inter-translatability are inconceivable.

---

domain is hardly translatable in terms of an experience which is possible within a different domain. And the relative functional codes are therefore in principle incommensurable and incommunicable" Zolo (my translation, 2002, 82).

(3) Therefore, either it is not possible to conceive of total untranslatability between different linguistic systems in terms of a radical divergence of conceptual
schemes, or one is presented with a case of total untranslatability, such as language spoken by an alien, which it is impossible to recognize as a language and
therefore as a conceptual scheme.

Argument (I) runs counter to the possibility of total failures of translatability.
Davidson supports this consequence by demonstrating that it is not possible to separate the notion of linguistic capacity from that of translatability in such a way that
something may be recognized as a language without being, at the same time, an
object of translation. In other words, what Davidson underscores is that it is contradictory to attribute a linguistic capacity to someone on the basis of the principle of
charity of interpretation[3] while at the same time declaring the impossibility of inter-
preting such utterances. If the notion of "linguistic capacity" is strictly dependent on
that of inter-translatability, wherever one recognizes the property of linguistic capacity, one is also obliged to admit the possibility at least of partial inter-translatability.
This leads directly to the consideration of Argument (II) which, in its turn, can be
presented as exhibiting the following structure:

(i)   Partial failures of inter-translatability are not sufficient conditions for the exis-
      tence of different conceptual schemes.
(ii) Partial failures of inter-translatability do not prove either radical incommensu-
      rability or total commensurability of the conceptual schemes.

According to Davidson, a partially incommensurable conceptual difference can
arise only when one presupposes, simultaneously, and as a background condition,
a common system of coordination. This is because whenever someone engages
in interpretive activity, she engages in the ascription of beliefs and concepts. According to this precept, which follows from the Davidsonian principle of charity of
interpretation, any interpretation implies the projection of one's own concepts and
beliefs and consequent adjustment and alteration of one's projections. Hence, any
ascription of belief, as well as the possibility of disagreement, presupposes a large
area of agreement (Davidson, 1984, 197). As a matter of fact, individuals or social
systems, can diverge in belief, for instance, with respect to the different referents
of their shared beliefs, but this simply means that concepts are used in different
ways, without implying radical incommensurability. In such cases of disagreement,
reciprocal understanding is still possible, since endorsement of a larger number of
undiscussed beliefs is not ruled out. The charity principle, while not implying that
we need to share all the beliefs of a different culture, establishes only that it is not
possible in principle to conceive of any difference in beliefs, without simultaneously
presupposing agreement over the majority of shared background beliefs.

---

[3] This is the principle of optimisation of an agreement on the basis of an attribution of true beliefs
to those whose speech is being interpreted.

But whereas Davidson seeks simply to prove that condition (i) concerning partial incommensurability is not sufficient to demonstrate the existence of different conceptual schemes and of schemes in general, I for my part intend to claim that, so far as the cognitive domain is concerned, this is due to the existence of universally sheared conceptual schemes and also that partial incommensurability does not prevent the possibility of an indirect epistemic access of what appears as incommensurable in the cognitive target domain. Indeed, just as an intuitive exemplification, one can take the case of a sentence S in a language L which lacks of a corresponding translation in a language L1, but even if so, speakers of L1 are not deprived of an epistemic access to the linguistic content of S in L.

This means that partial failures of inter-translatability are not necessary conditions of failures of epistemic access. Indeed, notwithstanding a lack of direct linguistic correspondence, it is still possible to provide an interpretation of the word in L, as well as of the beliefs and of the concepts connected with it. While one can still say that linguistic accuracy is lost in translation, it cannot be claimed that this prevents epistemological access either with respect to the linguistic meaning of the word or to concepts connected to it.

Following a slightly modified version of this argument against translatability, one could proceed by considering whether from the evidence of *actual* failures of interpretation it is possible to conclude in favour of the notion of cultural epistemic incommensurability. My conclusion is that not even in the extremely rare cases of asymmetrical epistemological inaccessibility, as for example in the case of two numeric systems, it is possible to conclude against epistemic accessibility. In particular, in the case of epistemic asymmetries, one may lack *present* access to a different numerical system without precluding *in principle* future access to that system. This implies that contingent diversity cannot be taken as preventing potential conceptual access to diversity itself and that cognitive competence can be maintained as something distinct from its individual linguistic and conceptual realizations.

One interesting implication of this view is that if grammatical constructions encode semantic elements, then "superficial differences" among languages are no longer easily reducible to linguistic structures but reflect differences of semantic categorization and of cognitive experiential categorization. Grammatical differences are thus differences in meanings experientially grounded, and the possibility of translating one language into another involves the possibility of having partially commensurable forms of semantic structures. If translation is possible, then one must admit the presence of some universal experiential frameworks structuring the cognitive domain.[4] The further relevance of this for the notion of externalism in

---

[4] "What kinds of concepts is one most likely to find as one surveys conceptual systems? First kinaesthetic image schemas: concepts like up-down, 'in-out', 'part-whole', etc. Second, basic-level concepts for things, states, activities in one's immediate experience: body parts, plants and animals, basic-level artefacts, basic colours, basic emotions, etc Third, metaphorical concepts based on universal experiences: thus it would not be surprising to find 'more' being 'up', or 'anger' being understood in terms of 'heat' or 'pressure'. There are a fair number of such things that one

meaning is noteworthy. Putnam has suggested that philosophers were mistaken in running together two points: first, that meanings are simply "internal", and secondly, that they are analogous to what one defines as beliefs (the latter normally identified through their relations to other objects and events "external" to the subject himself).[5] The short reply to this is that meaning is "experientially" based and cannot be conceived of beyond subjects' interaction among themselves and with the environment, or in any individualistic way. More in detail, Putnam (1981b, chap. 2) presents his idea through the example of Twin Earth: we are invited to imagine two persons with the same physical properties, and who are therefore identical as far as their restricted psychological states are concerned. One of the two, the person on Earth, has learned how to use the word "water" by watching water and playing with it etc.; the other, on Twin Earth, has learned to use the word "water" in similar circumstances, with the sole difference that the substance he refers to, even if apparently similar to Earth-water, possesses a different chemical composition. Even if the restricted psychological states of the two subjects are the same, the extension of "water" on Earth and on Twin Earth is different, thus "meanings are not in the head". What results from this version is a reduction of the authority of the first person, given that we could always be wrong about the meanings of the words we use without being aware of it. But simply from the fact that meanings are partially determined by external objects, it does not follow that they "are not in the head". Putnam's mental experiment nonetheless leaves open the possibility of an interactional construction of meanings which depends both on physical interactions with the environment and on interpersonal constructions of meanings. Therefore, while his explanation sheds light on the fact that the micro structural components of a meaning can obviously play a role, so that "water" in Earth and "water" in Twin Earth can be differentiated, this differentiation can occur only whenever interactional and experiential reasons require it. Until then, there is no possibility of a "view from nowhere", nor of a "God's point of view" under which uninterpreted substantial physical properties are the only pertinent elements to meaning construction. The idea is that physical properties do not escape conditions of *intentionality* and *indexicality* in meaning with the consequence of subordinating meaning validity to standards which can be either satisfied or violated with reference to a situated self.[6]

This revised interpretation of meaning construction is able to connect both the authority of the first person, the partial fixing of meanings by external objects, and the social character of language through the relevance given to the second person (I can judge you as following a rule if you proceed in the same way I would, or more generally if you make yourself interpretable to me).[7] Respect to the standard

---

would not expect to vary much. All of these are tied very closely to well-structured experience" Lakoff (1987, 336).

[5] Putnam (1975).

[6] For the presentation of a clear argument against externalism see Searle (2004, chap. 6).

[7] The thesis presented here is broadly compatible with the views recently expressed by Davidson (2001, 66–67 and 155ff), even if relevant points of difference can be found in the

against which other subjects are to be measured, there is no need to establish a criterion independent of the interpretative activity of those subjects themselves. As a matter of fact, this would simply constitute an infinite regress, and require an additional standard from which to interpret the former standard. Intersubjectivity relies, therefore, on the interactional interpretational activity of the community of speakers with the surrounding environment, bearing only a difference of degree, but not one of kind, in respect to the necessary capacities for the interpretation of another language.[8] According to this view, the environment comes to assume a regulative function which precludes any possibility of considering meanings in terms of a mere correspondence to an independently constituted world.[9] The quest

---

foundational role played in my analysis by the space-temporal categorization and the Davidsonian interactional perspective of category construction.

[8] On this point Davidson claims: "A creature may interact with the world in complex ways without entertaining any propositions. It may discriminate among colours, tastes, sounds, and shapes. It may learn, that is change its behaviour, in ways that preserve its life or increase its food intake. It may 'generalize', in the sense of reacting to new stimuli as it has come to react to prior stimuli. Yet none of this, no matter how successful by my standards, shows that the creature commands the contrast between what is believed and what is the case, as required by belief. What *would* show command of this contrast? Clearly linguistic communication suffices. To understand the speech of another, I must be able to think of the same things she does; I must share her world. I don't have to agree with her in all matters, but in order to disagree we must entertain the same propositions, with the same subject matter, and the same conception of truth. Communication depends on each communicator having, and correctly thinking that the other has, the conception of a shared world, an intersubjective world. But the concept of an intersubjective world is the conception of an objective world, a world about which each communicator can have beliefs. I suggest, then, that the conception of intersubjective truth suffices as a basis for belief and hence for thoughts generally. And perhaps it is plausible enough that having the concept of intersubjective truth depends on communication in the full linguistic sense. To complete the 'argument', however, I need to show that the *only* way one could come to have the belief-truth is through having the concept of intersubjective truth. I confess I do not know how to show this. But neither do I have any idea how else one could arrive at the concept of an objective truth. In place of an argument for the first step, I offer the following analogy. If I were bolted to the earth, I would have no way of determining the distance from me of many objects. I would have no way of determining the distance from me of many objects. I would only know how they were on some line drawn from me towards them. It might interact successfully with objects, but I could have no way of giving content to the question where they were. Not being bolted down, I am free to triangulate. Our sense of objectivity is the consequence of another sort triangulation, one that requires two creatures. Each interacts with an object, but what gives each the concept of the way things are objectively is the baseline formed between the creatures by language. The fact that they share concept of truth alone makes sense of the claim that they have beliefs, that they are able to assign objects a place in the public world" Davidson (2001, 103). It is quite clear that what Davidson admits he cannot explain is straightforwardly explicable if cognitive systems are afforded an experiential foundation.

[9] The internal connection between the notion of a world as a regulative concept and the notion of the validity of experience has been very clearly described by Harré and Krausz: "It is possible for an internalist, one who holds that all existential categories are created within theoretical contexts, to project these categories onto an external world, a world which exists independently of its being examined. From within an internalist framework, one can make intelligible the idea of something to which we can have no direct epistemic access. We can talk of the intelligibility and of the

for truth can be placed only within the horizon of experience, which comes to be the never completely exhaustible condition within which an internal critical process of dialogical reflection occurs.

A cognitive-relativist counter-argument against the idea of a general translinguistic accessibility might also take the form of *ontological relativism*, in particular as it results from the Quinean notion of *under-determination of translation*. Here the thesis assumes that, for two languages L and L1, there exists an infinite number of translation manuals from L to L1 all respecting the general condition C that each manual has to respect in order to be correct. Quine claims that if there is a translation manual from L to L1, then there exists an infinite number of translation manuals which are all correct in relation to C and yet incompatible with each other. If this argument is sound, then the reference of each translation manual could be different, invalidating the relevance of the notion of linguistic reference itself. Let's consider the following argument:

(1) If T1 is a correct translation of S, then T1 and S have the same reference.
(2) But since, according to Quine's argument, one can obtain a multiplicity of correct translations of S such as T1, T2 etc.
(3) Then, it is not possible to establish which is the reference of T, due to the multiple references exhibited by translations T1, T2 etc.

For the sake of elucidation, if on the traditional version of cognitive relativism, a sentence S is believed to have different truth-conditions operating at different social contexts, Quinean relativism avoids incoherence by admitting a multiplicity of valid translations that maximize and predict equally well the behaviour of the society in question. In the first version, relativism is supported by a notion of radical incommensurability and un-translatability, whereas in the second version, there are too many translations that are equally right. Indeed, the Quinean thesis on the indeterminacy of translation does not claim that singular translations are themselves indeterminate, since each translation is a determinate, equally valid interpretation of sentence S. But if Quinean relativism, on the pain of an infinite interpretative regress must admit that multiple translations of a sentence S are multiple determinate translations of that same sentence, then it must also admit in principle that there is a way of establishing whether a translation is more correct than another on the basis of a determinate meaning that the sentence translated represents. I believe that the crucial point in Quine's argument is the relevance assumed by the notion underpinning "the

---

inaccessibility of a particular or of a type of entity in virtue of a well-constructed theory, which posits the existence of the relevant type or particular. That is we might argue that it is necessary to assume the existence of a certain class of entities so that the phenomena which we know to exist should be possible. If there are to be electro-magnetic interactions there must be virtual photons. If there are to be earthquakes there must be tectonic plates. By the same token one may hold to a theory of truth in terms of a correspondence between discursively constructed cognitive objects and some aspect of the world, yet agree that one has no direct access to the world-in-itself, and so no way of making judgments as to the truth of particular hypotheses about the world beyond all possible experience" (1996, 139).

general conditions of correctness" according to which a translation manual should conform to in order to produce valid translations. This brings us back to the postulation of the notion of experience as a normative standard framework of our bodily experiences with the environment and the social world.[10]

This notion provides a common cognitive framework for the development of experiential meanings and conceptual scenarios. For instance, establishing relations of symmetry between parts of our body allows us also to assign negative or positive values to each of the orienting spatial vectors. If in many categorical spheres the bodily-cultural experience is variable, as concerns the space-bodily experience, such variability is reframed within a *framework of conceptual comparability*. This emerges clearly in cases of perceptive asymmetries which allow for an orientation choice that is reducible to front-back, above-under, raised-underlying.[11]

Such bodily-constrained conceptual elements can be taken as instances of the well known notion of "rational bridgehead" as introduced by Hollis (1982), and can be used for the defence of the necessity of a common core of equivalent perceptions and beliefs shared inter-culturally which allow for the inception of translation activities. Rational bridgeheads, according to Strawsonian terms (Hollis 1982, 75 ff), through their provision of a "direct attack on meaning available" and "a massive central core of human thinking which has no history" would break a vicious circle consisting both of the assumption of understanding a belief before being capable of translating it and on the prerequisite of translation before the possibility of understanding the meaning of a different linguistic system.

1.2 Epistemic Relativism Refuted

Moving now from the notion of translatability to that of truth and reason, the first observation is that relativism is neither a coherent nor a good explicatory theory. The central thesis of a certain epistemic relativism is that it is perfectly fair to

---

[10] More specifically: "From the commonalities of our visual systems and motor systems, universal features of spatial relations (image schemas) arise, whereas from our common capacities of *gestalt* perception and motor programs basic-level concepts arise. From the common colour cones in our retinas and the commonalities of our neural architecture for colour vision, the commonalities of colour concepts arise. Our common capacity for metaphorical thought arises from the neural projections from the sensory and motor parts of our brain to higher cortical regions responsible for abstract thought" Lakoff and Johnson (1999, 463).

[11] "[...] The correlation hypothesis implies that since P-space [perceptual space] is a human universal, it should condition L-space in every language. The L-space of each language should therefore exhibit properties that are consistent with the P-space as briefly described in this paper. This hypothesis does not imply that each language should have the same spatial terms (except for translation) or terms drawn from the same small inventory of spatial terms. Rather, the hypothesis implies that the possible rules of application – those spatial conditions presupposed by the spatial terms – should be universal. Since these rules of application can be combined in a number of different ways, many systems of other languages that I am at all acquainted will appear to be very similar to the English L-space" Clark (1973, 54).

defend the claim that there are cases where what is true for a culture X is false for a culture Y. This implies that, for the relativist, the truth of a sentence is relative to a group's assumptions and varies according to its characteristic truth-claims. This explanation of the variability of truth conditions is simply incoherent, since it relies on the false assumption that cognitive systems are reciprocally incommensurable. On the contrary, if one keeps in mind the earlier claim concerning epistemic partial translatability of different cognitive systems, it may easily be replied that truth conditions holding for one sentence S of a language L, when translated into L1, must be the same. But can the invariability of truth conditions in different contexts be backed by a variability of reasons according to different conditions? There seems to be a strict link here between truth and reason, since what is a reason for x must also be true of x. If this is right, then the invariability of truth conditions determines the invariability of reasons for holding true the same sentence both in L and in L1.[12]

My aim in the next two sections will not simply be that of refuting some possible versions that a theory of epistemic relativism might take, but of defending a view that, while taking into serious consideration some supposedly relativistic assumptions, is capable of offering a form of universalism within an enriched notion of rationality. In order to achieve this objective, I will first discuss some of the central assumptions that characterize epistemic relativism through the Wittgensteinian criticism of the idea of solipsism. Then, I will show how some relativist tensions can be identified also in accredited non-relativist authors who have shaped the contemporary debate on the matter. The general aim, which will be further developed in the next section, is to show how it is possible to maintain some of the relativist questions without necessarily falling into an epistemic relativist theory.

First, epistemic relativism can be defined according to two central hypothesis: the "standard-related" hypothesis for the validation of any knowledge, and the "no neutrality" hypothesis (Moesteller, 2006, 2ff). The standard-related hypothesis claims that any propositional truth "p" can be formulated only according to some standards "s1", "s2" etc., whereas the "no neutrality" hypothesis, claims that given a multiplicity of standards "s1", "s2" etc. there is no privileged neutral point of observation for evaluating the superiority of one standard in respect to the other (see Siegel, 1987, 6). From this definition of epistemic relativism several well-known self-refuting arguments against relativism might follow: if epistemic relativism is true, then there must be at least one non-relative true proposition, but since it is contradictory for relativists to produce a non-relativist meta-claim, then epistemic relativism cannot be proved to be true.

---

[12] As explained by Newton-Smith: "The fact that truth cannot vary across such contexts precludes the possibility that reason should vary. R is a reason for believing that p just in case there is an appropriate truth linking R and p. That my typewriter case looks white to me is a reason for thinking that it is white just because things that look white in the sort of circumstances that obtain at the moment are or tend to be white" (1982, 110).

Besides the extensive discussion which has already been produced for such arguments, a different route of justification for epistemic relativism can take the form of epistemic solipsism and claim instead that: relativist truths are simply a function of first-person dispositions to consider them truths for oneself (Putnam, 1992, 73ff). If it is so, then there is not a truth-claim to be justified universally, and therefore no relativist self-refuting argument that can be advanced.

The problem with such an argument is that solipsism in terms of purely private standards of propositional validity, or as a privatized world prevents in principle communication itself and, with that, a criterion of propositional validity even if within solipsistic constraints, that is, not just only towards the others. It is worth, at such regard, considering in some detail the Wittgensteinian reflections on the private language argument as well as his criticisms of any pretension for establishing the rules for a private language.

At *Philosophical Investigations* §258 Wittgenstein rejects the possibility of a private language. That the meaning of words can be essentially private is the thesis that we find implied in Locke and more in general in all those philosophers considering the mind as an inner space where mental phenomena are located. Wittgenstein's private language argument entails the rejection of the view of words as signifying inner ideas, and therefore the rejection of the mind as a box whose processes are accessible only to the subject himself. This picture of the mind is what, according to Wittgenstein, has obscured the understanding of language as a public practice. By not distinguishing between "following a rule" and "believing to follow a rule", it has considered sensations and meanings as locked up in the mind as if they were essentially and necessarily private. Wittgenstein's critical discussion of this point is aimed to present the extreme consequence of what the conception of a private language entails. A language whose meanings are essentially private does not simply prevent communication between two speakers, but it also contains words that are meaningless to the single speaker himself, and thus to any possible relativistic-solipsistic argument in thought and language. The aim of §258 is precisely a clarification of this point and a rejection of the idea of private sensations and private language.

Wittgenstein asks to imagine the case of somebody who wants to keep a record of one recurrent sensation. Each day he has this sensation he is supposed to write down his diary "S". "S" signifies by means of an inner ostensive definition. I concentrate inwardly on my sensation and I point to it by using "S". At this point Wittgenstein asks "what is this ceremony for?" in fact it seems that in this way we have not gained any definition of the sign since we have to rely just on the rightness of our memory for future uses. If that is the case then we could simply say that the only criterion we have reached is just that "whatever is going to seem right to me is right", and that would mean that we can't talk of rightness. Precisely because the Wittgensteinian argument presents some lacunae, its philosophical fortune has been so great that several interpretations have been proposed. In what follows I will consider only few, with the aim of clarifying what can be maintained and what can be dismissed of any solipsistic pretension in language and truth.

Some commentators have found in this passage an argument which makes use of a verificationist principle and distinguished between the possibility of a strong verificationist argument and a weak verificationist argument. Both arguments share the same premise, namely the no-independent check argument. This argument, which is claimed to be crucial in Wittgenstein's passage, states that if I introduce "S" as the name of a private sensation and later I check whether the occurrence of a new sensation can be called "S" again, I can rely on the rightness of my memory but I cannot actually check whether I have remembered correctly. This means that I do not have any objective independent criterion that I can appeal to in order to check if I'm applying "S" correctly. But the question is: how can we proceed from saying, as Wittgenstein does, that I don't have a criterion of correctness to saying that we can't talk of correctness at all? As a matter of fact it seems that from the fact that I don't have an independent criterion of correctness it does not follow that I can't talk of correctness at all. Indeed I might use "S" correctly even if I don't have an objective criterion for establishing it. Both the strong and weak verificationist argument try to fill this gap in the argument. The strong verificationist argument says that a statement is meaningful only if it is verifiable. Therefore, since in the case of a private language I cannot verify if I'm applying "S" correctly, it follows that "S" is meaningless. It can be replied to this argument that there could be a way to verify, at least indirectly, if my memory is reliable by memorizing a sequence of letter/colour on a card. If I can test the reliability of my memory in this case, I can then proceed to a justification of the rightness of my memory even in the case of a private language. The weak verificationist principle, in the version given by Glock (1996), says instead that somebody can be said to follow a rule only in the case there is an "operational standard of correctness" that can be verified. Therefore, since in the Wittgenstein's case there is no operational standard of correctness, we cannot say that the subject is following a rule. The objection that can be raised to this argument is that it seems intuitively plausible that we can be said to follow a rule even if there is not a standard of correctness that we can appeal to. We can be said to use "S" meaningfully, that is according to a rule, even if there is not an operational standard of correctness that we can check. If, for instance, I'm in a prison and I'm prevented from any linguistic interactions with other men, I can decide to write "S" in my diary for each day I see a rat. After few months, I might not remember what I used this "S" for, given that I did not express my rule in the form of "S = . . .", namely whether I used this sign during the days I saw a rat or during the days I have not seen any. Even in this circumstance I can use the sign "S" according to a rule, but this rule is not an independent operational standard for my use of the sign.

There are however at least two other interpretations that do not rely on a verificationist argument: Hacker's Circularity Argument (1972) and McGinn's Stage Setting Argument (1984, 1997). Hacker's Circularity Argument goes as follows: what Wittgenstein wants to attack at §258, is the view according to which the way we apply words makes use of an internal looking up process. If I want to know what "red" refers to, I look for a mental example of red in my mind and then I compare it with several objects until I find something of the same colour so that I finally know what "red" refers to. If that is the way "S" means too, we are making use of a circular argument. As a matter of fact, if I must know what "S" means by a mental looking up process, how do I know what mental sample I have to look for? If I already know what mental sample I have to look for, then I can already use the word and I don't need a mental sample. The point here is that the looking up process presupposes the same ability to use the sign "S" that it is supposed to explain.

A different version of the argument is the so-called simple stage-setting offered by McGinn (1997). According to McGinn the focus of the argument at §258 must be understood by reference to a previous passage at §257, where Wittgenstein says "[...] a great deal of stage-setting in the language is presupposed if the mere act of naming is to make sense". If we take the argument at §258 as pointing to the limits of an inner ostensive definition out of the context of a stage-setting, we can understand why Wittgenstein proceeds on to say that it is "an idle ceremony". If, for example, we use the word "tove" pointing to a pen, would we use this word as a proper name of the object? Or do we use it to refer to its shape, colour etc.? In other words in order to understand an ostensive definition we already have to be able to master a language, and therefore know the place this word has in the grammar of the language. This point is quite important, since it rules out the basic importance of the ostensive definition that also the Augustinian theory of language made use for. The Augustinian theory of language gives an explanation of how we learn a language as if our thoughts are already there in a well-structured form ready to be matched with words. But according to Wittgenstein this would be a circular explanation of how we learn a language, since it would presuppose the same ability it aims to explain.

It might seem that the stage-setting argument, in the way it is formulated, would rule out the same possibility of the start of a language, since any initial ostensive definition would lack a stage-setting. However, this difficulty could be solved by recurring to what I consider as the experiential grounding of semantics in terms, for instance, of kinaesthetic image schemas as a form of pre-conceptual experience directly emerging from our bodily interactions with the environment. If that were the case, one would also be able to understand the possibility of having an initial definition which is at the same time constitutive of a basic stage-setting. This point will receive full elucidation in the remaining sections.

As we have seen, all these arguments focus on a particular aspect of §258 without completely exhausting the argument itself. It may be claimed that Wittgenstein offers a series of puzzles condensed in just few lines, but even if so it is hard to make clear sense of all his points. Nevertheless, in pursuing the stage-setting criticism, other features emerge that connect some secondary aspects of the Wittgensteinian view on language to the experiential foundations of our linguistic and cognitive system.

Having dismissed the possibility of a private language as a chance of defending a solipsistic form of epistemic relativism, I will turn now to the philosophy of MacIntyre, who, while advancing an anti-relativist position, attempts to include within his views both a specific interpretation of the "standard related" hypothesis as well as of the "no neutrality" hypothesis introduced before. MacIntyre defines rationality as something inherently embedded in some traditional-cultural pattern: it is only when individuals participate in some socially established cultural practice that they can develop patterns of rationality (MacIntyre, 1998, 121). If the standard of rationality is always relative to cultural schemes, then it follows that there is no possibility of assessing two conflicting cultural standards from a supposedly neutral perspective. Indeed, MacIntyre seems to be committed to precisely this claim when he writes that: "There is no standing ground, no place for enquiry, no way to engage in the practices of advancing, evaluating, accepting, and rejecting reasoned argument apart from that which is provided by some particular tradition or other" (MacIntyre, 1988, 350).

If MacIntyre were simply to reduce rationality to cultural patterns of justification, then he would be clearly representing a case of epistemic relativism. But an important aspect of his argument affirms that epistemological explanations attached to one tradition or another can be defeated and replaced not only by epistemic resources available in that tradition itself, but also by epistemic explanations advanced by a different competing tradition: "a tradition can be rationally discredited by and in the light of appeal to its very own standards of rationality in more than one way" (MacIntyre, 1988, 365), and also: "It is in respect of their adequacy or inadequacy in their responses to epistemological crises that traditions are vindicated or fail to be vindicated" (MacIntyre, 1988, 366). Therefore, one may conclude that MacIntyre, while sharing some of the relativist positions such as the "standard-related hypothesis" and the "no-neutrality hypothesis", is not committed to a form of epistemic relativism.

One preliminary criticism of such a view might take into account that if rationality undergoes only an internal cultural criterion of validity, then it seems quite difficult even to understand how to establish when two cultural systems do indeed advance a conflicting claim. This point appears even more problematic by the further claim according to which not all cultural-relative patterns of rationality are equally explicative when facing epistemological crises, and that indeed one tradition can be proved superior to another without resorting to an external-independent criterion of rationality. But in order to make sense of a supposedly more extensive explicative force of one tradition over another, it is important to understand that the same possibility of epistemological crises and their eventual resolution through the adoption of different standards cannot be understood if not on the basis of the *transcendental anticipation* of a trans-cultural notion of truth forcing culturally embedded subjects into a process of self-criticism and self-transcendence that can take the form of an intersubjective evaluation.

The problem with MacIntyre's notion of the "situatedness" of a standard concerns its identification and conformity of the explicatory patterns of rationality to specific culturally embedded traditions. What is wrong with this kind of identification is that a similar step does not necessarily follow maintaining the "standard-related hypothesis" and the "no-neutrality" hypothesis. For instance, one can develop a subjective-universalist epistemological paradigm which, while context-related, is capable of expressing a form of validity trespassing the context itself. This is what can be referred to as the notion and the function of the "reflective judgment" of Kant's Third Critique, which in my view can take both an epistemic and a political reading, and which can be adopted as a universalist solution to the challenges of relativism presented in this work. Indeed, it is the same notion of reflective judgment which can be combined with the notion of a counterfactual anticipation of truth, and this latter can be intended as a regulative criterion of universal validity which does not commit to a supposedly neutral point of observation from which competing positions can be assessed. Reflective judgement, instead, allows for a process of epistemic universalization by demonstrating how each specific epistemic judgment is placed in a more fundamental epistemic condition of understanding assuming the form of aesthetic anticipation of the experience in general.

If one returns to MacIntyre's position, what seems extremely unconvincing is his philosophical explanation for the very possibility of scientific improvements within traditions, both when epistemological crises make appeal to internal forms of resolutions and paradigm-shifts and when, more importantly, no other supposedly superior epistemological frame can provide satisfactory answers to one's epistemological gaps. In such cases, once again, only the possibility of science to transcend its own rationally established patterns can provide a more adequate indication on how to improve the rational understanding of the world. Overall the proposal advanced by MacIntyre, while attempting an interpretation of the "standard related" and the "no neutrality" hypothesis in non-relativistic terms, seems incapable of escaping the very criticism of relativism. Indeed, if no criterion of transcendental validity can be advanced, it seems that in cases of epistemic crises each tradition-bound resolution can be validly justified only in accordance to culturally specific standards whose validity cannot transcend its contextual form of origination. Not dissimilar to this point is the position advanced by Rorty (1993) when he rejects the idea that justificatory practices can trespass the contextual validity from which they originate. According to Rorty, there is no possible transcendental anticipation of truth which could be in principle separated from actual justificatory patterns: for Rorty the idea of truth as warranted acceptability towards an ideal community does not make sense other than as a willingness to defend one's position to "[...] us educated, sophisticated, tolerant, wet liberals, the people who are always willing to hear the other side, to think out all their implications, etc." (1993, 451).

It might seem that admitting a transcendental criterion of truth could lead to the rejection of the standard-related hypothesis and, more seriously, to the inclusion of an objectivist paradigm within an apparently non-objectivist justification of truth. I believe, indeed, that the rejection of these two explicative components does not necessarily follow from the construction of an alternative paradigm following from the criticism of MacIntyre. My general idea is that the standard-related hypothesis can be proved to be more or less adequate according to a transcendental notion of truth based on the principle of subjective universalism and exemplarity. Such two features are indeed capable of preserving the "situated character" of the judgement and, with it, the standard-related hypothesis, but at the same time they allow for the opening of the same standards involved in a form of critical activity and confrontation in terms of adequacy towards a transcendental subjective standard of validity.

While, for instance, Putnam has recognized the relevance of transcendentality for the rejection of epistemic relativism when he writes that "reason is both immanent (not to be found outside of concrete language games and institutions) and transcendent (a regulative idea that we use to criticize the conduct of *all* activities and institutions)" (1981a, 234), his notion of truth as idealized rational acceptability (Putnam, 1981b, 55ff), as it is, introduces an objectivist explanation for the assessment of the different competing conceptual schemes. In what follows, I will try to show how transcendentalism can be combined with a notion of truth dependent upon an embodied perspective.

1.3 The Experiential Validity of the Cognitive System

The task of this paragraph is to define the link between conceptual categories and the external world by defending the central view of "conceptual embodiment". This notion holds that conceptual categories are constituted on the basis of specific bodily characteristics not detached from the physical constitution of individuals.[13] Following from this reasoning, the foundation of the conceptual system must be individuated in those types of structures that emerge directly from our preconceptual experience.

Remaining faithful to this assumption, one can find in the realm of preconceptual experiences at least two kinds of structures, namely: basic-level structures and structures of kinaesthetic imagine schemas, the latter constituted by the "[. . .] Convergence of our gestalt perception, our capacity for bodily movement, and our ability to form rich mental images" Lakoff (1987, 267). The first are categories placed at an intermediate level within a hierarchical scale, that is, at the most basic psychological level. As demonstrated by Rosch (1977, 1978) and Berlin (1968), Berlin et al. (1974), basic-level categories are constituted at the basic level of categorization. This is strongly conditioned by our way of interacting with the environment, which in fact allows us to access through gestalt perceptions the essential characteristics of a genus and to identify and distinguish it immediately on the basis of specific properties: "At this level, people function most efficiently and successfully in dealing with discontinuities in the natural environment" Lakoff (1987, 298).[14]

---

[13] "Experientialism claims that conceptual structure is meaningful because it is embodied, that is, it arises from, and is tied to, our preconceptual bodily experiences. In short, conceptual structure exists and is understood because preconceptual structures exist and are understood. Conceptual structure takes its form in part from the nature of preconceptual structures" Lakoff (1987, 267).

[14] The level determined by the "basic-level categories" has the following properties: (1) It is the level in which the members of a category have similar forms (2) It is the highest level in which an individual mental image can reflect the entire category (3) It is the highest level in which a person uses similar motor programmes for interacting with the members of the same category (4) It is the level in which subjects are extremely quick at individuating category members (5) It is the level with the most commonly used labels for members of the same category (6) It is the primary level nominated and understood by children (7) It is the first level to enter the vocabulary of a language during its history (8) It is the level with the shortest primary words (9) It is the level in which the words are used in neutral contexts (10) It is the level in which most of our knowledge is organized (11) It is the level in which most of our functions are defined. Additionally basic-level categories satisfy four additional criteria: (1) Perceptual: individual mental image, quick identi-

If some examples are considered, one rapidly understands that it is easy for us to compose mental images for things such as cat, table, but not for supra-ordered categories such as animal. In the same way, one has motor programmes for using cars etc., but no programmes for using transportation machines in general.

Psychological tests conducted by Rosch (1977, 1978) also show that basic level categories are poles around which we organize our knowledge. As a matter of fact, we have many notions for what is intended by the concept of gun, whereas we possess many fewer for what is intended, for instance, by the supraordinated category of weapon. The basic level is also that at which people categorize accurately real world objects. Berlin, Breedlove, and Raven (1974) and Hunn (1977), in studies about Tzeltal plants and animal names found that, at the basic level, popular terminology for plants and animals fulfils almost perfectly the biological taxonomy. Basic level categorization points to an incorporated and experientialist cognition, more than to a disembodied and objectivist vision of it. Nevertheless, if one takes into consideration the notion of image schemas, it must be concluded that they are fundamentally different from mental images as such, since the former behave as recurrent schemes of bodily experience.

One of the most relevant peculiarities of the schematic-imaginative functionalities consists in the generically abstract level of the structuring of perceptions, events and images to which such conceptual instruments lead. By virtue of such abstractness, imaginative schemas are distinguished from mental images, the latter characterized by abundance of visual data making them capable of diversified application in accordance to different experiential and epistemic domains.[15]

To illustrate this notion, one may consider the scheme attached to the notion of container as constituted by the relation of interior and exterior. Such a scheme defines the basic distinction of in-out. If we consider our bodies as containers through metaphorical projections in the sensible world, the resulting properties of the container scheme would be the following:

(1) Bodily experience: we have constant experience of our bodies both as containers and as things in the container (if, for instance, we are in a room).
(2) Structural elements: interior, border, exterior.
(3) Basic logic: for most image schemas, the internal structure of the image schema of the container is organized in such a way as to respect a basic logic. Everything is either inside or outside the container, additionally if the container A is in B and B is in C, then A is in C, and this constitutes that basic logic of the *modus ponens*.

---

fication (2) Function: general motor programmes, general cultural functions (3) Communication: brevity of words, the most used words and contextually neutral (the connotative function is null), the first learned by children and inserted in the lexicon (4) Organization of knowledge: most of the attributes of category members exist at this level (see Lakoff, 1987).

[15] Regarding the common share of image schemas and mental images, cognitive linguistics is in debt to Kant's thought, even if in Kant there is a clear distinction between pure schemas, such as that of triangle, and empirical schemas (Kant, 1999 [1781]).

(4) Examples of metaphors: the visual field is considered as a container; things enter and exit the visual field. Personal and interpersonal relations are also understood in terms of containers: one can be "in crisis", "exit from depression" and so on.

The basic logic of image schemas results from their configuration as *gestalt*, as structured wholes that are more than the simple sum of their singular parts. The underlying logical implications are therefore a consequence of their configurations. Such a way of conceiving of the image schemas is cognitive, and therefore quite distant from the approach followed by formal logic, where gestalt configurations are not taken into account. The cognitive uses of such structures can be those of structuring new domains of knowledge, furnishing a topological basis upon which it is possible to construct a category.[16]

A further property commonly shared by image schemas and basic-level categories is that of direct emergence of signification, which implies that one can understand such structures without further conceptual mediation, and only via direct and repeated experience based on physical and environmental characteristics. As already anticipated by the definition of the notion of "embodiment", the role of direct signification of certain pre-cognitive structures provides strong motivation against a merely propositional consideration of cognitive processes.

Even if it is possible to attribute arbitrary symbols to structural characteristics of images, this does not necessarily imply that they can be considered as cognitively neutral processes. If one considers the human capacity of transformation and manipulation of schematic images analogously to manipulation of physical objects, the use of a "mental space" (Fauconnier, 1985) and the ability to manipulate abstract structures together establish the non-propositional character of the implied processes.[17] Image schemas, then, in contrast to the fixity attributed to them by Kant, must be considered rather as a continuous structure for the organization of an activity (Johnson, 1987, 29).

Individuation of cognitive schemas has led to a noteworthy development in the understanding of the nature of mental processes, no longer reducible to a merely propositional form and, in linguistic terms, has also contributed to the cognitive-semantic interpretation of the meaning of words, as well as of the phenomenon of polisemy at synchronic and diachronic levels. This perspective gives rise to

---

[16] Newton (1996), in an analysis of general cognitive functions, individuates two of these three functions by reference to the distinction between "reflective" and "non-reflective" use of image schemas.

[17] As proof of such capacities activities including the following can be considered: *Focusing of the path and the final point*, where one must imagine following an object across a path, stopping where the object arrests; *Overlapping*, imaging two geometrical three-dimensional objects and then trying to insert the first in the second and then the second in the first and varying, each time, the reciprocal spatial dimensions; *From multiplicity to mass*, imagining first a discrete group of objects then, via a "visual" distancing from the group of objects, coming to see them as an indistinct mass.

substantial criticisms of the so called "objectivist paradigm".[18] As a matter of fact, if, for objectivists, human thought is disembodied, experiential cognitivism considers it as implying the kind of structured experience which derives from having human bodies, as well as innate sense-motor capacities. Wherever objectivism sees meaning in terms of a "theory of correspondence", that is to say, as an association of symbols with external objects, experiential cognitivism sees meaning as implying an imaginative projection (through mechanisms of schematizations, categorization, metaphor and metonymy). Finally, if objectivism sees cognitive processes as a manipulation of abstract symbols through the use of many well-structured algorithms, experiential cognitivism for its part poses a restricted number of general cognitive processes, whose application to abstract cognitive models contributes to the determination of the concept of rationality. The main thesis defended by objectivism can be synthesized as according to the following points:

(1) Algorithmic consideration of mental processes, that is, formal manipulation of symbols without regard to the internal structure of symbols and their meaning.
(2) Symbolic theory of meaning: arbitrary symbols can be significant through things in the world (where "the world" is considered as having a structure independent of the mental processes of any being).
(3) Cognitive metaphysics: as derived from the separation of symbols from their meaning, that is, from consideration of thought as an algorithmic manipulation of arbitrary symbols, indirectly meaningful, thanks to their association with things in the external world.

For objectivists, conceptual categories are generally defined as "classical categories", that is, as a group of elements that share a number of necessary and sufficient properties. Conceptual categories are represented by symbols that designate categories of the real world; the properties of such categories are therefore shared by all the members of that category. Recently, though, it has been understood that only some human categories follow the classical scheme of categorization, so that other non-classical categories have been admitted, as for instance *fuzzy* categories. Categories referred to, here, are rather characterized by a structure that cannot have any objective correspondence in reality, as in cases where imaginative aspects of the mind play a role in the nature of the categories: schematic organization, metaphor, metonymy, mental images; and also cases where the nature of the human body (perception, motor capacity) determines some aspects of the category.

In both cases, categories are not representative of natural objective aspects since what determines them are bodily and imaginative capacities. The role of the body in characterizing the meaning of concepts, as well as consideration of the imaginative human capacity as expressed by metaphors are only two types of experientialist

---

[18] This label is generally attributed to the predominant western philosophical and linguistic tradition, which considers meaning as reference, and truth as correspondence. Amongst examples of such theories are: the theory of Carnap, of Tarsky, and the referentialism inherited from American functionalism.

innovation. They draw from objectivism's failure concerning the relation between symbols and the world. What is needed therefore, in order to replace the objectivist vision of meaning, is a cognitive semantics capable of explaining meaning in relation to human beings, beyond referring to a metaphysical explanation of the reality external to human experience. The world experience is considered as connected to our active functioning and participation in the natural social environment. In this sense experience, our bodies, our innate capacities, motivate what is significant in human thought on the basis of a structure that is inherent in our experience, making a conceptual understanding possible.

On the basis of what has been said so far, it can be argued that the most abstract activity is founded upon topological schemas arising from experience.[19] As has been demonstrated, indeed, spatial relations of the "top-down" kind offer a structural orientation to large domains of knowledge and emotional states, an orientation that delimits and specifies our type of abstract reasoning. The value of the words we use for our most abstract concepts must be redirected to pragmatic factors and basic topological cognitive structures must be experientially motivated. This means that the link between pre-conceptual and conceptual structures respect to a specific physical and cultural environment precludes any attempt at framing the problem within objective and universal truth-conditions criteria. As a consequence, a "semantic of understanding" substitutes considerations of truth-values that are independent from human cognitive capacities.[20]

---

[19] As far as the distinction between abstract and concrete categories is concerned, the central idea is that of distinguishing between concepts derived essentially from physical experience and those abstract in themselves and not fully structured. The cognitive function of the metaphor will be made clear from the consideration of their inter-relation, that is, from the way in which abstract concepts are metaphorically structured on the basis of directly emerging concepts. As a matter of fact, even if, according to Lakoff, cultural presuppositions and beliefs always mediate our relations with the world, so that "every experience takes place within a vast background of cultural presuppositions" Lakoff and Johnson (1980, 57), it is nevertheless possible to establish a distinction between experiences that imply physical involvement, such as being in the erect position, from more culturally sensitive experiences. This distinction, at the experiential level, forms the basis of different conceptual categories. Lakoff defines concepts derived from the interaction of our body with the environment as directly emerging concepts, and the second as indirect concepts, the latter falling within a type of metaphorical structure. All our concepts of space, entity, temperature (warm-cold) – that is, concepts on the basis of which bodily states are defined – emerge directly from our interaction with the environment. Orientations such as top-down, front-back, inside-outside are functional to our disposition in space because they are the result of specific motor schemas. This differs strongly from the consideration given to the body in generative semantics: Chomsky (1991), for instance, considers experience simply as linguistic experience with the function of input in relation to the faculty of language. The problem of linguistic learning is thus reduced to the problem of finding which labels are used for pre-existing concepts.

[20] "The chief difference, then, between the Objectivist view of meaning and the non-Objectivist 'semantics of understanding' being proposed here can be summed up as follows: for the non-Objectivist, meaning is always a matter of human understanding which constitutes our experience of a common world that we make some sense of. A theory of meaning is a theory of understanding. And understanding involves image schemata and their metaphorical projections, as well

In the remaining part of this section, I wish to prove the relevance of an "integral view" of language, in order to demonstrate the pervasiveness of the experiential paradigm. This will further clarify the inadequacy of the generativist modular view of the mind, according to which the faculty of language works through an essential algorithmic manipulation of symbols. Generativism's basic principle lies in a double level of syntactic rules – deep structure and superficial structure –. This subordinates semantics to syntax, at the same time advancing the hypothesis that these two systems are completely autonomous domains.[21] If the separation between semantics and syntax has been a cross cutting issue conditioning the linguistic studies of the last thirty years, a crucial question it has helped to raise has been that of the type of foundation understanding possesses, that is, whether cognitive activity is a merely linguistic-syntactic endowment, or whether understanding is primarily a non-linguistic activity, upon which linguistic understanding is grounded.

In a well-known "mental experiment" called *The Chinese Room*, Searle (1980) imagined the emulation of the activity of a computer in the act of understanding an unknown language such as Chinese. According to standard procedures of elaboration, there would be a symbolic input of Chinese associated to other symbols through a programme of rules whose output consisted in the emission of further symbolic outputs. According to the theory of Schank and Abelson (1977), if inputs are questions over the story formulated in Chinese, and correct answers to the questions are obtained as outputs, it is possible to claim that the computer is capable of understanding the story itself (one could claim that this is just a new way of formulating Turing's experiment). Objecting to the reduction of the activity of the mind to syntactic-processes thus becomes Searle's primary objective. Searle claims that not only is it not possible to obtain an understanding of symbols by operating a correct manipulation of such symbols, but that it is not possible to consider syntax in natural languages simply as an explicative principle determining semantics. This leads to the hypothesis according to which human understanding, before being of the linguistic kind, is primarily of cognitive-experiential nature, so that grammar is a *non-arbitrary* result of activities grounded in experiential categorization.[22] The division of the semantic levels into lexical semantics, grammatical semantics and illocu-

---

as propositions. These embodied and imaginative structures of meaning have been shown to be shared, public, and -objective-, in an appropriate sense of objectivity" Johnson (1987, 174).

[21] "In many cases, the conviction that meaning can be more or less ignored in the study of language is clearly linked with a conviction that semantics is an independent field, which can be left to those who happen to be interested in meaning, while other linguists can devote themselves to something else – in particular, to syntax. Grammar in general, and syntax in particular, is seen as more or less autonomous of semantics, and can be pursued independently" Wierzbicka (1988, 1).

[22] "The basic idea behind the notion of 'grammatical semantics' is this. Every grammatical construction encodes a certain meaning, which can be revealed and rigorously stated, so that the meanings of different constructions can be compared in a precise and illuminating fashion, both within one language and across language boundaries. Grammar is not semantically arbitrary. On the contrary, grammatical distinctions are motivated (in the synchronic sense) by semantic distinctions; every grammatical construction is a vehicle of a certain semantic structure: and this is its raison d'être, and the criterion determining its range of use" Wierzbicka (1988, 3).

tionary semantics, together with their reciprocal interactions, explains the integral dimension of language-rules, for instance, speech act verbs such as "ask" can be said prima facie to belong to lexical semantics, whereas interrogative forms might be said to belong to grammar, whereas the meanings involved in both instances are of the same kind and therefore presuppose a common cognitive background from which they can be understood. One interesting implication of this is that if grammatical constructions encode semantic values, then "superficial differences" among languages, are no longer easily reducible to other linguistic structures, but reflect differences of semantic categorization and, indeed, of cognitive experiential categorization. Grammatical differences are thus experientially grounded differences in meaning, and the possibility of translating one language into another involves the possibility of having partially commensurable forms of semantic structures. If translation is possible, then one has to admit the presence of some universal experiences structuring the cognitive domain.[23]

One promising perspective of this kind is offered by ethnosyntax, that is, the study of the syntax of a speaking community in relation to its *Weltanschaung*. Starting from the premise of a substantial partial commensurability among languages, ethnosyntax attempts to investigate, by cross-linguistic comparison, beliefs underlying such different sets.

An example is provided by Wierzbicka (1988, 171ff), who examined actions directed to bodily parts within several European languages including French, Italian and Spanish. Propositions such as: "Pierre lui a lavé sa tête sale"; "Pierre lui a lavé la tête sale"; "Pierre lui a lavé la tête (*sale)" [Pierre washes his head], where the ambiguity of the referent "tête" in the first sentence can be solved by assuming a non co-referential value toward the subject, exhibit respectively different shades of semantic degree. In the first case, the result is that "the head" is intended as an autonomous bodily part which is not related to the person as according to the earlier introduced semantic vocabulary: "part of the body viewed as separate object, unrelated to the person"; whereas in the second case, even if the head is seen as an autonomous entity, the result is that it is also in relation to the person: "part of the body viewed as an object separate from, but related to, the person"; finally, the head as part of the body is seen completely as an aspect of the person: "part of the body viewed as an aspect of the person".

The three sentences constitute, thus, a sort of ascending semantic *climax* with respect to the degree of intimacy of relation between the person and the part of the body. Wierzbicka further considers that the same three possibilities of relation exist

---

[23] "What kinds of concepts is one most likely to find as one surveys conceptual systems? First kinaesthetic image schemas: concepts like up-down, 'in-out', 'part-whole', etc. Second, basic-level concepts for things, states, activities in one's immediate experience: body parts, plants and animals, basic-level artefacts, basic colours, basic emotions, etc Third, metaphorical concepts based on universal experiences: thus it would not be surprising to find 'more' being 'up', or 'anger' being understood in terms of 'heat' or 'pressure'. There are a fair number of such things that one would not expect to vary much. All of these are tied very closely to well-structured experience" Lakoff (1987, 336).

also in the case where examples of coreferentiality are considered between the agent and the receiver of the action. If this analysis is extended also to other Romance languages besides French, one would note some syntactic aspects are maintained unaltered. For instance, French, Italian and Spanish make use of the same syntactic structures for expressing indirect bodily action, whereas for what concerns the direct bodily action, Italian and Spanish take their distances from French, extending direct constructions also to contexts where French does not allow this: the French "Pierre pressait son (*le) nez contre la fenêtre", the Spanish "Pedro esta' poniendo la nariz en contra de la ventana", the Italian "Pietro sta schiacciando il naso contro la finestra".[24] From these examples one can infer that syntax not only proposes itself as a non-autonomous instrument of cognition in general, but that the same notion of "exception", too often adopted by generativists in the explanation of linguistic facts which cannot be explained on the basis of a general rule, can be largely dismissed.

The same approach can be fruitful regarding syntax.[25] Wierzbicka (1988) critically presents a study conducted by Cowan and Rakuŝan (1985), showing that syntactic exceptions are perfectly explainable under a semantic perspective. The argument under discussion concerns the relation between infinitive and subordinate propositions introduced by the particle *aby* [abi] in Czech. For instance:

Infinitive propositions

(1) Doctor se rozhodl viŝetrit yanu. (The doctor has decided to examine Jana).
(2) Eva xtyela studovat filozofiyi. (Eva has wanted to study philosophy)

Relative subordinate propositions

(1) Premluvia ysem doktora abi viŝetril yanu. (I have convinced the doctor to examine Jana).
(2) Matka rekla evye abi studovala filozofiyi. (Eva's mother has told her to study philosophy).

These are only a few of the possible examples, offering a general idea of the difference between the two types of constructions. Wierzbicka objects that if one had to translate into Czech sentences such as: "John has ordered Eva to do it", "John has prohibited Eva to do it", "John has forced Eva to do it",[26] one would expect subordinate constructions introduced by "*aby*" whereas, surprisingly, the correct translation considers infinitive syntagms, since in Czech verbs such as "to order" (naridit), "to prohibit" (zakarat), "to force" (prinudit), require this kind of construction. The semantic reason for such linguistic behaviour must be located in the fact that such verbs imply a high degree of control over the action to which they refer to. If, in general, one can postulate that, on the basis of a degree of determination of the action, the infinitive constructions are accompanied by coreferential subjects,

---

[24] Examples are taken from Wierzbicka (1988, 179).

[25] For a criticism of the generativist approach on cognitive basis, see Lakoff (1987, 470–471, 583–584).

[26] Wierzbicka (1988, 5ff).

whereas subordinate propositions introduced by "*aby*" follow non-coreferential subjects (since control is higher in the case it is oriented to determination of one's actions), then one can explain similar exceptions by recourse to their semantic structure. Finally, the semantic approach to grammar can be extended to the value distinction and function performed by adjectives and nouns. These two classes are not simply distinguishable by reference to their indication, respectively, of substances and qualities, but rather in the semantic structures they express. In the case of a sentence like "John is weak", the property described by the adjective "weak" is aligned with a potentially infinitive number of other possible properties attributable to the subject in question. In the case of "John is a weak", the substantivation of the adjective classifies John within a provisionally unique category hierarchically ordered above all the other possible classifications. The last point is directly linked to the notion of "kind" attached to the specific capacity of nouns, which in its turn has not to be seen in terms of compositional differential traits, as observed also by Putnam (1975). If the concept of "kind" is linked to the capacity of nouns to express a multiplicity of properties (as is relevant, for example, to the use of "smart", referring to a multiplicity of properties such as "being intelligent", "charismatic" etc.), then such multiplicity allows individuation of a well-defined class, whereas adjectives maintain only a descriptive function.

The web of knowledge associated with a noun behaves as the notional and cognitive background, thanks to which it is possible to obtain linguistic understanding. Without an intralinguistic and interlinguistic overlap of cognitive frames experientially grounded, neither communication nor mutual understanding would be realizable.

From the foregoing discussion it can be inferred that the emergence of a conceptual apparatus occurs in an interactive way, through person-to-person and person-to-environment relations. In the first case, one must take into account specific bodily and environmental properties which frame and structure higher processes of conceptualization, which in turn become increasingly dependent on the cultural and social interactional contexts of reference. Within this path of analysis, solipsistic or more generally disembodied approaches, are reinterpreted as grounded upon shared standards of physical interrelations with experience. In fact, the emergence of primary categorizations, such as image schemas, occurs only through an interactional bodily experience with the environment which, in due course, activates universally shared configurations of experiential conceptual frameworks.

As a consequence of this commonality of experiential conceptual frameworks, what have been named as conceptual bridgeheads must be understood on the basis of an embodied epistemic frame which reveals a cognitive and linguistic partial commensurability across cultural variations. Cross-cultural translation is possible thanks, for instance, to a limited choice of space-temporal options which also structure more abstract domains, though the content of the latter is more dependent on the cultural context. Given a shared system of space-temporal environmental relations where cultural variability is reduced to an *either-or* possibility of formal framing (in-out, up-down etc.), and given a widely shared basic level of categorization, it can be concluded that cognitive accessibility from divergent cognitive domains is unlimited, even in cases of partial failures of translation. Such a possibility, how-ever, occurs only within experientially significant categories which thus rule out any variant of the "view from nowhere" as a basis for assigning meanings.

1.3.1 Judgement and Truth

In the following section I will present one of the most crucial concepts developed in this work: the concept of judgement and the function it plays in relation to both an epistemic and a practical use. I will presently focus only on the epistemic func-tion of the reflective judgment, and will postpone an explanation of its function in political philosophy to later discussion. As will become apparent, however, while dependent on Kant my purpose is not that of proposing yet another reading of the *Third Critique*, but rather that of rethinking, in an idiosyncratic frame of reflection, several Kantian notions which I consider extremely useful for the understanding of the problems raised by epistemic and moral relativism, and of human rights, as will be clarified in the third chapter. Whenever required by expositive reasons, I will indicate my indebtedness to the work of Kant, even though his general con-tribution is to be read as part of a personal attempt at producing an independent argument.

In order to re-examine the problem of epistemic relativism, let us take the case of the Ptolemaic-Copernican diatribe, and see how it can be assessed without resorting to a neutral standard of evaluation:

C1 The earth is fixed and the planets move around it
(C1 is dependent upon standard S1)
Vs
C2 The sun is fixed and the planets move around it
(C2 is dependent upon standard S2)

Were one to defend a traditional-bound form of epistemic rationality, then claim 1 and claim 2 would remain reciprocally unassailable. Due to the impossibility of transcending one's own view according to a higher standard of epistemic validity exhibiting the same conditions in which both claims can be asserted, one would not be capable of trespassing the same condition of epistemic incommensurability and thus of relativism.

Nonetheless, the point which has been made thus far is that epistemic accessi-bility to epistemic schemes is never prevented, and that this leads to the possibility of projecting one's own truth-conditions into different and competing conceptual schemes when engaged in the activity of interpretation. Indeed, in the aforemen-tioned case, proponents of C1 and proponents of C2, in order to defend their own claims, must presuppose some sort of transcendental condition enabling each po-sition to claim legitimate truths. In other words each proponent, in order to be truth-pretending, must presuppose that her cognitive faculties and the achievement of the experiential truth be a transcendental condition whose possibility must be postulated *a priori*. But to admit such a transcendental condition for the possibility of truth is to admit also a notion for the "finality of the experience", which can be distinguished, according to Kant's view of finality, into a form of "subjective" and "objective" finality. The latter indicates the regulative understanding of the external world as if it followed an intelligent plan whereas the first is to be understood in terms of a transcendental condition for the validity of truth-claims "as if" our cognitive faculties were organized in such a way that the external world could be scientifically interpreted and that a notion of truth could be validly postulated as a standard to which our claims should conform.

Since the epistemic relativist also presupposes the form of transcendental finality of the experience, then epistemic relativism itself is refuted. Each competitor, indeed on the basis of such a regulative presupposition, is in the position of evaluating other arguments comparatively and then proceeding in the assessment of their explicatory force and insight in providing a motivated and internally coherent argument. In so doing, each would temporally transcend one's own interpretive frame while endorsing her reciprocal conflicting standard and consider it in view of an experiential regulative standard of validity. Due to the possibility of infinite epistemic accessibility among cognitive systems, in all such cases the competitor would be capable of moving into an extension of the truth-conditions for the validation of any submitted epistemic theory on the basis of a common presupposition based on a notion of experience as a regulative background and as a normative standard for the assessment of the validity of the truth-claims for any scientific model submitted to scrutiny.

It might be objected that such a view confuses truth with the notion of idealized warranted assertability and that epistemic agents placed in idealized conditions would invert what is to be ideally agreed because true with what is true due to an agreement reached in idealized conditions. The experiential epistemic approach allows the reformulation of this dichotomy by maintaining, in Habermasian terms, that "Although truth cannot be reduced to coherence and justified assertability, there has to be an internal relation between truth and justification" (Habermas, 2003a, 358). It thus recognizes that from within such internal relation, truth and belief can be separated so that from within a given context of justification arises the pragmatic necessity of postulating an unconditional counterfactual scenario of truth validity which, while exemplarily transcending its same context of origin, cannot but be postulated from a given context. The counterfactual anticipation of an exemplar consensus assumes, within the judgmental paradigm, a regulative function for those justificatory processes that are, on the one hand, always subordinated to fallibilism and possible revisions and, on the other hand, that are subordinated to validity conditions posed by the idea of an objectivity of the world which is itself subordinated to the transcendental finality of experience in its subjective and objective dimension.

Indeed, one can infer that there is an objective world out there only once she has assumed that if knowledge can be achieved, then this requires an experiential unity of the world. All this amounts to say that: from the assumption that I am epistemically enabled to produce a truth pretending knowledge of the world, I can assume that there must be indeed an objective world to be known. The relation between a truth pretending knowledge and the autonomy of an objective world is bi-directional, and it is this bi-directional mutual implication that is implied into the experiential paradigm. Instead, were one to postulate simply the transcendental objective unity of the world, then one would come to infer that from the necessary assumption of a transcendentally independent objective world out there, the possibility does follow of an objective reference and truth as according to a paradigm of internal realism. The point, although, is that the formulation of the assumption that an objective world must be postulated transcendentally cannot be assumed independently from an assumption about the epistemic possibilities of our faculties to know that something. In short, I cannot assume the existence of something which I cannot know at all since, in that case, I would rather postulate for the transcendental relevance of a chimera which would escape any process of argumentative validation.

I think Habermas saw this problem and in the development of his argument, he attempted to bend the presupposition of the objective unity of the world to the strictly entrenched intersubjective dimension of the understanding of something in the world, calling this interconnection of the objective and the intersubjective as an "unavoidable" condition from which we cannot step out (Habermas, 2007, 48). But, to my understanding, by not seeing the necessity of postulating both the objective and the subjective dimension of experience as pragmatic-transcendental conditions, the Habermasian model of validation of truth-claims remains unjustified precisely from the intersubjective perspective, weakening therefore the pretence of truth of the dialogical practice itself.

This point critically revises the Habermasian project for a detrascendentalisation of reason. Indeed, the required anticipation of the experiential finality of the world, both in its subjective and objective understanding, is prior to the Habermasian idealized presupposition of the objectivity of the world itself as a pragmatic transcendental premise of actors oriented to the formulation of epistemic judgments that enter a process of dialogical-argumentative validation (Habermas, 2007, 26ff). According to the experiential perspective, for epistemic agents, the very possibility of postulating a world of independently existing objects, that is, an identical world for everyone (Habermas, 2007, 31), is parasitic to the idealizing premise of a shared way of experiencing the world itself and of speaking of its truth conditions as according to the triangular dimension of subject to subject and subject to environment relations. Such experiential finality of the experience, which must be postulated as a pragmatic presupposition for the same possibility of providing a justification for epistemic truth, regulates transcendentally our epistemic orientation towards the world, submitting possible truth-claims to regulative functions played by the transcendental conditions for the finality of experience.

Coming back to the Kantian distinctions, whereas scientific judgments are to be constructed in conformity to the principle of finality used as according to its "objective" understanding, that is according to Kant, to its regulative function in relation to the chaotic multiplicity of the natural phenomena, from a transcendental point of analysis, the same teleological judgement relies upon a subjective condition of universality, that is, upon the notion of exemplarity of judgments as according to the "subjective" use of the principle of finality. This implies that the same scientific knowledge is dependent upon a non-logical condition, that is, upon an aesthetic dimension of our judgemental activity.

At the basis of the logic-scientific understanding of the world, there is thus a truly aesthetic transcendental condition for the validity of judgments which works in terms of an aesthetic anticipation of the experience in general forcing the judgmental activity to search for a universal rule not yet given.

In order to solve the difficulties encountered by epistemic relativism, I have claimed that relativist truth-claims can be understood only on the basis of a transcendental assumption of the finality of experience which must be presupposed as a universal condition for the possibility of the truth-validity of any supposedly relativistic assumption. And yet, if relativist claims according to their very declared pretension of truth must presuppose a non-relativistic condition of validity according to which each claim can advance a pretence of truth, then such supposedly relativistic assertions cease to appear as incommensurable standards of validity, and become instead a plurality of yet differentiated standards of rationality understandable from within the common presupposition of an *a priori* synthetic unity of the experience. Within such conditions, the notion of *sensus communis* as developed by Kant within his *Third Critique* postulates the requirement of an *a priori* consensus which can only be revealed, as far as it is possible, from an *a posteriori* condition of reflection. The notion of *sensus communis*, indeed, indicates the *a priori* condition of judging as members of a community, within an enlarged horizon of reflection – as a form of dialogical transperspectivity- through the consideration of other possible judgements. As Kant recognized, such form of judgment is characterized by the property of thinking autonomously, without the influence of prejudice, of thinking while keeping in mind other points of view in an "enlarged way" (*erweitert*), and of thinking coherently with one's own premises. The *sensus communis*, in as far as it is connected to the free play of imagination and intellect, produces a pleasure that is detached from specific interests and is independent from personal aims: due to the public status of such feeling of pleasure, the judgment pretends to a form of validity which, while being subjective, is nonetheless universally communicable. This position is strictly connected to the acknowledgement that the subject's capacity to grasp different points of view depends on her capacity to endorse a second-person perspective which, in turn, requires that *emotional recognition* of human fellows be categorically prior to the possibility of *cognition* in general, as Honneth (2005) has recently demonstrated. Honneth has provided an interesting combination of scientific data concerning autism and related deficiencies in emotional receptivity. An *ontogenetic* explanation of how and when children develop forms of empathy for the surrounding environment, as well as an explanation of the reasons why this is a prerequisite to cognition is there advanced. In his explanation, symbolic thought is strictly dependent upon the capacity of the subject to engage in emotional identification with others in a form of an "empathetic engagement or sympathy", so that in the case our recognition of another person is not, so to say, positive, there remains "a residual intuitive sense of not having done full justice to their personalities" (Honneth, 2005, 123). When the process of recognition is not activated, the resulting attitude towards others takes the form of a reification of ethical and cognitive categorization: "One could say with Dewey that in this case reification consists in nothing but this reflexive act of detachment through which we, for the purpose of attaining objective knowledge, extract ourselves from the experience of qualitative interaction in which all of our knowledge is always already anchored" (Honneth, 2005, 126). The pretence of an external point of observation falls short of a process of reification which, also in the case of non-human objects, produces a form of emotional and intellectual blindness (Honneth, 2005, 133). Hence, from this picture it emerges that knowledge is characterized by an interactional process with the human and the surrounding environment which offers an experiential grip on the world and which grounds interpersonal processes of language acquisition and learning. As previously mentioned, it is only once a transcendental presupposition of the unity of the world with the self, or in other words of the truth of experience in accordance to its transcendental finality is established, that the validity of judgments can be understood in terms of *transperspectivity*.[27] Transperspectivity implies reflective processes of evaluation of other perspectives, as well as of their possible integration, into a more articulated, justified view. This process involves acts of imagination which make possible the understanding of others' viewpoints and rational criticism of the proposed scenarios. Self-reflection is combined with reflection about others' perspectives: it is a two-way process, implying a moving back and forth between "us" and "others".

Within this perspective, also the classical objectivist notion of the self is reinterpreted in terms of an experientalist self that is not pre-established or fixed outside the realm of experience in which deliberations take place but is instead involved in a constant process of transformation aimed at the progressive definition of its own cognitive identity.[28] The possibilities for self-transcendence and imaginative transformation are always located within the presupposition of the unity of the experience, which hence sets conditions for the envisaging of yet new cognitive possibilities. Not all experiential events in one's life can be brought into coherence. Still, the constant endeavour to achieve a synthetic unity, on the pain of disintegration of the self, leads to the search for a meaningful narrative structure in accordance with the transcendental unity of the experience.

Once such transcendental unity of the experience has been presupposed, then the actual narrative structure of the self is thus evaluated from a contextual standpoint of observation through hypothetical normative structures of choice presented to us in

---

[27] Johnson (1993, 241).

[28] As Johnson claims: "A self-in-process, which is what each of us is, is a self that is continually both searching for its identity (i.e., trying to find itself in its ends, actions, feelings, moods, attitudes, experiences) and is contemporaneously trying to form itself in accordance with its imaginative ideals of what it might be" (1993, 149).

terms of descriptive analysis of options aimed at optimizing adaptive behaviours.[29] The experiential framework here defended, while rejecting an *a priori* determination of possible objects of knowledge in favour of contextualist and embedded learning process, does not intend to propose a naturalization of reason. Neo-Darwinist self-descriptions as rational beings struggling for adaptation in the environment are therefore re-understood in the context of a regulative idea of judgmental truth, so that the normative orientation of reason towards agreement precedes, logically, our instrumental and functional mechanisms of adaptation as natural beings.

---

[29] On the metaphorical and unconscious process underlying the notion of the self see Lakoff and Johnson (1999, 267–289).

Chapter 2
Beyond Moral Relativism and Objectivism

So far I have defended an epistemic perspective which rests between the two extreme poles of cognitive objectivism and relativism. While rejecting any approach that strays from a situated critical perspective of evaluation, I have also underscored the incoherencies arising from any theory which renounces the formulation of any normative force from within an experiential perspective of reflection. In this chapter, I further investigate my initial insights by extending the scope of the proposed approach to the moral and political realm. For this reason, in the following I consider the challenge that moral relativism and objectivism present to any pretension of universality in morality, while maintaining the objective of formulating an initial frame of understanding for a non objectivist and a non relativist justification of human rights principles. The beginning of this chapter is devoted to the clarification of the methodological difficulties that certain approaches face in the assessment of moral validity, and it is only with the final paragraph that a more precise alternative to the discussed views will be suggested. Indeed, as will be apparent from later discussion, the idea of the "ethical life" intersects both the moral and the legal domain from an institutional perspective, so as to assign a specific functional role to it, thus defining the contribution which a political philosophical approach is capable of providing. Those who see absolute incommensurability between moral codes implicitly assume that individuals or cultural moral systems are subjective practices whose validity relies on inherently private norms. This assumption entails an understanding of different moral systems as independent monads whose criteria of validity are neither transferable nor assessable from an external point of view. In some ways, this form of moral relativism recalls the previously discussed argument for the inadequacy of a private language. Here the inconsistency of the relativist argument relies either on the implicit contradiction between the assertion of a relativist point of view pretending to some truth or, in its more refined form, to the subordination of a normative "ought" to a factual motivation, as in the case of Harman's "quasi-absolutist" understanding of moral relativist statements.

In this case, as in the first chapter, the rejection of several forms of relativism does not necessarily lead to blind acceptance of competitive classical models of universalism. It is as if there were some unquestionable truths both in relativism and

C. Corradetti, *Relativism and Human Rights*, DOI 10.1007/978-1-4020-9986-1_2,
© Springer Science+Business Media B.V. 2009

in universalism which compels us to formulate a new paradigm for dealing with the difficulties arising in both cases. The seriousness of the claims advanced by both classical universalists such as Nagel and pluralistic relativists such as Wong can be appreciated in view, respectively, of the relevance that a criterion of validity has in moral reasoning and of the relevance of pluralism in modern societies. Indeed, while I reject Nagel's conclusion that moral validity favours impersonal reasons, I retain his considerations for a public assessment of competitive moral paradigms. Reversely, while I refute Wong's relativist conclusions excluding the possibility of establishing defeating arguments for moral assessibility, I incorporate his insights into pluralist universalism. As opposed to Wong's pluralistic relativism, my formulation of pluralism is inscribed within a single formal framework of conditions of communicative agency. Thus, while Wong's relativism maintains an external connection and coexistence between objective and relativist judgments, the form of pluralistic universalism that I defend accepts variation as morally sound only having fulfilled formal conditions of mutual recognition.

Thus, pluralistic universalism establishes a stringent interconnection between universal constraints and pluralist configurations, since it rejects a double standard of truth validity as internally articulated into an abstract universal standard plus a non universalizable contingent one. What emerges from such an enquiry is the necessity to admit certain unavoidable conditions of communicative agency through the formulation of a notion of mutual recognition. To this preliminary condition, it follows that the validity of pluralistic configurations advances a second standard, that of exemplar validity, which springs precisely from the reflective use of judgment.

The final paragraph attempts to underpin the dynamics of a dialectic of recognition within the public realm. The confrontation of publicly valid models of morality gives place to a dialectical movement as embedded within the same process of recognition. While this idea is fully developed in the third chapter, here I reconstruct its seminal relevance within some of the most indicative Hegelian texts.

2.1 Forms of Moral Relativism

Moral relativism can be thought of at three different levels: descriptive, normative and metaethical. Normative relativism claims that moral requirements apply to different moral agents or groups of agents since they are relative to the internal principles of such agents and groups. Normative relativism does not simply claim a *de facto* distinction based on observational data of the differences among individual and cultural moral systems; it defends instead the stronger view according to which peoples *ought* to follow their own internal individual or cultural principles. By claiming this, normative relativism seems to conflate what is *morally required* with what is *approvable* from an internal perspective, that is to say, it tends to *reduce* what is morally required to what is morally acceptable as a motivation to action.

Internalism of this kind considers psychological motivation as a source of moral reason, where moral reason cannot determine an action if it is connected only to a moral requirement. There seems to be confusion, here, between motivation and morally right action for an agent. Indeed, for any action, the fact that one does not have a psychological motivation for that action does not imply that it is not morally right. Variation in psychological motivations is not coextensive with variation in moral rightness: one can be obliged to act in a certain way even when there is no personal psychological motivation to act that way. While such two notions must be kept distinguished, they provide necessary and sufficient conditions for action only when combined.

Normative relativism can also be proved self-contradictory. This self-contradiction becomes apparent if one reconstructs what it amounts to when the notion of culture is limited to a source of moral justification:

(a) cultures are the moral sources for individual actions, so what is morally right is culturally context-dependent
(b) one must act in accordance with her own cultural context
(c) therefore, it is wrong to defend the universality of moral principles

The implied inference derivable from (a) and (b) is that cultural bias has a universal validity *per se* if considered from a third person perspective. This means that to conclusion (c) one can add a further conclusion:

(c^1) principle (b), according to which one must act according to her cultural context, has universal validity.

Evidently (c) and (c^1) are self-contradictory statements, and therefore the argument is unsound, and cultural ethical incommensurability cannot be defended on the basis of normative relativism. Certainly, there exist more sophisticated philosophical strategies for defending normative relativism, most of which would escape the above mentioned difficulties. Some of the most prominent ones, such as those recently presented by Harman and Wong will be considered along the next sections.

Normative relativism is distinct from descriptive relativism and metaethical relativism: indeed descriptive relativism is limited to the observation of pure differences between moral systems and does not express value judgments about whether such differences are normatively justified with reference to different cultural contexts; the second affirms the impossibility of defining the notion of moral truth *tout court*, favouring nihilist or emotivist positions.

As stated, descriptive relativism recognizes that cultural practices differ, but it also adds the stronger claim that such differences lead to a strong form of incommensurability conducing to fundamental moral disputes that are neither reducible to non-moral disagreement nor rationally resolvable. Descriptive relativism, in order to defend its claim, must therefore show that all sets of cultural practices amount to permanently not resoluble conflicting views. This point remains far from having been demonstrated, due to both methodological criticisms that can be advanced against supposedly "neutral" observations about what counts as relevant for differing cultural practices, and the fact that the same possibility of theorizing extensive disagreement implies agreement on a large portion of overlapping beliefs. As far as the first point is concerned, there seems to be, indeed, a kind of "empirical under-determination" in the claim advanced by descriptive relativism (Moody-Adams, 2001, 93–106). First of all, determination of what counts as relevant data in an empirical practice implies non-empirical assumptions concerning what is to count as an empirical evidence of that practice. For instance, empirical determination of the concept of truth – and relevant practices associated with it within a culture – presupposes in the observer a complex notion of what counts as relevant in framing the notion of truth, with the additional burden of proving this notion as valid towards possible divergent definitions within the observer's cultural domain. Moreover, empirical data apparently defining a cultural practice as incommensurably different often result from studies that have failed to consider the presence of internal criticism within that same culture which rejects that practice.

The approach to cultural diversity has led to the treatment of empirical differences as fundamentally irreconcilable practices causing fundamental moral conflict. But why should such conflicts be taken as fundamentally unsolvable? Descriptive relativists would answer that their thesis of the irreconcilability of moral fundamental cultural conflicts is proven by the presence of opposing evaluations for the same type of action. If there is an agreement on the properties of the action, but a clash over its evaluation, then the two views are incommensurably divergent. The point here is that if empirical under-determination is true of relativism, then it is not at all clear whether such a sharp distinction can be drawn,[1] or on the contrary, if evaluative disagreement is possible, then a large amount of agreement over the properties of the action must be presupposed. For this reason, even if one concedes to descriptive relativists that there is extensive moral disagreement, this does not imply that they are more widespread than possible overlapping agreements. Instead, it seems the opposite; that is, the same possibility of theorizing extensive disagreement implies agreement on a large portion of overlapping beliefs. Such consideration can take two different routes: an *a posteriori* argument according to which descriptive moral relativism is simply false (Walzer, 1994), or an *a priori* argument rejecting absolute moral incommensurability (Davidson, 1982).

As far as the *a posteriori* argument is concerned, such a reply advances a factual denial of the notion of a fundamental clash of beliefs among cultures (Walzer, 1994). It might be simply untrue that cultures present opposing views over central beliefs,

---

[1] "The problem is that it is profoundly difficult to construct a reliable description of the moral practices of an entire *culture* – a description of the sort that could license judgments contrasting one culture's basic moral beliefs with those of other cultures. To be sure, some of the difficulties in formulating the contrastive judgments needed to defend descriptive relativism reflect methodological obstacles that plague the construction of *any* reliable descriptive morality and not simply a description of the moral practices of a given culture" Moody-Adams (2001, 103).

such as the approval/disapproval of killing an innocent for fun. This line of argumentation takes the form of recognition of basic rational rules that a society has to promote for the survival of its members and of itself. If members live under conditions of strong physical insecurity, if no rules regulate relations among members of the society, if every form of prevarication escapes sanctioning, then there is nothing to gain in being part of a group, bringing society to collapse.

That societies in general, in order to ensure their own continued existence, must be structured around some central moral laws, constitutes a strong argument against the idea of a fundamental clash of beliefs between cultures as defended by descriptive relativists. If cultures do not clash in any fundamental way, then absolute moral incommensurability is ruled out, and if it is ruled out, incommensurability remains only partial.

This point bears important connections with the *a priori* argument against descriptive relativism. Indeed, if this argument were true, then also the Davidsonian argument against total incommensurability could become instructive for the moral sphere when applied to the case of moral schemes. In such cases, according to the Davidsonian lines of reasoning, the interpretative activity of the morality of a different culture can be successful only if a large portion of one's beliefs are projectable into the target domain. As already introduced in the first chapter, the "charity principle" indeed states that one must allow that the interpreted system satisfies a general standard of coherence and similarity of, at least, some of the features adopted for its understanding, on the pain of total failure of interpretation. Therefore, if intercultural moral interpretation is possible (since other moral systems are never totally alien to us) then at least partial commensurability in terms of an overlapping of values must be admitted.

The point now becomes whether the notion of partial moral commensurability, if taken seriously, can be used in order to defend a certain notion of commensurability within the moral domain, so that it would eventually be considered in accordance with its dependence upon such a criterion of commensuration. The Davidsonian argument, though, does not seem to be easily applicable in this case, not only because of the deep ethical disagreements existing among cultures, but also because of the same evaluative language implied in morality. Indeed, in the case of a *prima facie* shared belief such as "do not kill an innocent for fun!" further disagreements might arise when defining the meaning of what it is to be an "innocent" or of what it is "killing for fun". The outcome would be that no intercultural common practice would derive from a *prima facie* shared belief.

And yet, even if the Davidsonian charity principle cannot be useful in determining *directly* a possible commonality of comparable intercultural goods as such, it can nevertheless be *indirectly* confirmed when addressing what *common presuppositions* might be agreed as universal conditions of purposive agency, so that the specific views of the agents' goods might then be validly restricted and become partially commensurable as according to such agency presuppositions. According to the main distinctions presented above, it is possible to infer that even if descriptive relativism can be reconnected with anti-relativistic theories at the normative level, due to the fact that one can recognize empirical incommensurabilities without thinking that they are morally justified, meta-ethical relativism, in turn, can be re-joined both with positions of normative relativism and with positions of normative universalism.[2]

There are two main versions of metaethical relativism that must be accordingly distinguished: the first is absolute metaethical relativism and the second is moderate metaethical relativism. Absolute metaethical relativism is not simply a form of moral scepticism. Moral scepticism admits that even if one cannot presently know the answer to a moral question, it is possible that there is one correct moral answer. Absolute metaethical relativism, instead, denies that there are any moral truths to be known and believed at all, so that the impossibility of denying or confirming a moral claim is not contingently postponed but remains unassessable in principle. An immediate reply to this position is that it claims what it pretends to reject: if a moral statement is not subjected to any truth or falsity, then the same statement is neither true nor false and thus uninformative. Additionally, evidence in support of metaethical relativism is drawn from persistent moral disagreement. The point here is that the mere fact that there is a persistent disagreement between different moral views does not rule out, in itself, the possibility of admitting true objective answers to moral questions, and therefore the wrongness of views conflicting with such truths.

If absolute metaethical relativism claims that there are neither true nor false standards of validity for moral claims, and that, whatever moral judgment is thought to be true, there is no possibility of either confirming or disproving it, moderate metaethical relativism admits instead that in ideal conditions of deliberation, different doctrines might have the possibility of convergence over common valid standards of morality, or more specifically, moderate metaethical relativism claims that: "[...] there are at least *some* instances of conflicting ethical opinions that are equally valid" (Brandt, 1959, 275), and thus that forms of normative universalism can be admitted from within a metaethical criterion of validity.

A slightly alternative form of understanding of metaethical relativism consists in distinguishing two sub-thesis, one negative and one positive, the former denying any possibility of truth or falsity to moral statements as in the case of non-cognitivist positions, and the latter claiming that from the impossibility of establishing objectively valid universal principles it is still possible to justify these as true or false only relative to a cultural group or society. Positive metaethical relativism, therefore, bears some interesting connections with normative relativism, since it does not simply deny the truth-validity of any possible moral justification, but it suggests the possibility that moral principles can be validly conceived of only "in connection with" some cultural practices and that the standards of moral validity in such cultural practices differ so much that there is no rational common ground one can appeal to for solving such divergences.

---

[2] Normative relativism, instead, presupposes empirical relativism, since it does not make any sense to assert that one is justified in following his personal or group rule if it is not also admitted that moral systems are descriptively different as well.

One difficulty with such an argument is that it presupposes a clearly defined understanding of the separateness of cultural groups, and such a clear-cut differentiation seems quite naïve. Indeed, it is not only true that socio-cultural groups do indeed hybridize by importing and exporting cultural practices, but also that individuals themselves do often belong to different groups, each promoting opposite views on specific problems. Such mythological view of the absolute separateness of social embeddings seems thus inadequate for the understanding of the actual phenomena implied in the socio-cultural interactions. Indeed, were it true, it would also have to explain on the basis of which normative priority an individual belonging to different socio-cultural groups bearing conflicting moral insights would have to prioritize one group's moral authority over another. Above I have distinguished between absolute and moderate metaethical relativism and claimed that the latter does indeed admit the possibility of at least some irreconcilable moral divergences. One interesting implication of the distinction between such two forms of metaethical relativism is that since weak metaethical relativism is content with the minimal possibility of admitting at least *some* irresolvable moral conflicts, it indirectly claims that aside from some delimited cases it is nevertheless possible in many instances to assign conditions of truth validity. If the possibility of truth conditions is implied by weak-metaethical positions, then this means that whereas strong metaethical arguments can admit only non-cognitivist positions, weak metaethical theories are instead compatible with cognitivist moral theories. In the following I will consider the case of Rawlsian constructivism, and in particular some aspects of his reflective equilibrium, and evaluate how this form of moral justification can be interpreted in accordance with an idea of weak metaethical relativism. In order to critically assess the notion of reflective equilibrium, it is necessary first to reconstruct this notion in its full complexity. Reflective equilibrium is a theory of moral justification that seeks to find coherence in our moral views and theories. A distinction can be drawn between wide and narrow reflective equilibria.

While reflective equilibrium attempts to achieve coherence between: (a) a set of considered moral judgments, (b) a set of moral principles, (c) a set of background theories (Daniels, 1996, 22). Narrow reflective equilibrium seeks to achieve coherence only with respect to (a) and (b). Both are opposed to foundational methods of moral justification, which can be characterized by reference to the distinction between beliefs not requiring a justification because they are self-evident, and beliefs requiring justification, the latter being logically dependent upon the former. Rawls's approach in A *Theory of Justice* can be seen as being based on wide reflective equilibrium since different layers, ranging from moral, considered judgments to background theories are all present in his discussion.

With respect to the definition of considered moral judgments, substantially stronger and weaker criteria can be distinguished. According to Rawls, considered judgments best display our moral capacity without distortion since they must be those of which we are most convinced (Rawls, 1971, 47). This places a tighter check over such judgments being, in some way or another, mistaken. Weaker criteria for considered moral judgments, by contrast, refer only to the *circumstances* out of which one's judgments arise: for instance, if a person is "upset or frightened", or likely to "gain one way or the other" (Rawls, 1971, 48) her judgments will not pass the test. Thus, stronger criteria positively identify what can be qualified as "considered" via a critical assessment that filters out judgments passing the test. Weaker criteria instead fix negative constraints which exclude faulty judgments, with reference to the conditions under which they are proffered.

This analysis raises several problems. First of all, Rawls does not clearly define thicker conditions of evaluation for entering reflective equilibrium. It seems that critical assessment might consist in trying to universalise one's judgment in order to evaluate whether it is biased in nature, via the presence of a personal interest, for instance. Yet even a process of universalization which extends recognition of a personal interest in morality universally does not seem logically out of bounds. On the contrary: in some circumstances, it seems intuitively right to move from a third person neutral detachment to first-person interest in moral reasoning, as in the case of a strongly rational self-interest (personal survival) defeating the dictates of moral reason.[3] Further, there is an additional, and more technical, problem if we accept stronger criteria for considered judgments. Here, the point would be that if evaluation of the correctness of the belief formation process is initially undertaken by *self-evaluation* of how one arrived at a specific judgment, and if such a judgment can be universalised, then there would be no work of moving back and forth for reflective equilibrium to perform. This is because the task of comparing raw material with its possible universalization would be done *before* the activity provided by reflective equilibrium.

There is still another final point to observe. I have laid emphasis on the fact that the evaluative process for defining judgments as considered judgments is a *self-evaluative* process of analysis. I think that this characterization prevents the subject from understanding most of the social, educational and psychological factors contributing to her definition of what counts as "considered", in her view. *Self-evaluative* patterns of analysis are blind towards unconsciously acquired prejudices and cultural biases, whereas a dialogical and transcultural form of assessment can reveal such limits. Since Rawls's notion of reflective equilibrium seems to be founded on the stronger criteria approach, his analysis is exposed to the criticisms of foundationalism over coherentism: foundationalism would seem even more patent in the case that the constituent role of rationality is assigned to a restricted list of primary goods, which are taken to be objective goods governing the actual process of justification. Despite such difficulties, by subjecting considered judgements to revision, it is still possible to defend a weak version that is not committed to the notion of fixed points.

---

[3] As it is claimed by Brandt: "[...] a rational person's moral motivations might not always control conduct, even if they had the strength characteristic of a welfare-maximizing moral system. For this optimal welfare-maximizing degree of moral motivation might be weaker than self-interested motives in some situations. Just as it is uneconomic to punish a theft of one dollar by a twenty-year prison sentence, so it may be uneconomic for moral motivations to be developed adequately to ensure that the moral motivation will be superior in absolutely every case" Brandt (1979, 335).

One can distinguish between two readings: one that completely dispenses with the epistemic relevance of considered judgments, and another which treats them as "initial points of interpretation" (Daniels, 1996). The former hypothesis seems to be counterintuitive: it is difficult to see how one can arrive at acceptance of a moral standard by avoiding any form of consideration concerning her own deep beliefs. The second hypothesis appears more interesting, since it takes considered judgments only as initially plausible starting points that are subject to revision during the process of analysis.

However, even the latter case poses difficulties. It seems implausible that a person would be ready to reject her own deepest convictions if they do not cohere with a theory. Nor are the normative criteria by which one should decide to drop her own deepest commitments for a specific theory clearly identified. Indeed, this role cannot be assigned to the widest explicatory role of the theory, because it demonstrates an either/or choice, and not a wider explicatory advantage of the theory with respect to the starting judgment.

For a general assessment, one can reconsider the broad justificatory validity of the wide reflective equilibrium within the frame of the "original position" as a device for choosing just principles. I have already observed that this justificatory tool aims to bring into coherence a triple set of beliefs held by a person (considered moral judgments, moral principles, and relevant background theories), and that it encounters various problems. Now, I will deepen this criticism and show how wide reflective equilibrium can lead to a form of weak metaethical relativism. As already noted, wide reflective equilibrium fails to specify a substantive normative constraint capable of guiding modification of either considered moral judgments themselves, or moral principles and background theories, in order to maximize coherence within a triple set of beliefs. This produces three possible forms of criticism: (a) the still unsolved charge of intuitionism deprived of sound justification; (b) the possibility of two contradictory considered judgments leading to at least two coherent triple sets of beliefs; which leads to (c) the charge of weak metaethical relativism under specific circumstances.

It is possible to allow Rawls that considered moral judgments are subject to revision, and that validation of moral principles is not restricted to a circular notion of "best fit" with considered moral judgments (as it would be in a narrow equilibrium), if validation relies on an "independence constraint" which links specific considered judgments (a′) differing from those (a) linked to moral principles, in such a way that moral principles can be independently justified by coherence between a specifically different set of considered judgments (a′) with background theories (Daniels, 1996, 83). Nevertheless, this does not discharge Rawls from the duty to anchor his justificatory process in *actual convergence* rather than in *de jure convergence*, in such a way as to prevent *complete revision* of initial considered judgments after establishment of an independent constraint. In other words, even if the independent constraint allows a non-circular justification of moral principles, possible revision of considered moral judgments "cohering with" the principles cannot proceed beyond a certain limiting point. This leads to the second point, namely the impossibility, within the single subject, of taking a position as regards two contradictory considered moral judgments.

Indeed, were no answer available to the dilemma brought forth by two contradictory considered judgments, one would be allowed to construct two different coherent triple sets of beliefs, each of which would be perfectly unassailable from its own internal perspective, hence leading to normative and metaethical relativism, due to the justification for multiple reflective equilibria within an infra-systemic core of beliefs that it would offer.

One reply to this is that while this eventuality can be admitted in principle, it is hard to see it happening in practice, for example, because self-identity or epistemic constraints would force a decision in the direction of one option or another.

Still, even if one were to admit that, in practical terms, a subject always fixes on one, definite option, the problem then becomes that of isolating the overarching criteria by which one is allowed to select between conflicting options in such cases.[4]

Regarding the question of epistemic constraints, one could respond that a determination of which theory is capable of explaining more principles and intuitions could motivate an assessment between two contradictory reflective equilibria. If this is the ultimate basis of assessment of the best moral theory, it seems that the relational property of coherence exhibited by reflective equilibrium is a trivial qualification for the assessment of moral codes. Further, one would change a qualitative property of assessment into a quantitative one, coming to say that, all else equal, the greater the number of moral principles, considered judgments and background theories that are explained by one type of morality, the more this theory approaches validity.

However, this would seem to suggest the prospect of an exceptionally broad and abstract position opting for reductionism, oriented to the inclusion of a large amount of moral theories into a small core of central properties. In the case such a manoeuvre is not accepted due to its inappropriateness, then the consequence would be that of a notion of weak metaethical relativism rehabilitated precisely from within the Rawlsian notion of reflective equilibrium, since this latter would implicitly recognize the difficulty of finding a rational solution to all possible conflicting moral views.

An interconnected position derivable from metaethical and descriptive relativism is that presuming to draw the normative validity of tolerance from the general impossibility of rationally solving moral conflicts. According to such position, that one ought to tolerate moral diversity is a normative position resulting not simply from the descriptive evidence of moral incommensurabilities, but rather from the impossibility of establishing universal criteria of moral validity capable of solving all forms of moral conflict. The normative force of toleration, in this sense, is implied by the endorsement of descriptive and metaethical positions, and it constitutes rather a logical interconnected consequence more than a form of relativism in itself. To tolerate diversity, is not to be prevented from disapproval but to be obliged not to interfere with others' moral practices. Now, the point is whether it is correct to establish a logical implication from moral relativism to the normative

---

[4] I am indebted to a conversation with Ferrara for this point.

obligation of toleration. For instance, were one to uphold simply a descriptive form of moral relativism, then, from the assumption that moral disagreement is fairly widespread, it would not be possible to conclude that one *ought* to be tolerant. Similar difficulties can be advanced also in the case of any form of strong metaethical relativism which would result incapable of defending the normative universal validity of toleration due to the same impossibility of defending any form of moral truth. Accordingly Graham (2001, 226–240), claims that it is easier to establish a connection from toleration to objectivity in morality, once that it has been distinguished from absolutism, rather than to justify either the opposite relation or the connection of toleration with moral relativism. For instance, it is not clear why from the perspective of non-cognitivist or non-realist theories considering that nothing in morality can be established as true, it is possible to draw the conclusion that one ought to be tolerant. Indeed, from the fact that neither tolerance nor intolerance can be justified as true moral claims, it follows that there cannot be any relation of implication between relativism and tolerance. Whereas, on the contrary, if one keeps faith to the fact that objective truth might be the result of the assessment of conflicting positions in the public realm which ought to be granted the possibility of challenging any unreflectively accepted rule, then one would move from the normative necessity of establishing the validity of toleration, to the commitment to objective truth; to quote Graham's key passage at this regard: "If we think that the emergence of truth requires a process of conjecture and refutation and further think, as Mill does, that the validity of moral, religious, and philosophical doctrines requires the constant challenge presented by false competitors, we will have to allow social space for *some* false conjectures. Only by doing so will our grasp of the truth and that of others remain "lively", Mill thinks; more important, only by allowing the possibility of tolerated false conjectures can we reasonably look for the avoidance of error and the emergence of new truths, because 'The fatal tendency of mankind to leave off thinking about a thing when it is no longer doubtful, is the cause of half their errors' " (2001, 237. The quotation is from Mill, 1975, 54).

A more promising alternative for the justification of toleration, which avoids most of the difficulties presented above, is the one recently defended by Nickel and Reidy with a specific reference into the role played by human rights in the international scenario (2008). Such authors defend a notion of toleration on the basis of a defence of a principle of modest prescriptive relativism, which combines the normativity of toleration with the recognition of a list of objectively universal principles of human rights. First of all, in respect to the previous attempts trying to derive toleration from relativist moral positions, modest prescriptive relativism is connected with a form of thin moral objectivity. Also, it differs from strong prescriptive relativism because whereas this latter claims that "tolerance of moral diversity is the only value or norm for which there are good objective moral reasons of universal application", the former considers that there are "additional universally binding values or norms, but insist[s] that they are few in number and sufficiently narrow or abstract that they do not undermine the commitment to tolerating a very wide range of morally diverse values systems, cultures, ways of life, and legal and institutional arrangements" (Nickel and Reidy, 2008, 3). If absolute prescriptive relativism is an untenable position, due to the unconstrained range of application of the same principle of toleration even to morally intolerable practices, modest prescriptive relativism presents itself as a more defensible position. Toleration in this latter sense, occurs within conformity to universal objective principles of human rights whose vague formulation, within international charters of human rights, allows for states' self-determination as according to situational variation and implementation. Principled-constrained toleration of this sort, therefore, allows for balancing rights as according to contextual variation; it does so by harmonizing the universality of human rights with the states' value to self-determination and equality at the international level. So far so good. It seems that such a notion of toleration can save both moral universalism and cultural contextual variation. In any case, do we really now need a notion of toleration besides that in the a form of recognition matched by a criterion of exemplar validity of human rights judgmental evaluations? That is to say that: if each socio-cultural system, upon acceptance of some general principles of human rights, is allowed to produce human rights judgments in terms of a differentiated balance of rights in respect to a variation of circumstances, can't we simply claim that from whichever situated position we occupy, each of the well-produced judgments exhibit an exemplar validity in itself? It is not the case, then, that one has to tolerate diversity, but it is rather the more intriguing case of recognizing the validity, that is, the necessary exemplarity, of each normatively well-formed human rights judgment. I will return to this point later, when arguing for a theory of principled-constrained exemplar validity leading to a form of pluralistic universalism of human rights judgments.

Due to the several difficulties involved into the moral relativist arguments considered thus far, one might wonder whether morality can be best underpinned by a certain number of objective moral properties. For objectivist moral theories, indeed, facts exhibiting objective moral properties are taken to fix the preconditions for the establishment of a notion of rationality. According to such positions, facts are good or bad independently of the internal reasons an individual might endorse for their approval or disapproval even under an ideal condition of deliberation. Standards of rationality deriving from an objectivist consideration of moral facts imply that, once relevant objective properties are established, it is irrational to prefer the lesser good to the greater good, whatever is the present motivational set of the subject.

Even if such positions seem to be better placed when confronted with some of the relativist self-contradictory weakness, I believe that objectivism cannot be proved as it stands. Facts cannot be taken as good or bad *independently* of a subject, and the good and the bad are categories strictly interconnected with our interaction with the environment whose results provide us with an embodied notion of rationality. In the present chapter I will address only some of the difficulties which objectivists encounter due to their persistent separation of subjectivity from objectivity, leading to a "view from nowhere". Such criticism will then introduce a perspective which I will develop later starting from the analysis of the Habermasian theory for the normative validity of speech acts. As a result of such analysis, I will derive what are to be considered the fundamental experiential presuppositions for purposive action. It is indeed only from *the recognition* of such conditions that it will become possible, then, to formulate exemplarily valid judgments of human rights satisfying the condition of pluralistic universalism.

2.2 The Two Horns of the Dilemma: Relativism versus Objectivism

Moving from within a classical paradigm of philosophical analysis and once considered the conceptual inadequacies as in the above-mentioned forms of moral relativism, one might be tempted to think that only the defence of an objectivist perspective on morality might be capable of providing the most adequate alternative to the defence of the validity of practical reason. Indeed, objectivism in morality has traditionally been opposed to those forms of sceptical or of post-modern philosophies which have sought to prove as a metaphysical trap any attempt to solve moral disputes on the basis of an Archimedean point. Moral objectivism can be defined as a family of doctrines all sharing at least the idea that "there is or must be some permanent, a-historical matrix or framework to which we can ultimately appeal in determining the nature of rationality" (Bernstein, 1983, 8). From this, it follows that objectivism claims that moral validity constitutes a pre-given standard of truth which can only be discovered, not constructed, by rational investigation. Such pre-fixed structures of moral rationality, claim objectivists, provide us with an un-modifiable standard of validity whose ultimate foundation is subtracted from the changing conditions of our socio-political environment, and in particular from the perspective assigned to the subjectivity of each moral agent. Indeed, moral actions do possess objective properties which define the limits of what is to count as properly moral. If not from a naïve metaphysical perspective, objectivism has more often taken the form of an objective universal reason, whose laws ought to govern our practical actions. It is precisely this neutral point of observation as the grounds for objective practical reason which I will attempt to criticize when addressing more in detail some of the central elements of Nagel's moral perspective.

Philosophical discourse, historically, has often proceeded through progressive dichotomies, as for instance the dichotomies of subject and object, real and ideal, physical and metaphysical, the "is" and the "ought". The "dichotomist" method of investigation can be traced back to Ancient Greek philosophy's notion of the dieresis up to the Cartesian method and beyond. Perhaps, the first modern voice to have rejected the so-called "abstractions of the intellect" authoritatively was Hegel, in the course of his attempt to recapture unity underlying such distinctions, through the dialectical work of reason. However, even if Hegel's experiment still inspires some parts of current debate, in general, contemporary perspectives are still permeated by methods based on category oppositions, leading to a fragmented reconstruction of reality. I interpret objectivists precisely as perpetuating the classical separation of the Cartesian picture of the mind from the external world. Given that such a view is probably one of the most significant targets of the experientialist approach here defended, I will define all those perspectives attempting to overcome it as forms of a post-Cartesian philosophical approach.

For instance, Habermas, in his reconstruction of the philosophical discourse of modernity[5] concedes to Foucault that reason is "a thing of this world" and that the standards we use are embedded in social and communicative practices. While distinguishing Foucault's views amongst those of French post-modern thinkers, Habermas notes that given the "power-knowledge genealogy" Foucault adopts in order to unmask the essence of reason, he falls into a performative contradiction when making use of reason in order to criticize reason itself. Through the paradigm of communicative action, Habermas thus attempts to reconnect the notions of immanence and transcendence with that of validity, while defending a situated form of rationality which can be continuously criticized and revised by constructing, within context-bound everyday practice, a "moment of unconditionality".

As a starting point for the relevant part of its investigation, the present study accepts the Habermasian objective of criticizing a purely subject-centred reason (subjectivism) in favour of a reason understood in terms of communicative action. More specifically, though, it accepts the challenge of rethinking the mutual relationships between the following dichotomies:

(1) contingency and necessity
(2) incommensurability of life-worlds against partial commensurability
(3) the empirical and the *a priori*
(4) the body-mind distinction

But as will be clarified, the experientialist approach attempts at finding those pragmatic-transcendental conditions which ground purposive agency in general, of which communicative and instrumental agency are only a sub-species of such broader category. The experiential paradigm indeed, both at the cognitive-epistemic and at the moral level has to presuppose the unity of the subjective and the objective dimension within a unified paradigm of understanding – experience – as a dimension orienting our theoretical and practical categories. Thus moral experientialism does not ignore the subjective dimension for the validity of moral claims, but it rejects only those approaches reducing each standard to a relativist explanation, inscribing the former within a unified paradigm of reflection.

An important element, which can be here only anticipated, is the form of validity that, would follow from the general constraints on practical action. It is indeed the role that the Kantian *sensus communis* as a universalizable condition plays in respect to the moral validity of judgments of human rights, having to balance the opposition of right-mediated interests through the construction of an exemplar rule which is never given once for all. It is in this sense that the present perspective is connected to several relevant elements spread in Arendt's interpretation of Kant's *Critique of Judgment* (1958 and 1982) as well as Habermas' understanding of communicative

---

[5] Habermas (1987).

action (1984b). Indeed, the reconstruction of a unified notion of the judgmental activity capable of explaining both the cognitive-epistemic and the moral dimension of our human rights evaluations, situates itself in between the cognitive relevance of the Habermasian dimension of the practical discourse and Arendt's insights into the possible moral unfolding of Kant's reflective judgment. The form of validity promoted by the judgmental activity must take into consideration the perspective of those towards which the judgment is directed, but differently from what we will see as strongly defended by irreducible relativists, it does not advance a subjectively private form of validity, neither individual nor community internal. Rather, it aims for a universal agreement through what Kant and Arendt define as the "enlarged perspective" of thinking "in whose place" which reflective judgements give place to.

2.2.1 Harman's Inner-Judgments Relativism

As previously introduced, different levels of analysis can be adopted in approaching the notion of relativism, each focussing on a specific aspect of the problem. I have concentrated on a tripartite distinction, between descriptive, normative and metaethical relativism, and argued that one can reasonably defend different forms of moral relativism through the encroachment of the above-mentioned levels of analysis.

In what follows, I will consider a fairly well-established theory of absolute metaethical moral relativism, which has one of its most renowned representatives in Harman's relativist thesis of inner-judgments and quasi-absolutism. It has been observed that metaethical moral relativism must be distinguished not only from moral absolutism, but also from positions of moral nihilism. The latter positions move from the absence of any singular true morality to rejecting morality as such. To moral nihilism, Harman's form of moral metaethical relativism responds that "Relative moral judgments can continue to play a serious role in moral thinking" (Harman, 1996, 6), whereas to the former it replies that the rejection of moral absolutism can be achieved by showing the conventional nature of morality. It is indeed such conventional character of morality as based upon a bargaining activity of self-interested claims that is at the basis of each moral social framework and of morality in general (Harman, 1996, 23). Such bargaining activity is carried on by subjects instantiating different forms of power-relations that achieve a progressive balance by reaching compromises. Having established this, one can already infer that Harman's point is not that of denying the possibility of a self-interested compromise among competing positions, but rather that of denying that such compromise can at all take the form of a moral ought. And yet, even if non moral conventional agreement is what fundamentally justifies agreements, it is questionable whether such a contract starting from a *de facto* imbalance of competing positions can be justified in its first instance.

At any rate, Harman's argument proceeds by connecting the conventionality of morality to relativism, citing the incommensurable differences that such conventional arrangements reciprocally show as well as each conventional claim's inherent reference to its own specific moral scheme.

In *Moral Relativism* (1996), Harman's argument starts by drawing a parallel between the relativity of moral frameworks and the choice of space-temporal frameworks. An object can be taken as being either at rest or in motion, according to the chosen framework, and truth is relative to each particular framework, while lacking under the other. Objective superiority of one framework towards the other cannot be established, so no objective conditions of truth or falsehood can be set. Moral judgments, as well as scientific propositions, present themselves in an *elliptical form*, that is, with an implied "according to framework X", where X determines its truth conditions (Harman, 1996, 4–5).

On this basis Harman proposes his version of metaethical relativism under the premise that there is no way of assessing which of two moralities can better justify its own claims without falling into an objectivist explanation of the superiority of one moral theory over the other. Additionally, Harman's position is not simply that mere empirical differences constitute a sufficient justification for the validity of factual descriptive incommensurabilities. Indeed, what distinguishes Harman's position is his defence of relativism on the basis of the quasi-absolutist terms in which diverging standards can be uphold. According to Harman, quasi-absolutism claims that: "a moral relativist projects his or her moral framework onto the world and then uses moral terminology as if the projected morality were the single true morality, while at the same time admitting that this way of talking is only 'as if' " (1996, 34).

Quasi-absolutism is a thesis about linguistic meaning whose ambition is that of maintaining the imperative force of moral claims without admitting their objective validity. Quasi-absolutist claims express a speaker's attitude towards standards. If subject A says that X is wrong, and subject B says that X is right, they both communicate their differing attitudes towards practice X, without disagreeing on the respective claims but only on the *subjective attitude* of each towards each other claim. There is no problem in recognizing the other's point of view as a plausible one, according to her specific frame of reference; the contrast is instead in respect to the other's subjective attitude towards X (Harman, 1996, 37).

Such a view is then further integrated by Harman's logical consideration of the internal character exhibited by ought-judgments as a four-place predicates of the following kind:

Ought implies A, B, C, M, where an agent *A* has reason to do type of act *B* given considerations *C* and motivating attitudes *M* so that whoever proclaims an *ought-claim* must share with the addresses the same motivations Ms

This form of relativism combines agent-relativism with appraisal relativism, since it requires that those uttering an internal judgment and those to whom such judgment is addressed must have entered the same conventional moral agreement in order for such a judgment to be compelling. In short, Harman's thesis is that "the judgment that it is wrong of someone to do something makes sense only in relation to an agreement or understanding [. . .] it makes no sense to ask whether an action is wrong, period, apart from any relation to an agreement" (Harman, 1982, 189–190).

Normative "ought" judgments such as "A should do x" presuppose "certain motivational attitudes" (Harman, 1982, 194) on the part of the agent which must be shared by the subject uttering the judgment. This means that the same desires which provide a reason for doing x must be available not only to the speaker but also to the agent for an "ought" judgment to be compelling.

The subjects' motivational basis of "ought" judgments leads Harman to categorize them as "inner" judgments, due to their reference to the interior disposition of the agent. For Harman, "having reasons to do something" is to be explained by the possession of "goals, desires, or intentions" (Harman, 1982, 193–194). Inner moral judgments are only those of the kind: "A should have done x" or "A was wrong to have done x", where the motivating considerations are of a moral and not merely of a predictive or hypothetical nature of the kind: "if one wants to open this door, one should use this key". Harman distinguishes inner moral judgments from non-inner moral judgments and considers that non-inner moral judgments are not part of his relativist objective. The latter are types of evaluative judgments, which do not depend on the agent's being motivated by those moral considerations as the judging subject, as for instance in the case of: "the judgment that someone is evil or the judgment that a given institution is unjust" (Harman, 1982, 190).

But can one really draw such a clear-cut distinction and maintain that to claim that someone's actions are bad or unjust does not prevent us from maintaining a relativist position according to which nothing can be advanced of significant normative force in regard of what she *ought* or *ought not* to do? In other words, it is not clear why for Harman, while we are prevented from criticizing someone for not having behaved as according to a moral standard because of her lack of internal motivation, we are nevertheless allowed to impose on her evaluating judgments of the kind: "it is bad or it is unjust that you did such and such", and pretend that she agrees with us even if she does not share our same standard of goodness or justice.

As in the case of moral normative judgments, also evaluative judgments, in order to be action motivating, must be referred to a shared standard of what is "good" and therefore can be subjected of being relativized to in the same vein as those normative judgments concerning what is right or wrong. But if this were so, then we would be even in a worse position, since there would be no possibility of imposing either a normative duty or an evaluative consideration upon someone who does not already share our same motivational set.

If this position were true, then the immediate consequence would be that there would not be much to reply to Harman's claim that there is no way to criticize even Hitler for the extermination of the Jews other than the manifestation of a statement relative to one's own standard. However, if this were so, then such a statement would not be strong enough for providing enough reasons to Hitler's set of internal reasons: "Suppose Mabel takes Hitler's actions to be a great evil and also believes that Hitler's values were sufficiently perverse that they provided Hitler with no reason to refrain from acting as he acted [. . .]. Although she judges Hitler to be a great evil, she may find that she is no more able to judge that it was wrong of Hitler to have acted as he acted [. . .]" and this would not be enough for providing Hitler with a reason to modify his personal beliefs (Harman, 1996, 60).

It seems that Harman's position of inner judgments and relativism amounts basically to the following point: in order to be motivated to act as according to a certain standard conventionally agreed, there must be an actual desire or disposition in the motivational set of the agent. But this seems simply to reduce a moral ought to the presence of an existential condition "is", subordinating moral normativity to the factual presence of a motivational set of already existing conditions. To this, a Kantian might reply that it is instead from the same autonomy of the moral imperative that a *sui generis* feeling can be derived in terms of a sense of respect for the moral norm, that is to say that the motivation to moral action must be seen as the result of the autonomy of the moral imperative and not the contrary.

Harman might reply that, due to the conventional character of morality, there is no normative force that morality *should* have, since it never had it in the first place: "According to moral conventionalism, morality must be seen as lacking any objective absolute normative force, of course, because according to the moral conventionalism there is no such thing as objective absolute normative force" (Harman, 1996, 28).

It seems though that in order to attempt a first answer to Harman's relativism, an initial consideration might be oriented to the underscoring of his lack of consideration of the *form* of what it means to be motivated to act, that is, to the sameness of the structural patterns of underlying the dynamics of what it is to be motivated to action *qua* dispositions, desires and so on are present within the agent's internal motivational set, and that from such formally universalized consideration it becomes possible to derive some general preconditions of agency as necessary pragmatic-transcendental constraints.

Were one to admit the binding force of general conditions of agency, then Harman's internalist perspective would collapse. Rather than surrendering in front of internal motivations not subjected to a form of universalization, were certain pragmatic-transcendental constraints of agency recognized from within our experience as purposive agents, then on the pain of a pragmatic contradiction, each agent would have to act in accordance to those same universal constraints which only guarantee for the possibility of acting as according to her preferred purposes. It is from the same recognition of such universal conditions of agency which one's own internal motivational set is compelled to be critically revised accordingly, due to the fact that any motivational pattern violating those same presuppositions of agency would prevent any future possibility of action. This process will be explained more in detail in the next two chapters in terms of the inherent interconnection between the experiential conditions of communicative agency and the exemplarity of the reflective judgment. Such interconnection is indeed aimed at providing an interpretation for the internal/external reasons debate by trespassing such radical opposition and claiming that while moral reasons exist independently from *de facto* motivational sets of individual subjects, they are not nevertheless detached from the general motivational patterns that subjects might have were they following certain conditions of validity in the constructions of their judgments, that is, were their judgments exhibiting conditions of exemplar validity. Indeed if, on the one hand, the pragmatic-transcendental conditions of purposive agency do fix the conditions of transcendental liberty for the individuals, on the other hand, their specific configurations and situated validity achievable through the use of the reflective judgments translate such transcendental constraints into political principles capable of providing motivation to action for socially and politically embedded subjects.

So far, I have attempted at showing how a refined version of moral relativism such as that presented by Harman fails to meet certain conditions of experiential validity. This failure, though, should not necessarily lead us to think that the only valid alternative to moral relativism is provided by an objectivist and universalist form of moral validity. In order to prove how objective moral universalism is also an inadequate form of explanation for the validity of moral judgements, I will concentrate the next paragraph on one of the leading positions in contemporary moral universalism.

2.2.2 The Limits of Nagel's Objectivism in Morality

In several writings, Nagel views morality as bound to a system of cross-cultural universal and objective reasons which compels everyone. In *A View from Nowhere* (1986), for instance, he concentrates on the notion of normative objectivity of values. Such a notion, in Nagel's view, is strictly related to that of normative realism, with the latter claiming a notion of propositional truth and falsehood about values as established independently, through critical scrutiny, of appearances in the world. Nagel does not claim that all values must be objective, but only that if moral objectivity is true, then at least *some* values must be taken as objectively true. If values are objectively valid, then it is also possible to look at them from an impersonal perspective: that is, as having an action-guiding force independent of specific subjective perspectives. If objective reasons for actions can be found, then they must be generally valid and not tied to specific justifications.

The objectivity of moral values is to be defended against the increasingly widespread view which considers cross-cultural variation of moral codes as a sign of their dependence on socio-cultural factors. Nagel's answer here is that the possibility of reaching, at least in principle, an agreement on objective answers, indicates that when people distance themselves from particular positions, they activate a *common evaluative faculty*, guaranteeing the same overall output, which is supposedly free from subjective bias. Disagreement, according to Nagel, is only a consequence of distorting factors (such as social pressures, personal interests, lack of rationality) which yield biased results. To overcome this problem one must transcend oneself, so to become capable of reordering, somehow, one's internal life.

Nagel claims also that even when a desire is present as a reason for action,[6] it cannot establish a causal relation with the action itself, but it supplies rather a

---

[6] Nagel (1986) specifies that there are also cases, such as those of prudential and altruistic motivations, where desires are respectively projected either into the future or in the recognition of other's desires and interests.

motivation for action by providing a *reason* for doing that action. For instance, in the case I want my pain to disappear, it is this same desire which gives me a *reason* to act for a resolution of the problem. This means that I act not because of a desire, but because of a reason moved by a desire. Hence, the point is to establish whether pleasure and pain are simply agent-relative, or if they also provide agent-neutral reasons for action. In other words, if reducing pain provides an agent-neutral reason, there is a reason for all people to reduce both their own pains and those of the others. Nagel claims that pain is not only "rejectable" for the subjective self, but also for the objective self. The experience of pain is something one recognizes as terrible not only for oneself but also for having an autonomous life in general.

Pain thus seems to gain an objective autonomy going beyond the authority of the subject that endures it. One can recognize the brutality of pain externally from a simple subjective point of observation, as if there were reasons for rejecting pain that transcend the specific interests of the suffering subject. This does not rule out subjective recognition of pain and pleasure, but only subjects them to the authority of an objective self and to its impersonal neutrality. This agent-neutral perspective becomes even more apparent when it confronts deontological agent-relativity. Nagel asks the reader to imagine a car accident happening in the middle of the night. Passengers travelling in the car are seriously injured and only one can save them. Nearby is a house, without a telephone, but with a car. Inside the house, there is only an old woman watching a baby. One passenger tells the woman what has happened, but she does not trust the stranger and frightened, runs upstairs, locking herself in the bathroom. The old woman is ignoring the request, and the reader is asked whether she believes she might be convinced that it were necessary to twist the baby's arm. Should one do it?

Taking a consequentialist, agent-neutral perspective, one would compare different states of the world, and decide to adopt that which, impersonally, is the best one. This is the objective self's "perspective from nowhere", divorced from any specific agent. According to this perspective, one is allowed to perform some evil if the ultimate result is morally good. If there is no privileged subjective position, then any possible decision-maker – even she whose welfare is to be sacrificed – must agree with the agent-neutral output once she has transcended her idiosyncratic position. By contrast, from a deontological perspective, one may not twist the baby's arm, or produce pain for the sake of greater pleasure. Nevertheless, says Nagel, it is hard to see how agent-relativity can be combined with deontology. As a matter of fact, deontological reasons, distinctly from reasons for autonomy linked to the realization of optional projects, are compulsory. This means that if it is admitted that the agent-relative reason of not being subject to harm must be respected by the agent, then one has to accept that the interest of not having his arm twisted must be generally taken into account. If this is so, then it is not clear why this is an agent-relative and not an agent-neutral reason that everyone is bound to respect. Deontological reasons are compulsory upon everyone, and cannot be restricted to agent-relative reasons.

To evaluate critically the claims made by Nagel, I will concentrate upon the notion of a "common evaluative faculty" as a method for reaching agreement, and then

I will analyse the consequences which this implies in particular for the notion of the objective self. Then I will proceed by re-examining the notion of pleasure and pain as something objectively recognizable – that is, recognizable *independently* of any reference to the subjective self – and defend the idea that such a step is experientially incorrect.

Regarding the first point, Nagel imputes the existence of disagreement to the active role of distorted interests in moral deliberation. Removing all biased interests, by contrast, leads to activation of a common pattern of reasoning, in turn yielding univocal deliberative output. From the beginning this methodological description of moral agreement seems unsatisfactory. Not only is one left without criteria for biased interests. Even if one treats as subjective interests only those interests which are non-generalizable, it is not possible to recognize all those general interests that are equally biased. In other words, one can construct a general biased agreement. Furthermore, the total removal of subjective interests, instead of the separation of the normatively valid ones from the normatively flawed, yields a substantively empty moral space in which nothing can be recognized as a reason for action. Indeed, Nagel's treatment of the notion of "common evaluative faculty" is ambiguous: it does not necessarily entail an objective, agent-neutral capacity. If Nagel's common evaluative faculty assumption were integrated with preconditions of formal equality (such as reciprocity of subjects, for instance) one might obtain an inter-subjective universalist model of deliberation, leading to agreement on a rather different basis. This possibility would indeed be left open by the very method adopted by Nagel. Consequently, reasons achieve validity only if they pass the test comprised by the process of inter-subjective generalization of interests, which is something different from "reasons objectively valid *per se*".

Under this suggested perspective, the agent-neutral/agent-relative dichotomy can be overcome and reinterpreted through the notion of *agents-community*. This replaces the fiction of an objective-self, detached from her social life and personal relations, with that of a socially embedded self, submitting her personal interests to a counterfactual scenario where necessary conditions for agency would have to be found. Nagel's notion of the objective self not only seems not required by the methodological framework he proposes; it seems also incorrect once the phenomenology of "being in pain" is reconstructed. The generalization of the notion of "being in pain" starts exactly from the recognition, in someone else, of one's experienced emotional status of being in pain. There is no objective detachment here. Instead, there is a subjectively universalizable feeling of recognition that I project in all beings in this condition.

Further support for these criticisms can be derived from analysis of Nagel's texts. If one is prepared to take seriously the ambivalence Nagel manifests through his rejection of agent-relative positions, one must further conclude that Nagel's position, overall, is incapable of reconciling the divided self. The problem is how to unify the limbs of this dichotomy and this, I believe, cannot be satisfactorily achieved within Nagel's framework. This difficulty becomes even clearer after *A View from Nowhere* (1986), namely in *Equality and Partiality* (1991). Here, Nagel's principal aim is to find a perspective under which a moral and political theory which overcomes the tension between the personal and impersonal standards, the subjective and the neutral self, can be justified.[7] Internal competition between these two perspectives within the self takes the form of extreme positions: on the one hand, in the case of self-centred positions failing to recognise claims of other selves, whereas on the other hand, in the equal consideration to the other selves, who are recognized as counting in exactly the same way as oneself.

The search for unanimity represents, then, the "third stage" in ethics, that which assumes the Kantian question of "what, if anything, can we all agree that we should do, given that our motives are not merely impersonal?", and which substitutes the former question with another, that is: "what can we all agree would be best, impersonally considered?" (Nagel, 1991, 15). In analysing Kant's categorical imperative, and in particular its formulation in terms of contradiction of the will, Nagel recognizes that even Kant's formulation is incapable of mediating the personal with the impersonal standpoint in order to achieve reasonable unanimity (1991, 41–43). Nagel then canvasses a possible solution in the following terms:

> The desire for a solution to our conflicts that at some level everyone must accept is another expression of the recognition that, important as one's life may be from the inside, one is only one person among all those who exist. But in this case the recognition does not manifest itself through the detached perspective of impartiality, but through a universal identification with the point of view of each individual, and a consequent desire to find a way to live which can be endorsed by everyone, partly but not entirely out of impartiality. Pure impartiality cannot guarantee this sort of Kantian unanimity, because it does not act alone. The initial opposition between impartiality and personal aims is somewhat modified by the internalization of impartiality as an individual motive. The well-being of his fellow humans becomes in this way important to each person, part of what he wants. But unless impartiality replaces the individual's purely personal aims completely (which is neither possible nor desirable) the mixture of impartiality and the personal that is the usual individual configuration will continue to generate conflict among and within persons. Nagel (1991, 47).

Yet the critical question Nagel needs to address here is: how can one achieve the internalization of an impartial standpoint, if one is not ready to leave behind a frame which prevents the entry of subjective preferences into an inter-subjective frame of reasoning so transforming subjective preferences themselves into reasons shareable by a community of peoples? The solution cannot be found within the self, nor can it be found in the normative division of labour to be realized by the state, since conflicting preferences, within it, would endanger the stability of the institutional order.

If subjective preferences are not transformed through public discussions towards externalized processes of inclusiveness, then the ideal of "a set of institutions within which persons can live a collective life that meets the impartial requirements of the impersonal standpoint while at the same time having to conduct themselves only in ways that it is reasonable to require of individuals with strong personal

---

[7] "My claim is that the problem of designing institutions that do justice to the equal importance of all persons, without making unacceptable demands on individuals. Has not been solved – and that this is so partly because for our world the problem of the right relation between the personal and impersonal standpoints within each individual has not been solved" Nagel (1991, 5).

motives" (Nagel, 1991, 18) would certainly collapse. Additionally, if transformative action over subjective preferences is not realized precisely through a process of inter-subjective recognition of the different weights reasons acquire within a social community, then what it is "unreasonable to reject" remains a concept without effectiveness: I would still have reasonable reasons "to resist a reasonable aim", as Nagel recognizes at the end of his work (Nagel, 1991, 172).

This means that the aim of universally shareable reasons must be justified by a different route. It must start by recognising my individuality as relationally constituted, on the pain of not being able to move from a purely solipsistic pattern of reasoning. But if this is so, the process of transformation of my personal aims into generalizable ones is socio-political.

It is in my own social interrelations that I learn to consider intrinsically subjective reasons as subordinate to those publicly justifiable, in a way that the space left for personal ambitions is, strictly speaking, subordinated to inter-subjective justification. That Nagel occasionally sees the problem in these terms is clear from passages such as this: "Somehow the standards for justification to individuals either in ethics generally or in political theory should emerge from an assessment of the importance of personal motives which has general validity and can therefore be impersonally acknowledged: What is reasonable in personal motivation is itself the object of a general ethical judgment" (Nagel, 1991, 31). Three points arise. First, the strategy adopted by Nagel here differs from that proposed in *The View from Nowhere*, where the emphasis lies with the abdication of subjective reasons in order to obtain a neutral point of view. Second, it is a *non sequitur* to accept the general validity of personal reasons while not recognizing an inter-subjective scheme of deliberation. Thirdly, it is not possible to move from what can be *generally* accepted to what is *universally* valid. If universality is one's ultimate goal, then stronger conditions are needed to transform subjective preferences into universal principles.

Finally, one can observe that, so far, Nagel has left us with a double standard of reasoning: on the one hand, Nagel recognizes that a completely agent-neutral morality is not a plausible human aim, whereas on the other, he specifies that personal projects and motivations should not compete for the achievement of valid principles. Agent-relative reasons are to be confronted, instead, with the most fundamental interests and needs of others as objectively valid reasons. And yet, Nagel's position is still more complicated. He also recognizes that it would be a sign of un-correctness (but not of incoherence) if a morality sacrificed any personal special relationship or life-plan for merely impersonal reasons.

Even if it is possible to take a rigorous route and claim that we are morally required to attain impersonal standards and revise our personal reasons to them, Nagel affirms that neutral standards have to define their threshold in order to be compatible with the complexity of human beings, where impersonality is only one aspect, not all, of what characterizes humans. What seems reasonable is to find equilibrium between personal and impersonal reasons, but such a compromise would be realizable not necessarily through the extremely compelling reconstruction of new men converted only to neutral reasons, but through a division of the normative labour occurring thanks to the political and institutional reshape finalized to the realization of agent-neutral objectives. This would leave individuals, including those running public institutions, free to realize personal goals and ambitions that do not find space within the sphere of state neutral reasons.

But if one were to take such route of justification, then agent-neutral reasons would be left to the state, without any direct participation of citizens in the determination and enforcement of such principles for action.[8] Thus, the result would be that of a state constructed independently of inter-subjective democratic processes of participation and civic solidarity, with agent-neutral principles remaining detached and, worse, not required within the face to face relations of the social sphere. This seems counter-intuitive, and diminishes the role of participatory rights, which we would expect to exert in multifaceted human relations. A hint at a possible revision of this position can be found in some of Nagel's later work. In *The Last Word* (1997), Nagel claims that both a purely personal and a purely impersonal position, are unsatisfactory for several reasons. As far as mere subjectivism is concerned, I can recognize a reason which pertains to me as including others, only if what concerns the others is relevant for my own interests, and therefore only in terms of means to my own ends. With respect to the impersonal position, everyone is objectively deprived of a specific value, and one does not have any specific reason for asking others to give his own case particular consideration. The latter perspective, says Nagel, is quite unreasonable and hard to accept, since the belief according to which it is irrelevant that I die, for instance, cannot be peacefully accepted by me as merely egoistically motivated. I will later develop a view which will attempt to find a solution between the purely subjective and the purely objective perspective

---

[8] Besides the too-demanding effects of principles of redistribution for the well-off, Nagel rejects criteria based only on the guaranteed minimum since they do not favour convergence from the side of the worst-off. His suggested solution for this dilemma – which underscores the separation between individual and state responsibility – can be found in the following passage, which fails to construct legitimation and stability in the social sphere, while not passing on the task to the political one, either: "First, it clearly is a desirable feature of a social order that within it, people should not be too constrained in the pursuit of their own lives by constant demands for impartial attention to the welfare of others. A limited morality of non-interference; respect for life, liberty, and property; and mutual aid only of the most basic sort embodies this idea effectively. But this is an adequate individual morality *only within the context of a societal framework that does much more* to satisfy the claims of impartial concern which other lives make on us [...]. The second point is this. When we follow those rules within an acceptable social system, it is part of the freedom they confer on us that we do not have to feel responsible for everything that happens which we could have prevented [...]. We are responsible, through the institutions which require our support, for the things they could have prevented as well as for the things they actively cause. That is why the worse off, under the guaranteed minimum, are being asked to sacrifice for the benefit of the better off, just as surely as the better off are asked to sacrifice for the benefit of the worse off under an egalitarian system. If sacrifice is measured by comparison with possible alternatives rather than by comparison with the status quo, the situations of possible winners and possible losers are symmetrical. So an acceptable societal framework for apportioning negative interpersonal responsibilities is a condition of the moral acceptability of strict limitations on negative responsibility in the rules of individual conduct that govern personal relations within it" Nagel (1991, 84).

on values and interests, so that from within an experientialist approach such two dichotomies become entrenched into one single model.

2.3 Wong's Mixed Position: the Idea of Pluralistic Relativism

One intermediate model worth considering is constructed on the combination of elements derived from both classical relativist and universalist paradigms. I will define these models in terms of "mixed positions". Mixed positions hold that neither relativism nor objectivism can alone be explicative of the moral life. Following from such unsatisfactory radical opposition, similar theories have generally attempted to construct theories combining both the objectivity of some moral judgments with the recognition of relativist truth-conditions. Mixed positions can be distinguished into universalist mixed positions such as that of Foot (2001), Scanlon (2001), Nussbaum (1993) and relativist mixed positions as in the case of Wong (1986, 2006). I will here consider Wong's position as the most representative approach of relativist mixed positions. If my criticisms are well founded, I will have accomplished the task of ruling out as possible forms of justification not only strict relativism and objective universalism, but also mixed forms of relativism. The *pars destruens* characterizing the first half of this book then will be complete, and my enquiry will proceed by constructing a specific notion of pluralistic universalism which clearly falls within what I have just referred to as mixed universalist positions.

The critical point for relativist mixed positions is that while certain judgments can be either true or false as according to certain circumstances, there exist other kinds of judgments which, independently from given circumstances, do indeed maintain their truth validity in a universal way. With reference to the above distinctions between weak and strong metaethical relativism, relativist mixed positions do place themselves within a form of weak metaethical relativism, since they also claim that certain moral disputes can be universally solved through the appeal to criteria of moral validity. In this sense, weak metaethical relativism can accommodate both constructivist positions, as for instance Rawlsian constructivism as according to the interpretation provided before, and mixed relativist positions as those here presented.

In what follows, I will take into account only a specific instance of relativist mixed positions, that is, Wong's pluralistic relativism. Wong defends his notion of pluralistic relativism through the endorsement of a position of moral naturalism which claims that: "The root sense of naturalism that is opposed to the supernatural and the ontologically non-natural is a belief in one single natural world, in which human beings and other purportedly radically different beings must be situated" (Wong, 2006, 29). The specificity of methodological naturalism consists in a refusal of the reduction of moral properties to natural ones and in the maintenance of a criterion of normativity in morality, even though the rejection of the possible reduction of moral wording into non-evaluative terms does not prevent considering morality as bearing normative force without exhibiting irreducibly moral properties.

Moral naturalism, thus, rejects the validity of *a priori* principles regulating our moral life and it defends, instead, an evolutionary theory based upon the general function that morality displays in the fostering of social cooperation.[9] Regarding this point it differs quite broadly from the notion of experientialism which has been defended so far, since naturalism misrecognizes the role that the transcendental unity of experience has in providing the conditions for the validity of our cognitive and practical life.

If relativism is defined as the view that any morality is as good as any other – that is, as a purely subjectivist view that does not distinguish between better and worse moralities – then Wong's pluralistic relativism does not fall within it. Pluralistic relativism holds, instead, that there is an irreducible form of "moral value pluralism" but it admits that such pluralism falls within constraints underpinning the adequacy of moralities and that such criteria do allow for a plurality of moralities which are all true.[10] But if this is so, then the question becomes that of specifying why Wong's theory can be labeled as a form of true relativism and not instead as a form of simple pluralism since, from the examples provided, one cannot prove that the contrast between right-based versus community-based moralities can lead to an instance of contradictory true moralities. Let's suppose that the criteria adopted by Wong do allow for the possibility of two contradictory but equally true moralities. If this were the case, then one would wonder whether Wong's criteria are rather instances of vagueness rather than of truth since, as for any principle, to allow for the possibility of "p" and "non-p" provides a sufficient condition for being self-refuting.

In the construction of his idea of pluralistic relativism, Wong begins his reflections by addressing the point of moral ambivalence and pluralism which supposedly would, according to the author, pose difficulties to any pretence of moral universalism: "moral ambivalence is the phenomenon of coming to understand and appreciate the other side's viewpoint to the extent that our sense of the unique rightness of our own judgments gets destabilized [. . .] the most discomforting kind of moral disagreement [. . .] is also a disagreement in which coming to the other side brings along an appreciation of *its* reasons" (2006, 5). Moral ambivalence thus implies that cultural values are at least partially commensurable and that what differs are the specific priorities which can be assigned to values when facing controversies, together with the criteria adopted for the determination of such priorities, as for instance in the case of deontological versus consequentialist theories or in the priority that either the individual or the community must assume (2006, 20). With this specification,

---

[9] "One such methodological theme holds that philosophy should not employ a distinctive, a priori method for yielding substantive truths shielded from empirical testing [. . .] Rejection of the a priori arises from the insight that powerful explanatory empirical theories have frequently overturned claims that seemed logically or conceptually true at the time" Wong (2006, 30).

[10] "Pluralistic relativism accounts for the plurality of values and for moral ambivalence by holding that the universal limits on adequate moralities do not narrow the range of such moralities to just one. The possibility of setting different priorities among values corresponds to different ways of regulating interpersonal conflict of interest and providing direction to the individual" Wong (2006, 65).

one can better understand what Wong's relativism is based upon; that is, rather than on values *per se*, ambivalence is based upon the presumed impossibility of providing a defeating argument for the moral criteria adopted by different cultural systems, or even within each system itself, in the assessment of moral controversies. Moralities, according to Wong, do indeed possess many commonalities, which in their turn form a shared core of duties including binding rules of reciprocity as well as duties of special relationships. But since such universal constraints of moralities do not restrict the number of adequate moralities to just one true morality, then a plurality of adequate moralities represents alternative and equally justified ways of fulfillment of the general functions of morality and in particular of the function of enhancement of social cooperation.

One might wonder why there would be the necessity of duplicating the criteria of moral validity by introducing also locally contingent criteria to the universal normative standards for adequate moralities. Wong's answer is that universal criteria are simply "a skeleton of a morality, insufficiently rich in content to be action guiding [...] the selection of specific priorities among conflicting values is underdetermined by such a general function of morality and by the relevant features of human nature and of the human condition. That is why specific priorities must be established by local criteria within the truth conditions for moral judgments" (2006, 81).

This implies that local criteria are optional for societies "from the purely metaethical perspective defined by the tenets of pluralistic relativism, one is not rationally *required* [...] though one is permitted [...]" (Wong, 2006, 82) to embrace one morality over another, whereas from a normative first-order perspective one is allowed to consider as repugnant the norms of a different morality conflicting with one's own norms.

Pluralistic relativism bears important connections with the idea which I will later develop in terms of pluralistic universalism, even if it differs profoundly in the relation of consistency and subordination of moral variation respect to what I define as the universal constraints of agency. Whereas for relativist mixed positions, truth-conditions of certain judgments, are independent from universally valid procedural constraints, pluralistic universalism claims that only those views subordinating moral variation to the universal conditions of agency seen in terms of *mutual recognition* as purposive agents, can advance a plurality of truth-configurations from *within* the necessity of conforming to certain implied parameters of purposive action.

Thus, whereas relativist mixed positions maintain an external connection and coexistence between objective and relativist judgments, pluralistic universalism accepts variation as justified only when allowed by the formal conditions of mutual recognition. Pluralistic universalism, thus, fixes a more stringent connection with the universal constraints that it advances, since it does not admit a double standard of truth validity as distinguished into an abstract universal standard plus a non universalizable contingent one. Instead, it inscribes within such general conditions for agency (recognition) a plurality of exemplar configurations springing from the reflective use of judgment as engaged both in the construction of exemplary valid human rights principles and in the exemplar balancing of possible conflicts of rights through the use of the notion of the finality of rights.

Pluralism regards, then, only those different configurations of rights and of rights maximizations, whose differentiations are justified on the basis of the different cultural and contextual circumstances in which judgments are constructed: that is, on the basis of the assumption of a *sensus communis* which situates the exemplarity of reflective judgments within the borders of what is to be thought as valid for "us". Such assumption, though, is itself dependent upon a further condition, which is the fulfillment of the principle of recognition of otherness as a normative requisite for the construction of a meaningful common sense.

Such condition brings a universal formal standard of validity within an exemplarily pluralist model of justification. The interconnection between the fulfillment of the condition of recognition with the form of exemplar universality of the reflective judgments, not only subordinates the acceptability of cultural variation to universal standards, but it allows for the possibility of a subjective universalization of situated claims while respecting the same constraints of agency. Indeed, situational complexity can never be resolved by the application of one single right over its possible violation. Situational complexity leads us very often to judge cases where two or more rights do conflict, without there being the possibility of taking on justified basis a one-sided decision. Reflective judgment, when dealing with infra or inter-rights conflicts is called to balance rights on case by case as well as on context by context basis, without the possibility of obtaining one single rule validly applicable for all possible scenarios. All these points will be readdressed more extensively later, but before entering into the details of my model, I wish to introduce the general background framework within which my version of pluralistic universalism falls. This will be obtained by referring to a certain interpretation of Hegel's ideal of the ethical life, and to his philosophically stimulating idea of "recognition".

2.4 Discursive Dialectic of Recognition: for a Post-Metaphysical Justification of the Domain of the Ethical Life

Within the philosophical discourse for the legitimacy of the political order, the institutional "facticity" of the modern state has been often evaluated in terms of an external normative standard of correctness, an ought, placed autonomously from social context interaction. Attempts have been devoted to the definition of "free-standing" models of political legitimacy with the aim of establishing neutral standards for political stability. Besides the contestability of several details contained in such models, such as for instance the function of "primary goods" in Rawls's original position, I will here concentrate upon the methodological inadequacy that a certain reading of Hume has produced in the political philosophical approach to social facts in general. In other words, I will attempt to show the incorrectness of a clear-cut separation between a factual "is" and a moral "ought" as a philosophical premise for a theory of political legitimacy.

Whereas the rejection of such point has found the engagement of several contemporary authors,[11] few have made reference to Hegel's idea of the ethical life and recognition as a primary source for a rejection of the reciprocal insulation of the normative and the factual dimension.[12] Indeed, the domain of the ethical life is the privileged context for the emergence of justice within institutional concretisations in Hegel's *Philosophy of Right*. Rather than being simply subordinated to a moral standard, the ethical life "contains" within itself both moments of abstract law and morality as its main dialectical components. Within such sphere, interpersonal relations are established on the basis of a relation of recognition which, in the state, reach a full rational awareness.

Recognition is, for Hegel, the primary bond of intersubjective connection between the members of an ethical community. And yet, its link to the dialectical movement remains merely external, as in the case of the Hegelian relation between the family, the civil society, and the state. The primary aim of this work is that of reconstructing some central concepts of the Hegelian understanding of the right and of providing a post-metaphysical reinterpretation of the notion of recognition in terms of a dialectical process, granting fundamental rights within the context of an institutional discursive model of rationality.

Hegel's philosophy, indeed, represents the most systematic attempt to supersede those "Enlightenment dichotomies" of the intellect on the basis of a dialectic process of self-understanding. Specifically, with reference to his notion of the ethical life (*Sittlichkeit*), it might be claimed that he intersects a conceptual domain conjoining the abstract normative universality of (Kantian) moral freedom with the "facticity" of an institutionalized process of law production. To understand such extreme poles through the lenses of the ethical life, means to commit oneself to the idea that modern institutional structures, in as much as they are a product of the right, represent rational concretisations of life-forms oriented to the social reproduction of liberty. Concrete institutions represent a medium term of dialectic synthesis, solving within

---

[11] See for instance Putnam (1981b, chap. 6) and Oakeshott (1978). Oakeshott, in particular, says that "The absolute discrepancy lies only between 'what is here and now' *as such*, and 'what ought to be' *as such*. And while the mode of being signified by 'what ought to be' is certainly discrepant from that signified by 'what is here and now', 'what ought to be' may without contradiction occupy the same world as 'what is here and now' " Oakeshott, (1978, 281). If the mere "ought to be" were purely a "not being" period, something untranslatable into practical experience, it would not only constitute a meaningless command, but also an inadequate evaluation of the real potentialities and transformative actualizations of experience. It would also represent a contradiction of the being and not being what ought to be. Indeed, if something which ought to be is such that due to its same nature it cannot be predicated of a being, then this would contradict the internal necessity of its becoming an a property of which can be predicated. But while what ought to be exhibits the potentiality of becoming a predicate of one something, it maintains also its normative autonomy. Since, even if what ought to be is not yet a predicate of something being here and now, it nevertheless is a type of being in the value-system it represents.

[12] Important exceptions are Habermas (1996a), Honneth (2008a and 2008b).

themselves the indeterminacy of a purely subjective moral norm and the anomy of a non-rationalized – non-articulated – objective substance, as is for Hegel the case of Spinoza's substance. Through the reflective activity of a self-conscious subjective rationality opening itself to the investigation of the rational content of institutional arrangements, a true meaning of being at liberty can arise. The rationality exhibited by institutional settings mirrors the form of a rationality achieved by a self-determining will, so that: "What is rational is real; And what is real is rational".[13]

The Hegelian co-implication of the rational and the real is in fact dependent upon the understanding that there subsists a mechanism of mutual interdependence between rationality and socio-political constructions, that is, between the development of a capacity by the subjects to think and act rationally and the instantiation of such rationality within the political institutions of a constituent body. The domain of the ethical life, is detected therefore as a level of intersubjective interaction and reflection in which, the intertwining of rationality and being, becomes the point of departure for a political reflective activity of normative-critical thinking.

Following from the observations above, then, Hegel's domain of the ethical life comes to be determined in view of the construction of political sociality and of sociality *tout court*. And yet, in order to achieve such a result, Hegel introduces the principle of recognition as a way to overcome the strict opposition between self-identity and alienation advanced by jusnaturalistic theories for the entering into a legitimate political order. This corrects the conceptual contradiction of contractualism grounded on the pretence to derive political obligation from an individualistic view of political action. As a consequence of such privatistic foundation of the political order, the same idea of a contract as the root of public legitimacy collapses, not only because of its inadequacy as an instrument of private law transferred into the public domain of regulation, but also because of the conceptual impossibility of its fulfilment without prior commitment to reciprocal recognition of subjects as contractual parties of the contract itself.[14]

Therefore, recognition represents a conceptual *prius* to the hypothesis of an original contract among people, and the goal becomes that of understanding the nature of such a concept. In this regard, Hegel favours a non-naturalistic understanding of the grounding of law. The right cannot be rooted in pure individualism since no interaction nor the formation of a common will can be derived by an atomistic understanding of the legal-political order. Negation, through the form of a responding other, thus becomes a necessary step for the achievement of a superior moment of self-conscious intersubjective recognition.

Within the domain of the ethical life, Hegel's *Philosophy of Right* distinguishes between three spheres of interaction: the family, the civil society and the state. With the partial exception of the civil society, to each corresponds a specific characterization of intersubjective relations of recognition which, as Avineri claims, represents "[. . .] three alternative modes of inter-human relationship . . .[that is] particu-

---

[13] Hegel (2001 [1821], 18).

[14] Hegel (2001 [1821], §57n).

lar altruism – the family; universal egoism – civil society; universal altruism – the state" (1972, 33–34). Indeed, whereas in the case of family relations, love grounds an *immediate* form of intersubjective ethical relation of recognition where each is "itself in the other",[15] upon the entry of the educated children into the civil society, the ethical unity of the family collapses. Civil society represents mostly a negative moment of the ethical life, a moment which is characterized by the self-realization of individual interests in the medium of abstract right. And yet, through the role played by the "*Staende*" in terms of associations of interests, proto-forms of interrelations of ethical recognition are constituted from within the sphere of the civil society itself.[16] The inherent condition of intersubjective misrecognition characterizing the non-ethical relations of the civil society finds a primary partial reconciliation in the aggregative role played by the *Staende*.

Finally, within the structure of the state, a mediated relation of recognition is re-established through a non-external medium of "right" and within the condition of a full realization of the ethical life. In the state, the institutionalized spirit of a nation transforms the abstract freedom and rights of the subjects in the civil society into an individualized and concrete freedom.[17] Within the state, the relation of recognition overcomes its internal contradictions and becomes a universal conscience, a universal will, incarnated within the spirit of a people. The rationality of the mutual relations of recognition is here dependent upon the mediating role of the law, which is now seen as representing the institutionalized *ethos* of a people.

And yet, were one to follow the *Jenaer Systementwürfe*, it would be necessary to admit that ethicity arises from misrecognition, struggle, that is from "not seeing oneself in the other".[18] While the immediate form of recognition leads to the constitution of family relationships, the mediated form of recognition through the negative moment of "the struggle for recognition", leads to the achieved awareness that the subject is the depositary of a sphere of rights. The pervasivity of the role that the struggle for recognition has in Hegel's philosophy, is something central even within his *Philosophy of Right*. There, the negativity of the civil society (as a place of the experience of danger of death of starvation or violence) represents an essential moment for the development of rational relations of recognition, as demonstrated by the counterbalancing force of the *Staende* in the suppression of the negative effects of the civil society:

> The corporation provides for the family a basis and steady means (§170), by securing for it a subsistence varying according to capacity. Moreover, both security and capacity are in the corporation publicly recognized. Hence, the member of a corporation does not need to certify his capacity or the reality of his regular income to any larger outside organization. It is also recognized that he belongs to and has active interest in a whole, whose aim is to promote the welfare of society in general. Thus in his class he has honour. Hegel (2001 [1821] §253).

---

[15] Hegel (2001 [1821], §167–168). Hegel speaks of "a loss of the ethical life".

[16] Hegel (2001 [1821], §253 and §254).

[17] Hegel (2001 [1821], §260).

[18] Hegel (1968 [1802–6], 218).

Such dialectical negativity of the process of recognition, while distancing Hegel from Fichte's conception of recognition for the transcendental deduction of law,[19] links the generation process of the ethical life to the "struggle for recognition" and to the fear of death dominating the self-interested relations of the civil society, since only by facing the annihilation of the natural determinations can man raise to a level of self-consciousness.[20] Within the civil society, which remains at a state of "external necessity", recognition itself is characterized in terms of its externality. The object of recognition in such dimension is ownership, and subjectivity is recognized only as much as it can be identified through ownership. However, the same possibility of access to ownership within the civil society can occur only through the "corporations" (*Stände*), and thus Hegel's reference to the recomposition of the process of recognition within the corporation as in terms of honour is explained. Honour is a particular specification of the relation of recognition which, differently from the ancient immediate concept of recognition, refers to a mediated form where the element of mediation is provided by ownership.

In the attempt to reformulate the Hegelian idea of the ethical life and recognition, as well as the rationality of the institutionalised reflective moment, it is important first to consider that institutional designs oriented to law production cannot be seen anymore as ontological instantiations of logical moments belonging to the development of a "universal history". Along post-metaphysical lines of philosophical reflection, it appears rather that after the Holocaust no philosophy of history as a "theodicy" can be provided and that any meaning of commonality can be reconstructed only from within any given social experience. If the Hegelian ontological understanding of logical forms is rejected as being dialectically embedded within historical concretisations – "the rational is real" – a post-metaphysical understanding of the rationality of states' institutions must reconsider the phenomenological status of Hegel's notion of recognition and reformulate it in terms of a socio-institutional discursive structure for the generation of legitimate communicative actions.

Let's address this point by referring first to Hegel's mechanism of political representation within the civil society and the emergence of public validity from an institutionally based deliberative conception. In Hegel's *Philosophy of Right* (2001

---

[19] Fichte (2000 [1796]).

[20] Fichte considers that the same possibility for the unity of the subject and the object that the process of self-consciousness should demonstrate, must presuppose an *a priori* unity of the consciousness itself. From this perspective, it follows that "determination" and "self-determination " are part of the same intuition, and that mutual recognition can be established only within reasonable peoples who set limits, reciprocally, to the exercise of their own freedom towards the other beings. The interdependence of one consciousness to another establishes man's rights as rights of a generic being who is inherently constituted by intersubjective relations. One's freedom depends upon its recognition by someone else, so that one's free will presuppose an intersubjective form of limitation preventing arbitrariness. I will later investigate Hegel's distinction between immediate and mediated recognition. On the difference between Fichte and Hegel of such point see also Wildt (1982, 312–365).

[1821]), the *Staende* place themselves as a form of intermediation between the individual and the rational will of the state. Accordingly, states assembly takes bicameral form, an higher and a lower Chamber, the latter subordinated to electoral process on the basis of corporative affiliation (Hegel 2001 [1821] §306–7). This system of electoral procedure is already, for Hegel, a form of initial rationalisation of individual arbitrary: if elections are based upon corporative groups, then society is not atomistically resolved into individuals (Hegel, 2001 [1821] § 308). This point is useful to our purposes in highlighting what has been too often ignored in Hegel's conception of the state, namely that a form of pluralism within the deliberative functions of states' public assemblies is part of his design. But besides the mechanical design of a pluralist transmission chain of interest mediations within the state, Hegel can even be considered as anticipating a proto-dialogical form of discursive argumentation. Indeed as already noted by Avineri (1972, chap. 8), the addition to para. 315 of the *Philosophy of Right*, contains an explicit reference to the emergence, through public deliberation, of virtues and attitudes determining the validity of political orientations. Outside an institutionally constrained public debate, for Hegel, public opinion is certainly endowed with the substantial principles of justice, but such elements are connected with all the accidentality springing from the lack of information and the false conscience of the case. Therefore non-institutionally constrained public opinion is both to be evaluated and deprecated at the same time (Hegel, 2001 [1821] § 317). One should not be too severe in criticizing Hegel for the low consideration of the so-called *vox populi* because at that time few people had access to relevant information and political debates. What can, instead, be retained from such a consideration is the conviction that were people sufficiently informed and enabled to form their own opinion regarding political issues, public agenda would be fixed from a bottom-up deliberative approach.

Having clarified this textual point, it might be claimed that from within an Hegelian perspective, the confrontation of diverging opinions in the public realm must be rethought in terms of a discursive form of recognition.

Recognition, thus, can become a discursive *dimension of dialectical recognition*, a dimension whose achievements always represent revisable outcomes for the critical self-understanding of a political community. Since institutions are no longer rational instantiations of the historical progression of the "Idea", their rationality can no more be measured in view of a capacity to mirror a particular form of achievement of the "Absolute". Rather, the role of institutions is limited to the functional capacity of exhibiting the most extensive guarantee of a *pluralist argumentative inclusion*. The dialogical form of dialectical recognition can in fact proceed in its tasks only upon the condition that the ethical life is cohabitated by a plurality of doctrines, and that institutional arrangements are oriented to the maximal dialogical inclusion of its parts.

In virtue of an inherent negative moment which accompanies the dialectical process of recognition, no mediated form of coordinating principle can be mutually achieved without a prior moment of (argumented) discursive mis-recognition. Signs of dialogical mis-recognitions occur when a critical "no" is advanced on the request of actions coordination. The Hegelian dialectical reconciliation of the "to be with itself in the other", is thus a condition posed through the median moment of a critical (determinate) negation.

A difference here must be drawn between absolute and determinate negation: as in the *Science of Logic* (1969) [1812–16] the Hegelian passage from absolute being and absolute not-being *does not constitute* a dialectical process, since the transition to the determinate being is defined as a "falling" into a "calm result". In a parallel way, within a discursive form of dialectical recognition, absolute dialogical refusals to a proposed illocutive claim prevent any form of dialogical reasonability. Upon the condition of recognizing the interlocutor as a legitimate bearer of coordination claims, negation takes the form of a critical and determinate refusal which, far from leading to a total conversational break, opens up to a higher reflective moment of agreement (ethical recognition).

When confronted with other discursive models oriented to action coordination, the dialectic notion of recognition here proposed considers mutual agreement as a *mediated result* of argumentative confrontation among agents. The initial intuitive presupposition of action coordination is only a starting point for the development of an idea of public acceptability which gains its legitimacy only having surpassed the test of pluralist criticism. The discursive dialectic of recognition, indeed, offers full legitimacy to an internal process of argumentative disagreement in the public sphere seen in terms of a necessary moment for the achievement of action coordination at a higher ethical moment. Disagreement is something embedded within the same process of discursive recognition: through its internal dialectic it favours a truly conversational improvement among participants. Such inherent dialectical "negativity" of validity claims is the guiding force of a truly dialogical enterprise of coordinating action. Indeed, as I will show in the next chapter, differently from the Habermasian model of communicative action, it is only when communicative agents engage in the critical overcoming of particularly situated exemplar judgments that concrete universality, as Hegel would put it, can arise.

This explanatory model takes the dialogical interrelation among agents as a pragmatic-transcendental condition for the characterization of intersubjective rationality. This means that we cannot avoid the dialogical condition for the constitution of ourselves as rational beings and that any monological-strategic position is conceptually derivative from the dialogical dimension. In a word, any negation of the dialogical dimension presuppose as its same condition the dialogue itself. If this is a preliminary characterization of what I mean by discursive dialectic, then, an immediate implication of this scenario concerns the situatedness of the speakers. More specifically, if the dialogical dimension cannot be avoided and if whatever one claims is part of a specific context of formulation and argumentation, then one cannot see herself as advancing an objectively neutral detached position. On the contrary, from the situatedness of every speech act, it follows through intersubjective dialectic confrontation, a reflexive form of understanding of those same conditions of the dialogue itself which can never though be completely at disposal of the speakers. The conditions of possibility of the same dialogical activity can be grasped from within the dialogical activity of intersubjective argumentation. Such conditions provide the formal parameters of a universal structure of rationality which awaits to be vivified by actual argumentative speeches. While they truly represent the classical kind of formal universality as the one represented by the Kantian moral perspective, it is only once the plurality of reflective judgements confront at the public level that ethicity, as a discursively argumented form of mutual convergence, can arise.

In the following chapter I will characterize the transcendental and formally universal structure of the dialogical activity as the formal system of human rights liberties. These are only the preconditions for the realization of human rights exemplar judgements, but their status as unavoidable conditions for the dialogical activity must be presupposed as necessary conditions for the actualization of human rights discourses themselves.

Part II

Chapter 3
Human Rights and Pluralisitc Universalism

This chapter opens the second part of this enquiry with the aim of modelling a new frame for the understanding of the validity of human rights. While in the first two chapters I investigated the difficulties arising from relativism and objectivism in morality and knowledge, and proposed possible directions of investigation therein, here I consider how a normatively acceptable judgmental activity on human rights can be advanced without falling into the two aforementioned competing extremisms. I do so by highlighting how the generalized condition of purposive agency implies that of communicative action, that is, I elaborate how the condition for the realization of one's goals requires a preliminary condition of social coordination in order to be fulfilled. The central core of my proposal therefore takes its structure from a critical evaluation of the Habermasian notion of communicative action, and in particular a reading of the Searlian investigation into illocutive speech-acts.

In this chapter, the overall picture of the interconnection and the formal analogy between our moral and cognitive faculties will find a point of reference and an organic articulation in the understanding of the validity constraints of illocutionary speech-acts theory. Indeed, in my view, any illocutionary speech-act raises different kinds of validity claims; that is, from a first meta-claim of validity consisting in the condition of understandability or meaningfulness of that which is communicated, there follows the condition of normative correctness (which I take as being further articulated into truth and rightness), and of truthfulness (sincerity/veridicity). While the aim of the first chapter has been that of clarifying the meta-notion of *understandability* and of *epistemic truth*, as well as that of considering whether both the epistemic prerequisites of "mutual understanding" and of "mutual agreement" can resist relativistic challenges, here I rejoin such elements within a public use of judgemental activity on human rights. Needless to say that were relativistic challenges successful, the construction of a notion of public reason would be prevented within democratic deliberative processes on human rights.

Let's further clarify my explicative model. Here, we are interested in the condition of normative correctness because it concerns the notion of rightness. Through the examination of Gewirth's idea of necessary goods and Rawls' complex reconstruction of the relevance of primary goods, I claim that the right is a conceptually

C. Corradetti, *Relativism and Human Rights*, DOI 10.1007/978-1-4020-9986-1_3,
© Springer Science+Business Media B.V. 2009

supraordinated category to that of the good. In a regime of pluralism as the one of modern societies, conflicts arising from the diversity of the goods can be solved only through a form of adjudication which takes into account what is ethically right for that society to do. The relevance that the Hegelian notion of "recognition" acquires within my reformulation of the theory of communicative action reinforces this point.[1] The recognition of the other as a purposive agent grounds a metacondition for the validity of any speech act as well as its dialectical movement. Thus it follows that human rights and, most of all the right to freedom from which I take the other rights to be derivative specifications, are instances of a formally normative condition of recognition. And yet, this first check does not exhaust the process of validation of human rights. From this, in my view, follows a second parameter of validation which is represented by the idea of exemplar validity. Human rights judgments oriented to the meta-reflection of the conditions of validity of illocutive speech-acts are also subordinated to a substantive notion of "exemplar validity". While the form of universality represented by the notion of recognition is merely procedural, oriented to maximal recognition of otherness, the standard of exemplar validity attempts at producing a contextually situated judgment on the basis of a form of subjective universality. The form of universality which is pre-given in the use of reflective judgment is only a procedural one, whereas its substantive configuration is yet to be found. This point exhausts the conditions of normative validity that are embedded within illocutive speech-acts and completes my revised model of communicative action.

What results from the present model is a notion of "pluralist universalism" within the public sphere. Pluralist universalism allows for a certain number of valid and competitive configurations in the realm of the public sphere. In such cases, which belong to a normal public running of debates in modern democracies, what is required is the formulation of a *second-order judgmental construction* capable of overcoming interpretive conflicts and supposedly mutual mis-recognitions. Such collective form of second-order judgmental construction takes place within a process of a *dialectically mediated form of recognition* among those reasonable positions placing themselves in competing rivalry. I will not consider which institutional forms can best grant such an outcome. I believe that there must be a division of labour between the contribution that normative political philosophy might allow with what political science can suggest. My argument, therefore, will be limited to the construction of a theoretical model, leaving the institutional task to be assessed by a different form of enquiry.

---

[1] It might be claimed that to ground a theory of human rights upon the condition of the recognition of the other as a purposive agent might exclude a certain number of fundamental rights that ought to be recognized for instance for animals or for the environment. My answer is precisely that this book is devoted only to the construction of a theory of human rights as such and that, while compatible with further developments including also animal rights, as it stands, it is not concerned with such problems.

3.1 From Purposive Action to Communicative Action

Along the first two chapters I have proceeded by ruling out several competing positions to my defended approach to human rights. This preparatory work has been conceived in order to pave the way for the construction of a normative framework of human rights universalism which concedes a certain degree of variation at different levels. As will be explained, I define this approach in terms of "pluralistic universalism". And yet, before proceeding more specifically to the arguments in support of this view, it is important to critically analyse some of the most relevant philosophical positions which have been recently advanced for the justification of human rights. From the inconsistencies of the discussed views but also in a sort of "family resemblance" with them, I will derive my own model. By this I mean that the theories which I take into consideration are, so to say, "internally connected" to my defended view and my attempt is that of constructing a competing alternative on the basis of the weaknesses exhibited by these positions. I will begin my analysis by taking into account Gewirth's notion of "purposive agency", which I take as one of the most promising views in contemporary debates and then proceed to evaluation of the Habermasian notion of "communicative action".

Within the reflection upon the conditions of purposive agency, one interesting position is that developed by Gewirth (1981, 1982, 1984, 1996). Gewirth argues that all forms of human intentional actions presuppose some substantive moral views on the part of the agent. In other words, the very concept of agency requires an agent to make certain substantive moral claims on pain of contradiction. In what follows, I reconstruct Gewirth's general argument, while also providing some integrative elements. Gewirth states that: every rational agent must regard his purposes as contingently good.

If this is true, then every rational agent must regard as a *necessary good* the general necessary conditions for successful agency, since they provide the conditions of his acting to achieve his contingent purposes. Thus, every rational agent must regard as a necessary good the general necessary conditions for successful agency, so that the general necessary conditions for successful agency are freedom and basic well-being. Thus, every rational agent must regard as a necessary good freedom and basic well-being. Gewirth's argument relies on a distinction between two kinds of good. On the one hand, an agent regards x as a *necessary good* if (1) the agent regards x as good; and (2) it is not possible for the agent to regard x as not good. On the other hand, an agent regards x as a *contingent good* if (1) the agent regards x as good; and (2) it is possible for the agent to regard x as not good. From the distinction between contingent and necessary good, Gewirth deduces the category of Generic Rights, as follows:

(1) My freedom and basic well-being are necessary goods.
(2) If (1) is true, then I, as an actual or prospective agent, must have freedom and basic well-being.
(3) If (2) is true, then I, as an actual or prospective agent, require that other people refrain from interfering with my freedom and basic well-being.

(4) Therefore, as an actual or prospective agent, I require that other people refrain from interfering with my freedom and basic well-being.

(5) If (4) is true, then all other people ought to refrain from interfering with my freedom and basic well-being.

(6) Therefore, all other people ought to refrain from interfering with my freedom and basic well-being.

Thus, the agent who is committed to (1) is, on pain of contradiction, logically committed to (6).

Now, supposing the agent who is committed to (6) denies that "I have rights to freedom and basic well-being", through the following chain of reasoning, this will lead to contradiction:

(7) It is not the case that I have a right to freedom and basic well-being.

(8) If (7), then it is not the case that all other people ought to refrain from interfering with my freedom and basic well-being.

(9) Therefore, it is not the case that all other people ought to refrain from interfering with my freedom and basic well-being.

But (9) contradicts (6). Thus, (6) commits the agent to the claim that she has rights to freedom and basic well-being. Since (1) commits the agent to (6), (1) also commits the agent to the claim that she has rights to freedom and basic well-being.

Gewirth defines the rights to freedom and basic well-being as "generic rights". For the moment, he has proved these rights as necessary only for merely prudential, and not yet moral, reasons. Indeed, it has only been shown that the agent is committed to claiming that *she herself but not others* have rights to freedom and basic well-being. To establish that these rights are moral, we must also show that the agent is committed to the claim that all other human beings have these rights as well.

According to Gewirth, to apprehend that the agent is also committed to this further step, one must consider that the conclusion that "I have a right to freedom and basic well-being" is generated by the general claim that "I am a prospective purposive agent". Hence, on pain of contradiction, I must recognize that all other prospective purposive agents have these same generic rights. In other words, if I am entitled to the right to basic well-being and freedom because I recognize myself as a purposive agent, then everyone who is recognized as a purposive agent will hold the same rights. Now since the claim that "A has a right to X" entails that "every person ought to refrain from interfering with A's enjoyment of X," my recognition that "every other prospective purposive agent has a right to freedom and basic well-being" commits me to the claim "every person has a duty not to interfere with the freedom and basic well-being of any other person." As a result, on pain of self-contradiction, every agent is logically committed to what Gewirth defines as the Principle of Generic Consistency (PGC):

Act in accordance with the generic rights of your recipients as well as of yourself.

The Principle of Generic Consistency can thus be derived from the notion of rational purposive agency and plays the role of a supreme principle in morality.

There are several objections and possible suggestions of modification that can be raised against Gewirth's argument here, the resolution of which supports the advancement of an enriched reformulation of Gewirth's thesis.

First of all, Gewirth's definition of liberty and basic well-being as necessary goods recalls the Rawlsian list of primary goods in *A Theory of Justice* (1971, para. 68), where Rawls undertakes to clarify the terms of the differentiation of "the good" and "the right". The contrasting features of "the good" and "the right" are accompanied by a general criticism of utilitarianism, as guilty of having extended "to society the principle of choice for one man", and consequently of subjecting "the rights secured by justice to the calculus of social interests". Utilitarianism conceives of justice in consequentialist terms,[2] whereas justice as fairness aims to be a deontological theory, under which "the good" is not established independently from "the right", and the latter does not have to maximize "the good". When addressing the difference between "the right and the good", Rawls's first point is that, whereas the principles of justice and right are in general chosen within the original position, "the principles of rational choice and the criteria of deliberative rationality are not chosen at all" (Rawls, 1971, 446). It seems, thus, as if there is a first contrasting feature here, based upon *de facto* acceptance of the criteria of deliberative rationality and *de jure* acceptability of principles of justice in an idealized deliberative situation which establishes the validity of "reasonable constraints on arguments for accepting principles and that the principles agreed to should match our considered convictions of justice in reflective equilibrium" (Rawls, 1971, 446–447).

If there is no need to look for agreement regarding the great variety of principles of rational choice "since each person is free to plan his life as he pleases", what a theory of justice must assume, according to Rawls, is that "in a thin account of the good, the evident criteria of rational choice are sufficient to explain the preference for the primary goods, and that such variations as exist in conceptions of rationality do not affect the principles of justice adopted in the original position" (Rawls, 1971, 447).

Is Rawls saying here that, notwithstanding irreconcilable differences in subjective preferences as to life choices, there is still enough ground to admit that we can all agree upon "a thin notion of the good" based on a list of primary goods? And if so, what is the relevance of such a list within the idealized deliberation concerning the principles of justice in the original position? Can one infer from list of primary goods within the definition of justice as fairness that Rawls implicitly the draws a distinction between goods whose justifiability rests inherently on a subjective level, and goods that are publicly justifiable, just so that rational agreement can be achieved?

---

[2] It must be said that utilitarianism includes a quite complex web of doctrines and that while consequentialism is a constituent part of most of the utilitarian positions, as is also in the case of act-utilitarianism, consequentialism is not a necessary property for any form of utilitarianism, as for instance in the case of rule-utilitarianism.

If one takes into consideration the Rawlsian notion of a "thin knowledge of the good", as Rawls presents it, one might think that Rawls is introducing undemonstrated presuppositions constraining rational deliberation about principles of justice. In other words, in his account, "primary goods" are taken as setting the same conditions from which principles of justice can be agreed upon just by restricting, substantively, the range of possible justificatory configurations that might arise from the original position, thus lifting the "veil" for *ad hoc* purposes.[3]

Primary goods are defined by Rawls as necessary requirements for any conceivable rational plan. Income and wealth, opportunities, liberty, and the social basis of self-respect are universally desirable goods and, Rawls concludes, primary goods, on this basis. Primary goods are also desired in greater rather than lesser quantity; and they establish strong conditions of rationality, that is, they set conditions for the rationality of any individual's plan of action in life.

These far-reaching criteria raise important questions: how can Rawls conceive of these goods as required for any plan of life if neither specific life plans, nor a society structured according to any particular economic arrangement is allowed to play a role at this stage of his theory?

Let us consider, for instance, the notions of income and wealth. Why should one consider as irrational a society whose social arrangements are not based on these? The claim that the "basicness" of the goods involved is an unproblematic assumption does not seem entirely convincing. Can one take these two as prerequisite to a society's rationality? It seems they cannot: it seems plausible, for instance, that a community where income is not considered primary cannot be labelled uncontroversially as an irrational social arrangement. Social arrangements based on "solidarity brotherliness", to the contrary, can represent extremely rational forms of social relations. Further criticisms might be addressed to other subsidiary aspects of the primary goods mentioned, such as the vague quantification of the amount of them required in any social context or by any individual in order to achieve their purported life goals. Rawls even takes their status as primary goods for granted, but their abstract and rigid characterization prevents the possibility of variation in the quantity of their allocation according to contextual and individual differences.

Rawls has several arguments replying to my objections and in later writings he clarifies and reformulates the relevance of primary goods within a political theory of justice. In chap. 5 of *Political Liberalism* (1996a) Rawls claims that the good and the right are complementary concepts and that they have to be combined even if the right has to be given priority over the good. This implies that the idea of justice as fairness tells us that the principles of justice establish limitations to the variability of the ideas of those goods admissible in the public domain. The first restriction is that the ideas of the good are *political* ideas, and that therefore no possible community of brotherhood can be introduced in order to criticise his list of primary goods.

---

[3] The concept of rationality of goods in terms of realization of a plan of life is provided by Rawls in para. 66 (1971).

Further, such political ideas must: (a) be shared by free and equal citizens and (b) not presuppose any partial or total comprehensive doctrines. This means that those restrictions to the ideas of the good refer to the respect of the limits of a political view of what is good for a fair society. Conditions (a) and (b) are satisfied by five ideas of the good which are typical of the idea of justice as fairness, that is: the idea of the good as rationality; the idea of primary goods; the idea of the comprehensive view of the admissible goods; the idea of political virtues; the idea of the good of a well-ordered political society. With this characterization Rawls intends that a fair political society can include only rational plans of life as well as the pursuant of only rational ideas of the good. Therefore rationality will act as the basis of a public justification of political justice. Goodness as rationality provides a criterion for the formulation of a list of primary goods and the overlapping convergence upon primary goods takes its moves from within a political perspective of justice. In fact Rawls claims that primary goods must be combined with a political conception of citizens as free and equal. It is therefore crucial to develop a political conception of citizens which does not rest upon a comprehensive view. The agreement upon a number of primary goods establishes for each citizen the typology of those pretences that each can socially advance as well as the way in which this can be made. According to Rawls free and equal citizens would advance the following open list of primary goods: (a) fundamental rights (b) freedom of movement and of choice of occupation (c) powers in the institutions (d) income and wealth (e) the social basis of self respect. Primary goods define a public domain of interpersonal comparisons grounded upon objective properties within a background scenario of reasonable pluralism. Such primary goods must be congruent with a political conception of justice as fairness established as a focal point of an overlapping consensus. In as far as my previous objection concerning contextual variability is concerned, Rawls would reply that a list of equal distribution of primary goods would certainly be an unfair form of allocation, while his point simply refers to a list of basic moral capacities which can be exercised only on the basis of such goods and in view of the realization of equal terms of cooperation. And yet the reformulated arguments that Rawls introduces in *Political Liberalism* do manifest some inconsistencies. For instance, in para. 4 it is said that those conceptions of the good that violate fundamental rights cannot be admissible within a theory of justice as fairness. If one were to take this point seriously, then two possible objections might be raised. The first is that fundamental rights assume an ambiguous characterization, since they are treated both as primary goods *per se* and as criteria for the evaluation of admissible primary goods. Secondly, if the normative weight of the admissibility of the goods in the public domain relies upon criteria established starting from a list of fundamental rights, then, once that these parameters have been fixed, it follows that the same choice of these goods results as a philosophically irrelevant point. Rather, what seems relevant for our purposes is a procedure of justification of those same liberties that must be granted in order to obtain a fair political society. As will be apparent from the strategy which I develop hereafter, the discursive dialectic of recognition previously introduced gives priority to a procedural criterion that leaves the idea of primary goods as a contingent element of a political self-determining society. According to my defended view, the decision of which list of primary goods must govern a fair society is the outcome of a deliberative procedure which, if normatively valid, places itself in between a criterion of recognition and the exemplarity of reflective judgment.

In this section, therefore, I will try to justify a thick notion of liberty which, far from being considered as a primary good, will be derived from the criterion of recognition and defined as a form of enabling condition to agency, that is to say, as a transcendental condition for the pursuing of the good *qua* good is chosen. This idea rests upon the conviction that the plurality of goods as those advanced by modern societies does indeed advance forms of partial incommensurability, whose common root can be understood only with a reference to what the enabling conditions are giving place to, namely, pluralist configurations of the good life.

The rejection of any idea defending the priority of universal goods over all forms of considerations is extremely relevant for the dismissal of the wide-spread idea of human rights as intrinsic, or ultimate, necessary goods. For instance Raz, starting from a concept of "autonomy as achievement" *versus* "autonomy as capability", postulates the relevance of ultimate intrinsic values and claims that: "At least some of the social conditions that constitute such options [choices leading to autonomy] are collective goods", hence the notion of "intrinsic duties", as that of saving from deliberate destruction a Van Gogh's painting. Besides the reduplication of the right-duty correlation in terms of intrinsic goods-duties which contradicts Raz's criticisms of what he calls "narrow moralities", the problem remains that of producing a valid argument justifying intrinsic goods within a regime of pluralism (Raz, 1985, 50–52). But such an argument seems difficult to produce without a previous formulation of a concept of "autonomy as capability" which enables subjects to choose supposedly intrinsic goods. If this is the case, however, then Raz has to admit that rights grounding autonomy as capability must be logically satisfied before a subject can choose intrinsic goods and become capable of autonomy as achievement, as for instance in the case of a right to unpolluted air precedes logically the possibility for the subject to claim to his government an industrial politics safeguarding the environment.

Once dismissed the undemonstrated presupposition of primary or intrinsic goods in general, and of Gewirth's consideration of liberty as a necessary good – which does not consider the plurality of goods in modern societies and thus of the plurality of forms that liberty as a necessary good might take – let us turn to other possible objections to Gewirth's argument.

As far as a preliminary observation is concerned, it can be claimed that, having based his argument upon "prudential rational agency" premises, Gewirth is compelled to provide an argument as to why the relationship of necessity between human rights and agency is the only option that can be maintained as a condition for purposive agency. According to Gewirth's argument, one is compelled to show that the agent would contradict himself, were he not willing to recognize the conditions of human rights (freedom and basic well-being) as necessary universal conditions. Hence, it is necessary to specify conditions of purposive agency in terms different than those "factual elements" characterizing Gewirth's purposive agency, that do not rule out other possible candidates such as, for instance, the attribution of rights on the basis of personal merit.

There are two further specifications which such objection might take, namely: (i) to what extent the notion of agency can be conceived of and (ii) to what extent the notion of an agent's purposiveness can be assumed, in order to justify the rights to freedom and basic well-being as necessary rights.

Concerning the first point, if one remains once more within the perspective of an empirical purposive agent, the extension of human rights to those who, for instance, are in a permanent vegetative state, becomes problematic: the individual concerned lacks capacity to act as a purposive agent. If we subordinate, as Gewirth does, the notion of duties (ought) to that of an actual agency capacity (can), we would be forced to conclude in favour of a degree of variation in the distribution of rights according to the capacity of subjects to claim them. But, then, in so doing the outcome would seem to result in a very unsatisfactory theory of human rights.

Let me clarify this point. One weakness of Gewirth's argument concerns precisely his interpretation of the is-ought relation outside the realm of an institutional framework of the ethical life as previously indicated. By adopting the is-ought relation in purely individualistic terms, and by subordinating the ought to a factual is, Gewirth concludes that: from the fact that I'm a purposive agent, I ought to praise a certain kind of basic goods. It seems that if rights are argued this way, then different degrees of allocation of rights must be provided to agents in accordance to the amount of their factual capacity of being purposive. It is thus important to reverse the concept of proportionality defended by Gewirth in the allocation of rights, according to the agent's actual capacity of being purposive.[4] Indeed, if proportionality of this kind were defended, one would not be able to grant full rights to people suffering undeserved poverty or unjust imprisonment, for instance; rights would be distributed simply on the basis of a *de facto* acceptance of any undeserved human condition. If this were true, then human rights would lose their property of universality. It is true that to this Gewirth might reply that "[. . .] the point is not that something is an object of a right only if it is actually claimed, but rather that if one has a right to something then one has a justified basis for claiming that something from other persons" (1986, 335), but then rights allocations to defective purposive agents must be granted independently from an actual capacity and be allocated as if they were fully purposive agents. Only by presupposing a general idealizing condition of mutual recognition as purposive agents, it is then possible to agree with the factual observation made by Gewirth according to which: "Children and other persons who are unable to make claims for themselves can be represented by persons who can make claims for them, and this gives the not fully mature right-holders a status that normatively compels other persons to take account of the right-holders' interests for the latter's own sakes and as something which is owed to them" (1986, 336).

---

[4] Gewirth (1985).

That a rational agent must be committed to equality in enjoyment of human rights seems to recall idealized circumstances of purposive agency, according to which a purposive agent is required to make decisions under uncertainty. But if this is so, Gewirth would not need to speak of an "actual" agent moving from an "is" to a moral "ought": instead he would need to assume an idealized notion of agency which, under conditions of uncertainty, would select the safest options from amongst the range of possible outcomes in the "lottery of life". In order to address this point, I begin with a reconstruction of the Rawlsian notion of human rights and then proceed towards a more extensive discussion of the Habermasian human rights institutionalization of the discursive model and of its procedural-transcendental conditions of validity.

In *The Law of Peoples* (1999), Rawls dedicates some pages to the role that human rights play within the "society of peoples", and in particular to their function as necessary conditions for the definition of minimal conditions of social and political cooperation among the members of a society (Rawls, 1999, para. 8.2). Since human rights establish the socio-political cement for the cooperation of individuals, they come also to define the minimal conditions of "decency" of peoples in general, and with that, of the minimal conditions for an international agreement upon the eight principles characterizing the original position as extended to the non-liberal states. Upon careful scrutiny, besides the *prima facie* restricted Rawlsian understanding of what counts as human rights within his theory, that is essentially the right to life, liberty from enslavement, of conscience, religion and thought, the right to property and the right to formal equality (Rawls, 1999, para. 8.2, 2a), Rawls does not limit the relevance of universal human rights only to their negative constraints as rights. Indeed, within Rawls's specification of what the right to life indicates, the concept of the means of subsistence as well as of personal security are also introduced. A further element indicating a more complex view is contained in the footnote, where an even more specific reference is made to Shue (1980) and in particular to his interpretation of the right to life as encompassing the guarantee of a minimal socio-economic threshold of subsistence, not to speak of the more complex notion of "freedom from" Rawls seems to uphold when specifying the types of freedoms men should be granted universally, recalling quite clearly Sen's definition for the principles of human rights.

It is true, though, that even if Rawls provides many functions human rights must play within the international political scenario, such as those of placing limits or burdens to the internal sovereignty of states, as the suspension of the international duty of non-intervention into third-states, or the role of limiting the notion of pluralism among peoples etc., no contractarian argument is provided for the acceptance of the principles of human rights within the second original position, so that the suspicion of a *de facto* natural law bias for their justification can be rightly advanced (Ferrara, 2003, 4).

Nevertheless, it is possible to suggest an alternative reading for the explanation of how Rawls conceives of the status of human rights, and this could make reference to the idea of a "decent hierarchical consultation" characterizing, indeed, decent peoples. If decent peoples are mainly connoted by a decent form of hierarchical consultation, then this means that human rights as socio-political conditions of cooperation cannot be detached from a form of "proto-democratic" regime of legitimation, and that if this is so, then human rights are in a way co-original with such proto-deliberative form of consultation. If a similar reading is admissible, then liberal and decent peoples coming to reach an agreement in a second original position already possess an extensive notion of human rights so that their task is merely that of refining a commonly sheared perspective on what should be binding at the international level. But such non-ideal perspective for human rights legitimation would simply postpone without providing a solution to the problem for the justification of human rights. Since if, as Rawls extensively claims, human rights, whatever they are, must be taken as universally valid principles, whenever their legitimation is conceived of in terms of democratic or proto-democratic forms, no morally binding force can be defended against those undemocratic out-law peoples who being ruled by despotic governments, would never come up at recognizing the "co-originality" between democracy and human rights. Or better, if the Rawlsian argument for human rights can take such a form, then its plausibility would rather rely upon an idealized perspective for a mutual co-dependence of human rights and democracy as that developed by Habermas. In the following section, I will reconstruct some critical elements of the Habermasian co-originality thesis for human rights with specific attention to its linguistic insight.

As our investigation has indicated, from the dynamics of purposive agency oriented to the achievement of rational goals, it has resulted that each instrumental action requires the fulfilment of necessary presuppositions of human rights, as conditions granting action-coordination. This clarifies the subordination of rational egoist actions to the postulation of universal agency constraints conceived of as in terms of human rights. The agreement upon universal constraints of purposive action, therefore, is a pre-requisite for the realization of rational instrumental actions. These latter owe their same conditions of legitimacy only in conjunction with the respect of the unavoidable constraints of human rights. However, whereas in Gewirth there is an inversion between an actual capacity from which rights are claimed and an idealized scenario from which they must be justified, which subordinates universal justification to factual purposive capacity, in Rawls the "democratic-discursive" principle is implied but not fully developed. For this reason, I will turn to the Habermasian validity claims raised by illocutive speech acts which are aimed precisely at providing an idealized dialogical definition of the conditions for action-coordination oriented to agreement. The Habermasian project for a "detrascendentalisation" of rationality presuppositions – which proceeds in parallel to the development of the post-modern condition – finds one of its most interesting exemplifications in the famously argued argument for the co-originality of popular sovereignty and human rights (Habermas, 1996a).

In order to proceed to the analysis of such argument, it is necessary to begin by addressing, first, some elements connected to the discourse theoretical principle

(principle D),[5] and to its higher level of abstraction respect to the moral principle as a principle of universalization (principle U). In Habermas (1996a, 107), the validity of claims is measured with reference to the discourse theoretical principle "D". Principle "D" is reformulated as a purely procedural principle that is neutral towards morality. "U" comes into play when "D" is applied to moral discourses, whereas when directed towards law discourses, it takes the form of the principle of democracy. Such distinctions allow Habermas to maintain the realm of law as not subordinate to the moral realm, as strong natural law theories maintain, but in a relation of reciprocal integration. The formulation of the discourse theoretical principle precedes the distinction between morality and law, specifying itself into such two domains only once that different action types are justified respectively in terms of face to face individual relations (moral principle) and in terms of a process of legitimate legislation among citizens. Whereas moral norms exhibit a weak action coordinating power since no one is obliged to fulfil moral duties unless everyone else behaves in the same way, law proposes a stricter integrative standard for post-traditional societies due to its sanctioning power for non compliance. It is law, as a concretization of the discourse theoretical principle into the democratic principle, which paves the way for the legitimation of post-traditional societies. But legal procedures, while not subordinated to morality, bear with them a form of mutual co-originality and internal relation: legal procedures, in order to achieve validity, must embed moral constraints so that the relation between the two becomes complementary. This means also that in order to achieve valid communicative action oriented towards agreement, agents entering into pragmatic discursive interaction are bound to respect normative constraints of the kinds, "the best argument wins", and "everyone must be allowed to speak", in such a way that the pragmatics of speech acts is normatively constrained by such standards. Discourse practice, in order to produce valid claims, is constrained by the possibility of universalizing subjective claims through the test of rational acceptability of the consequences that any given principle might produce for potential participants in an ideal communicative situation: consensus can only be achieved about propositions that incorporate universalizable interests (Principle U), but propositions incorporating universal interests result from the activity of deliberation (Principle D), as constrained by communicative presuppositions.

Particularly interesting, for purposes that will be set out later, is that the Habermasian process of universalization does not rest on any ultimate *a priori* principle. By not relying on an ultimate form of justification or *a priori* knowledge (Habermas, 1990, 95–98), "U" is itself falsifiable by the activity of deliberation carried on by subjects, who arrive at different, but nonetheless valid, conclusions. Additionally, it seems, with respect to the application of his principle of universalization, Habermas accepts a contextualist orientation, which takes into consideration

---

[5] The discourse theoretical principle claims that: "(D) Just those action norms are valid to which all possibly affected persons could agree as participants in rational discourses" Habermas (1996a, 107).

the imperfect and contingent nature of knowledge. This acceptance results in a more flexible version of the formalization of the principle of universality: "A norm is valid when the foreseeable consequences and the side effects of its general observance for the interests and value-orientations of each individual could be jointly accepted by all concerned without coercion" (Habermas, 1998b, 42). Such ideal speech conditions are linked to the notion of democracy, the latter viewed as an institutionalization, through law, of the elements of rational deliberation, specifically, via the legal right of each individual to participate in discursive processes of production of legal norms. Both moral and legal norms are seen as derived from the ideal discursive process; discourses concerning the latter are institutionalized in complex structures in a democratic society.

According to Habermas, the democratic procedure is the only post-metaphysical source of legitimation through which law is created. It guarantees, on the one hand, a factual realization of norms through sanctions whereas, on the other hand, it grants legitimate conditions for the production of the self-same norms. From the point of view of the theory of society, law performs the function of social integration; it provides an abstract structure for face-to-face relations between strangers. It also stabilizes behavioural expectations, favouring simultaneously symmetrical relations of recognition between holders of subjective rights. Structurally, this bears similarity to the conditions of legitimacy of the model of communicative action, where the community is constituted not by a hypothetical contract, but by a discursively achieved deliberative consultation. Within an idealized democratic model, the entire democratic process carries the duty of legitimation, and the sources of legitimation are drawn from amongst communicative presuppositions. In this sense, human rights are not prior to law and to an idealized democratic will. According to the Habermasian perspective, they are instead co-original with the notion of democratic self-determination, in respect to which they are presuppositions.

Just as the creation of a legalized system requires the institution of subjects holding basic rights, in that, without liberties, the institutionalization of the private and public autonomy of juridical subjects would not be possible, the juridification of an equal distribution of rights is dependent upon the existence of a self-determining democratic power. Human rights are themselves co-original with the self-organizing deliberative activity of a society governed by judicial procedures. Accordingly, everyone must be granted the right to equal participation in the democratic process of deliberation, thereby bringing the public and private sphere into mutual co-implication.[6] If, on the one hand, the political right to an equal communicative participation is a presupposition for the valid self-determination of a political body, on the other hand this implies that its guaranteed public autonomy presupposes a condition of individual freedom granting agents' private autonomy. Within such frame of mutual dependence between private and public autonomy, the public and the private sphere are in a continuous tension for their mutual redefinition. Inasmuch as public autonomy is required for the legitimation of privately endorsable

---

[6] Habermas (1998a).

claims on the basis of the general principle of modern law according to which whatever is not forbidden is allowed (Habermas, 1996a, 120), private autonomy has to consent to a public the delegation of its prerogatives and redefinition by a collective will.

If so, then the private and the public are not only co-original, but mutually influencing and legitimating their respective domains of competence. The private cannot be defined without a public approval of what its scope must be like, and the public in its turn cannot decide without the recognition of a privately held sphere of individual liberties. Within such a circular process between human rights and a collective self-determining will, citizens become both the authors and the addressees of political legislative outcomes. But if human rights are, according to the Habermasian argument both necessary presuppositions and political outcomes of a collective body, then in order to avoid a *petitio principii* one must recognize that human rights as presuppositions must differ from those political fundamental rights established through a collective process of will formation.

Indeed, it seems that within the medium of law, deliberating constituent subjects regulate their juridical coexistence through the postulation of a reciprocally recognized "system of basic rights" as a system of not yet internally articulated juridical categories: private liberty rights, civil rights, due-process rights, political rights, welfare rights. Such formal categories of juridical rights are not on an equal level. There is indeed in Habermas an internal logical implication of priority between the right to political participation and that of individual freedom.

And yet, anticipating a juridical system of human rights to a specific articulation of rights as an outcome of a self-legislating body, seems still quite an unsatisfactory move for the avoidance of a vicious circularity. One critical element of the Habermasian communicative presuppositions of a self-legislating body, is that juridical categories are already outputs of an autonomous collective will formation. As presuppositions of communicative freedom, therefore, they must be justified on a different *pre-juridical* ground than as in terms of legal frames. If one wishes to avoid a vicious form of circularity, then the presuppositions of a legitimate self-determining body cannot be considered as themselves products of a not yet validly habilitated deliberating community. The Habermasian co-originality argument between human rights and popular sovereignty must be reinterpreted thus in terms of a hyper ordinate presupposition of habilitating conditions for the exercise of a legitimate political will formation. It is only once such presuppositions are recognized as unavoidable habilitating constraints for legitimate political will formation, that legal discourse can anticipate universally valid legal categories of human rights whose internal substantive articulation is then left to the political self-constituting power of a community of legal agents.

In what follows, I will readdress some of the aforementioned points against Habermas, considering how specific constraints to normative validity do indeed emerge precisely from the analysis of linguistic interaction. My understanding is that also in this case, it will be possible to propose a revised version of the Habermasian model for communicative action, by considering the centrality of those moral enabling conditions for purposive action.

Within a model of communicative action, Habermas argues, drawing from J.L. Austin (1975) and Searle (1969), that every speech act can be identified by its *propositional content* (locutive part) referring to the expression of a state of affairs, by its *illocutive function* as expressed by performative verbs such as "declaring that", "denying that" etc. and concerned with modality by words of making a promise, an order etc. and by its *perlocutory function*, concerning the strategic effects that the speaker aims at reaching on her auditors. Each speech act mode, is but a dominant form of speech interaction which can always be accompanied by any of the other forms as in the case of unconsidered perlocutory side-effects of an illocutive utterance.

Speech acts, by instituting an inter-subjective relationship, guided by rules, advance validity claims which can be either accepted or refused according to reasons possessed by the interlocutor. From a first meta-claim of validity, comprised by (a) the condition of understandability or meaningfulness of what is communicated, there follow three further conditions; namely, (b) the condition of truth (c) the condition of normative correctness with respect to given values and norms (rightness), and (d) the condition of truthfulness (sincerity/veridicity).

Now, in the case of perlocutionary speech act modes none of the aforementioned validity conditions are fulfilled. Perlocutions are actions oriented towards success, and they therefore advance a form of strategic interaction respect to the surrounding interlocutors. On the contrary, according to Habermas, communicative action as a form of action oriented towards reaching understanding, is advanced by dominant illocutionary speech acts which in their turn can produce either a form of "weak" communicative action, where the condition of normative correctness is not satisfied, or a "strong" communicative action, where all three conditions are fulfilled. The hearer's acceptance of all three validity claims advanced by a speaker through a speech-act do indeed realize the possibility of agreement and social coordination which must be logically antecedent to the rational self-realization conducted on the basis of purposive agency.

One might wonder how, once admitted the possibility that among all different types of speech acts only the illocutive ones do satisfy all three validity conditions, a specific form of action coordination can be advanced on the basis of the agreement produced by illocutionary speech acts. That is, due to the modality of speech interaction underscored by illocutionary speech acts, it is interesting to know how validity claims cannot be advanced but by starting from a specific form of communicative interaction. Differently from J.L. Austin (1975) for whom the validity of a speech-act is strictly dependent upon the propositional truth exhibited by an utterance so that different illocutive forces can be externally related the same propositional content (Habermas, [1976], 2003c, 66), Habermas claims that the meaning exhibited by illocutions is itself a linguistic component of the general meaning expressed by an utterance: "[. . .] we do not oppose the illocutionary role to the propositional component, seeing the former as an irrational force and the latter as that which grounds validity; rather, we should conceive the illocutionary role as the component that specifies *which* validity claim a speaker is raising with her utterance, *how* she is raising it, and for *what*. With the illocutionary force of an utterance, a speaker can motivate a hearer to accept the offer contained in her speech act and thereby to enter into a rationally motivated binding and bonding relationship (Bindung)" (Habermas, 2003d, [1981], 110).

Within the Habermasian framework of explanation, one might argue that the form of normative correctness, truthfulness, and truth considered of an illocutive speech act must be strictly connected to the specific *situational power-relations* raised by such speech act modality, so that the validity claims raised remain contingent upon the agent's situational role. Given this limitation, then, the coordinating force of communicative understanding would rely on the specific modality showed by each illocutionary speech act, and each validity claim raised would be eventually satisfied accordingly.

For instance, in the case of an illocutionary act of the kind "I order you to bring me some water" uttered by a restaurant customer, a waiter can possibly agree with the fulfilment of all three validity claims raised only once she has agreed with the situational power-relations established by the role assigned within such context. In other words, she must have *preventively agreed* with the situational meanings and roles springing from the activity of serving in a restaurant, before considering that all three validity claims are satisfied. But this would subordinate, for instance, the normative validity claim to already established power relations and patterns of actions which are socially expected within a defined agency context. Indeed, such Habermasian conceptual inversion for the explanation of the fulfilment of normative validity upon previously reached agreements on *de facto* situational power-relations, is evident in the case of "[. . .] *the conditions of the agreement* [. . .] to the obligations relevant for the sequel of interaction" (Habermas, 2003d [1981], 134). Habermas claims that in order to agree with an illocutive speech-act this declaration must have an imperative mode of the type: "The hearer fully understands the illocutionary meaning of the imperative only if he knows why the speaker expects that she can impose her will on him. With her imperative, the speaker raises a *claim* to power; and this holds only under the condition that S knows that her addressee has reasons to yield to her power claim. Since, to begin with, we have understood imperatives as sheer expressions of will, these reasons cannot lie in the illocutionary meaning of the speech act itself; they can reside only in the reservoir of potential sanctions that is externally connected with the speech act" (Habermas, 2003d [1981], 134).

The point can be made even clearer with the case of a disruption of communicative understanding performed by the refusal of a hearer to take as valid the illocutionary act of a speaker. As an illustration of this point, one might recall that there has been a time when political terrorists rejected any form of trail interrogation entrenching themselves under the formula "I consider myself a political prisoner". This form of absolute rejection of the legitimately constituted power breaks irremediably any further chance of action coordination, since it prevents the entering of both parties into the same linguistic game. The example, though, is mostly indicative of how the legitimacy of contextual power-relations must be previously agreed by agents in order to achieve communicative understanding, and indeed Habermas recognizes that "It would be completely impossible to explain how everyday processes of consensus formation repeatedly succeed in overcoming the hurdle posed by the risk of disagreement built into practices of reaching understanding in the form of criticizable validity claims were we not able to take into account the *massive preunderstanding* of participants in communication; this preunderstanding resides in the self-evident features of an intuitively present, prereflexively known form of life that is presupposed as unproblematic – features that have become culturally habitualized for the participants in communication and into to which they have been socialized" (Habermas, 2003e [1986], 208–209). The not disposable embeddings of subjects into a shared life-world prevents communicative agents from raising linguistic validity claims oriented to the reformulation of a background scenario legitimating communicative action. Even in a less dramatic case, considering what would be a "critical no" proffered by the hearer, the possibility of reaching understanding would not depend on the critical modification of those situational background conditions granting a *de facto* experiential validity to the linguistic validity claims raised by illocutive speech acts. Indeed, were someone's (legitimate) claims *not recognized* at all, then the rejoining of action coordinating functions with the normative validity of the illocutive speech act, would not possibly overcome the appeal to already existing conditions of legal validity. The same would hold, I believe, for all extra legal contexts making appeal to normative claims within the communicative action model.

If this is true, then the need arises to move from a communicative to a meta-communicative level of action coordination, a level which would ground a fundamental relation of intersubjectivity in terms of *recognition of the generalized other*. That the validity of the standard of normative correctness of speech acts, in order not to be subordinated to a factual element, must rely upon a meta-communicative condition of validity, is something that sporadically results also from some Habermasian passages pointing to a moral practice of reasons justifications, as for instance when it is claimed that "Someone who resists a directive is referred to prevailing regulations and not to the penalties that can be expected if they are not followed. And one who doubts the validity of the underlying norms has to give *reasons* that challenge the legitimacy of the regulation, that is, its claim to be right or justified in a moral-practical sense. Validity claims are *internally* connected with reasons" (Habermas, 2003d [1981], 136). And yet, such deferral to moral presuppositions for the justification of the validity of linguistic claims remain underdeveloped and secondary explanations respect to the previously mentioned arguments.

The above analysis indicates that "normative correctness" cannot be subordinated to illocutive speech acts purposes. If validity claims advanced by speakers were attached to the illocutive function of their speech acts, then agreement would be no more than a matter of behavioural conformity, submitting coordinating action to power-relations rather than to normative validity.[7] The objective then becomes that

---

[7] This point integrates the procedural strategy of the "discursive theoretical" model by providing the substantive conditions for a qualitatively high level of deliberative discussion and assessment: "The formal requirements cannot in themselves answer the question of how the needs and views of the various actors may influence the final decision. It is not enough that there are equal

of individuating normatively valid experiential constraints, that is, intersubjective constraints which, by legitimating power-relations, do provide a justified contextual background for the action coordinating force of illocutive speech acts.

Only once such experiential constraints are individuated will it be possible to draw a clear distinction between discourses oriented to normative agreement and those oriented to a strategic-prudential agreement. Indeed, on the one hand, speech acts raise not only truth claims that are validated on the basis of the presupposition of an experiential unity of cognitive rationality as the one presented along the first chapter, but also they raise validity claims of authenticity/sincerity as well as claims of normative correctness, the latter to be assessed in relation to formal constraints of human rights. As I will explain in the next section, the inescapability of supposed human rights constraints is dependent upon a *process of recognition* which incorporates, in itself, the very idea of pluralism of perspectives and which, while not owing its normative validity to any specific context of life-forms, it remains an autonomous form of standard validity. Action-coordination, thus, can result only from a previous fulfilment of a meta-communicative criterion of recognition, one which once satisfied subordinates all strategic intentional actions to normative validity.

3.2 The Priority of Recognition and the Formal System of Basic Liberties

Recently, the suggestion has become fashionable that rights and human rights in particular, arise from the experience of "wrongs". Attached to this idea is the conviction, shared by many authors, that if the notion of the good is so contested and agreement cannot be found between so many incommensurable conceptions of what it means to live a good life, the same does not hold as regards humankind's general understanding of "evil". It is as if there is an asymmetry comprised by the possibility of finding an intuitive, shared, convergent "experience of evil" and, contrariwise, the impossibility of bringing into unity radically divergent notions of the good, which underpin what is the post-modern condition known as "the fact of pluralism" (Rawls, 1996a [1993]).

Amongst the most prominent thinkers defending this view are Dershowitz (2004)[8] and Ignatieff (2001). Before critically discussing this view and advancing a partially alternative reading, I will recapitulate the reconstruction of Ignatieff's main thesis. The notion of the priority of evil can be resolved into three main postulates, namely:

---

opportunities to participate and discuss; we must also make sure that arguments are heard and taken into consideration, i.e. that the debate is good" Eriksen and Weigård (2003, 208).

[8] Dershowitz, for example, claims that his " [...] approach to rights first identifies the most grievous wrongs whose recurrence we seek to prevent, and then asks whether the absence of certain rights contributed to these wrongs. If so, that experience provides a powerful argument for why such rights should become entrenched. This bottom-up approach builds on the reality that there is far more consensus about what constitutes gross injustice than about what constitutes perfect justice" Dershowitz (2004, 82).

(1) a historical-normative claim, according to which human rights represent a reply to the historical evil perpetrated by some humans against others, so that human rights claims are a response to such historical events; (2) a minimalist-prudential claim, according to which it is more adequate to dismiss the possibility of cultivating a possible convergence upon a shared notion of the good and to start, instead, from a more easily shareable experience of the evil, connoting rather common disvalues than values; and, finally, (3) a pragmatic claim, as embedded in the language of human rights, which "prioritizes" the removal of evil upon realization of the good. In other words, the immediate pragmatic result of such position would foster practical action oriented to prioritize the removal of the evil rather than the realization of some common good.

Even if the thesis of the priority of evil appears to contain something interesting, if incomplete, at point (2), claims (1) and (3) entail several dubious corollaries. These, latter, limitations become useful, however, in completing the assertion contained in point (2).

Let us start with (1), the historical-normative thesis, and its reference to the fact that atrocities have been a persistent accompaniment to the existence of humanity over the course of time. According to Ignatieff, the language of human rights has arisen as an answer to the tremendous brutality of events disclosed by history: human rights claims have an historical, and not metaphysical, status; they are grounded in the experience of evil. This hypothetical explanation is supported by Ignatieff's confidence in the possibility, as an epistemological question, of determining as atrocities certain events in an *objective factual* way, *independently from* any contested conception of the good. But in reality, the question is whether the notion of "evil" is a factual or rather an evaluative concept and how, if evaluative, it can be defined through reference exclusively to descriptive initial assumptions.

Secondly, and this touches on claim (2), if the notion of "evil" is itself an evaluative notion, then a connection must be found with what can be defined as the notion recognition of among purposive agents.

From this, it follows that the notion of "evil", as an evaluative concept, is co-original and not prior to the notion of "enabling conditions for agency", and that its understanding and definition cannot be pursued without a parallel improvement in what must count as the conditions of agency.

Even allowing for the correctness of such preliminary observations, one can still hold that there is, probably, further room for convergence of our intuitions concerning the notion of "evilness", and therefore on the notion of "injustice", rather than electing one type of good upon which a theory of justice can be constructed. But also in this case, a relation of reciprocity between what counts as "just" and, by contrast, as "unjust", must be maintained, and the hypothetical closeness of the notion of "injustice" and "evil", as compared with the distance separating "goods" and "justice", does not eliminate the relation of complementarity between these two relational concepts.

Moving, then, to evaluation of point (3), that is to say, to the priority that the eradication of evil must assume with respect to the realization of some good, the notion of negative liberty, as Ignatieff's minimum requirement, seems to demand some scrutiny. The priority for pragmatic removal of "evil" follows from the conceptual priority that this notion has over that of "the good". Since "evil" coincides with disrespect of negative freedoms, the minimal, and prior, task of a human rights policy is to remove obstacles to the exercise of negative freedoms. The problem, though, is how the notion of negative freedom is to be understood: that is, whether it is to be seen in purely negative terms, as prevention of interference with human rights or whether, while staying faithful to a negative definition, it may also include positive duties with respect to third parties or, finally, if it consists in a broader category of "liberties from", that requires several and differentiated positive measures for its realization.

In the first case, one could say that, if negative liberty were seen only in terms of "refraining from" interfering with one's actions, then the notion of liberty would be in many respects inadequate, if it is claimed as guaranteeing a sufficient basis for realization of one's preferred "good", as Ignatieff seems to maintain. This is because the notion of liberty is related not only to the two-place structure, but also to positive action for protection, rather than on a purely negative "refraining from". This is clear for instance, in the case of the "liberty from hunger", where a fair system of redistribution is needed for the equalization and activation of peoples' fundamental capability of accessing food resources.[9]

In view of the above-mentioned difficulties, it seems that rather than searching for exemplar experiences of the evil as possible sources for the justification of universal human rights, it is more appropriate to try to understand those general common conditions enabling agents to the formulation of their preferred goods, *qua* goods are chosen within certain constraints. This would indeed advance the consideration of such parameters of action validity precisely into the justification of some chosen goods, since it would subject such goods to the respect of certain standards of non-performative contradiction in respect to certain purported enabling conditions for purposive agency. It is therefore on the basis of agreed action parameters that an indirect partial commensurability of the different views of the good would become possible. Accordingly, I will propose a model for the inference of the conditions of purposive agency seen in terms of supra-ordinate constraints to the advancement of any purported good, that is, as rights constraints of communicative action.

If one refers to the partially incommensurable plurality of the view of the goods which individual or collective purposive agents might advance, then the conditions for achieving goods depends precisely on the right-framing of those conditions of purposive agency which logically antecede any specific choice of the good or of any

---

[9] The term "capability" will be later reinterpreted in a more stringent way than how it is deployed by the capability approach. Indeed, some of the problems encountered by this theory and in particular by Nussbaum's version of it are that: "There are [...] two basic objections to the theory of capabilities. The first is that capabilities are natural facts, and thus morally neutral and potentially morally bad: imagination, for example, can be used to create works of art or novel methods of torture. We require a different moral theory to distinguish good from bad capabilities. The second objection is that the theory gives us no guidance when the meeting of one need conflicts with the meeting of another (Gray 1986, 47–9)" Freeman (2003, 67).

comprehensive plan of life.[10] Generally speaking, moral incommensurability can be defined as the position which considers that, at any given two or more goods, no common measuring value can be found capable of establishing that either one of them is better or equal to the others. Given that epistemic accessibility to the moral content of a value can be always reached, as claimed in the first chapter, the issue with moral incommensurability then shifts from that of the Davidsonian "optimization" of cognitive beliefs to that of individuating valid principles of ethical comparability. Goods can be taken as incommensurable in as much as they are refused the status as scalar unities sharing a third common property in different degrees. But if, contrary to this insight, an argument capable of showing goods' subordination to an higher form of hierarchical ordering can be provided, in terms of a lexical ordering, then the problem for their total incommensurability vanishes. Higher ordering values would then seem to resubmit the problem of total incommensurability at a different level. Respect to the potentially unlimited kinds of goods which can be chosen, basic rights as enabling conditions do restrict the range of possibly morally allowed goods to the extent that these latter do not infringe the same enabling conditions of choice; and in terms of their hierarchical relation to goods, enabling basic rights do resubmit a form of incommensurability as a lexical ordering between them and other purported goods: in this sense, human rights "trump" any consideration for the maximization of the good.[11] If goods are intended as subordinated to a system of basic rights bearing a hierarchical relation of status to them, then any possible attempt of partial commensuration among goods in such system would first evaluate whether any purported good constitutes a possible infringement of basic enabling rights. In as much as goods do not contradict basic enabling rights, then they can be said to be indirectly partially commensurable to a background system of enabling rights.

In a pluralistic social community ordered through rights, there is no valid paternalistic advice which can be tolerated as a moral guide to action. There are rather spheres of liberties and of mutual responsibilities within which any citizen can freely cultivate her own passions and life-styles without having to bear the weight of any moral burden for the possible public justification of the right-protected choices. The disjoining of such two levels opens thus to the development of two parallel and conflicting standards of moral reasoning which do proceed, respectively, by confronting what is due reciprocally as a matter of intersubjective duty with what is morally due in face to face relations.

Let's recapitulate some of the points of Habermas's speech-act theory. In Habermas,[12] the example is made of a professor asking one of his seminar participants to bring a glass of water. The validity of this request, says Habermas, can be criticized

---

[10] Within this picture, Waldron's "right to do wrong" (1993, 63ff) then refers to a different level of understanding, a level pertaining rather at the standard of moral criticism than that of rights-analysis.

[11] Dworkin (1977a, xi).

[12] Habermas (2003d [1981], 141).

as according to several speech-act validity claims, as for instance to its truth-validity (there is no water tap nearby), to its truthfulness (this request is just to reach perlocutory effects by putting him in a bad shadow towards other participants) or, finally, to its normative rightness (you are not entitled to treat me as a your employee). In this latter case Habermas claims that: "[...] what is contested is that the action of the professor is right in the *given normative context* (emphasis added)".[13] Now, what is unconvincing about this explicatory strategy is that normative contextual validity is here claimed without its conformity to any previously established criterion of validity set either dependently or independently from any given context. It is true that the Habermasian central concern regards the non subordination of any communicative action to possible instrumental finalities of speech-acts, but it seems rather difficult to achieve such a goal without allowing subjects with some logically prior counterfactual argument grounding the normative rightness of communicative speech acts before any possible life-forms contextual structuring. In the above mentioned example, in fact, the agreement between the two interlocutors would be at most achieved in terms of *socially convergent behaviour* as conducted within a given life-form and not as an argued form of normative rightness that remains autonomous from given contexts. It seems therefore necessary to reformulate, while maintaining the general features of a model of communicative action, those same constraints for normative rightness as well as to provide an argument capable of setting certain experiential constraints as preconditions to be attained by any illocutive speech act aimed at achieving understanding in all normatively valid language-games.

In the attempt of reformulating the Habermasian normative validity condition of communicative action, I will claim that illocutive speech-acts aimed at reaching, through understanding, action coordination force do raise two interconnected forms of normative rightness: (a) a formal universal *intersubjective claim of recognition*; (b) and an *exemplar* form of normative validity mediating between the counterfactual validity of universal recognition and the contextual appropriateness of practices embedded within any given life-form.[14] I will begin with the first point and leave the explication of the second to the next section.

Illocutive speech acts raise, first, a form of normative validity in terms of a counterfactual scenario setting the conditions for purposive action. Within the linguistic practice, such counterfactual conditions are presupposed as a form of a *commitment to the recognition of otherness* in terms of her capacity to self-determination.[15] The

---

[13] Habermas (2003d [1981], 141).

[14] The notion of experience, in this sense, is much more similar to the mediated and the structured understanding of experience advanced by Hegel than to the immediate certainty of the objects advanced by Hume. On some further characteristics the Hegelian notion of experience see Adorno (1994).

[15] On this point I follow Honneth's insights on the concept of recognition as grounding the legitimation of a legal order: "If a legal order can be considered to be valid and, moreover, can count on the willingness of individuals to follow laws only to the extent to which it can appeal, in principle, to the free approval of all the individuals it includes, then one must be able to suppose that these

idea of a commitment to the recognition of subjects as self-determining agents relies on the idea according to which individuals, by acting purposively, behave as if an agreement on equal terms of cooperation were anticipated. The preliminary commitment to an intersubjective dimension of validity is therefore raised by the same pretence of normative validity of any linguistic speech-act, it regards the mutual commitment of communicative agents to the definition of the boundaries of social interaction. Such commitment, viewed in terms of a meta-condition of communicative action, binds all purposive agents – acting for the satisfaction of different conceptions of the good – to presuppose, necessarily, a mutual recognition of the most extensive system of equal freedoms. Indeed, it is only by assigning priority to an intersubjective relation of mutual recognition, that each individual can become the depository of a system of formal enabling liberties which in their turn allow for the realization of her preferred goods: recognition indeed grounds an equal *right to have liberty-rights*. But from the establishment of such immediate intersubjective relation, which any speech-act that is oriented to social coordination must presuppose, it follows that its locutive aspect can always be criticised by the hearer who raises certain elements of exemplar relevance. This introduces the negative element discussed in the previous chapter when I addressed the dialectical dynamics of a discursive form of recognition intersecting also the notion of exemplar universality. The immediate form of recognition which is advanced by an illocutive speech-act aimed at reaching social coordination does establish, provisionally, a relation of reciprocity, but while advancing such an hypothetical and formal claim, it specifies substantively how this or that right is to be understood for a "We". Here there are two interconnected notions of counterfactuality at play: an abstract one, as that grounding recognition of all potential participants to discursive practice and an "indexical" one, that is, the pragmatic anticipation of a situated self entering into the dialogical process of exchange of reasons.[16]

Such a process, while declaring the specific form of exemplar universality that a discourse must take, it leaves open the determinate option of critical rejection to the other communicative agents, so that negativity enters discursively within the process of recognition itself. What is to be re-established is a form of an "identity of identity and difference", so to use an Hegelian expression, where each is recognized as an end in itself and where subjective wills merge dialectically into a universally concrete will. Such movement of being "in oneself" and "for the other" is what constitutes the domain of recognition within the domain of the ethical life, and consequently what transforms the natural law community of moral individuals into a political community. Since an overcoming of the abstract autonomy of the

---

legal subjects have at least the capacity to make reasonable, autonomous decisions regarding moral questions. In the absence of such an ascription, it would be utterly inconceivable how subjects could ever have come to agree on a legal order. In this sense, because its legitimacy is dependent on a rational agreement between individuals with equal rights, every community based on modern law is founded on the assumption of the moral accountability of all its members" (Honneth, 1995, 114).

[16] Within this second understanding of counterfactuality, the "indexical" one, we have to place all Searle's internalist considerations about intentionality adopted in the first chapter.

moral subject occurs in the intersubjective decentering of the self proper of the identity/difference movement, the affirmation of the general will cannot but take place within an institutionally grounded domain of social reflection. Within this higher form of recognition, the self relation to myself is mediated by the other, which is not anymore seen as an external element: this is, instead, an intersubjectively *mediated We* that arises and determines a parallel intersubjective mediated form of autonomy. The notion of mediated autonomy is clearly a re-elaboration of the Kantian notion of autonomy. In the latter, particularly according to the *Second Critique*, the categorical imperative, through obligation, reduces manifest freedom to conscience. It is through the moral law that freedom is discovered as an element of our self-conscience. Through such a step, then, the subject becomes aware of his autonomy. However, Kantian moral imperative and autonomy in general, in order to function, must presuppose itself the idea of an intersubjective community as a community of ends. The intersubjective paradigm of autonomy here defended, intersects precisely this level of enquiry, adding a dialectical moment as the possibility of outcome revisability despite an immediate form of intersubjective agreement. The self-affirmation of the other as different is an essential component for the overcoming of the abstract form of universality that one would obtain simply at the stage of immediacy of the formal We. Therefore the dialectical re-joining of the self and the other is necessary for the construction of a determinate universal as a concrete universal, where differences are assimilated within an higher form of universality which I will define later as exemplar universality.[17]

Once an anticipation to intersubjective recognition is made intersubjectively, then, a community of ethical agents is constituted. Within such a community, the reciprocal potentially unlimited extensivity of purposive self-determination gets negatively segmented in terms of non infringements of the self-purposive determination of the others. Now, to be free is always to be capable of pursuing or not pursuing a *desideratum* once that any sort of impediment, restriction, barrier to the realization of a purported plan is removed. To use a formula introduced by Mac Callum, liberty is a three-place concept; that is, it is a triadic relation which always includes the idea of an agent which is not impeded from realizing one's desired goal.[18] That the notion of liberty includes the removal of the obstacles preventing an agent from realizing her desired purposes means that both negative and positive freedoms are strictly interconnected. It is only at this point that liberty, through the emergence of a public domain, divides itself into a private and a negative sphere of individual purposive agency – protected by any unjustifiable intervention by the others – and by a public domain of self-determination through political participation.

---

[17] In explaining how the dialectical unification of the opposition works in Hegel's theory of recognition, Siep notices that the relation between two self-consciousness transcends them, since each is dependent not only from its relation to the other, but also to the self-understanding of the other, so that any change in oneself is also a change in the relation to the other (1979, 137ff).

[18] Mac Callum (1967).

This means that, in order to satisfy the fulfilment of the preconditions of liberty as the possibility to realize one's desired projects, one has to be put in condition – enabled – through the removal of intentional or foreseeable unintentional obstacles preventing the positive exercise of freedom. But if liberty is considered as interconnected to the removal of disabling conditions which lead to the exercise of self-determination, then, a basic condition of well-being is to be satisfied in view of a full exercise of private and public freedoms. Indeed, to be free to realize one's own desired purposes depends upon the agent "not being deprived from", or of "not being impeded from" pursuing one's desired goal. If it is so, then, one's impediments to purposive action are not only relative to deprivation of freedoms as such, but also and very often to forms of disability due to conditions of destitution or of health impediments. In this sense, the notion of basic well-being falls precisely within an enlarged notion of freedom as a triadic relation where, for instance, the right to be free from starvation is functional to the positive exercise of self-determination both in the private and the public realm. The rights to basic well-being, therefore, get justified in view of the possibility of the agents being capable of autonomy as purposive agents. And since the quantitative allocation of goods and services, in order to be enabled to the exercise of one's positive freedom, is functional to the contingent individual and societal conditions, a more precise criterion for the normative allocation of the required means to well-being can be only established through a situated judgment. The judgmental activity, which will be addressed later, would consider the allocation of services and goods not simply as a relation to the median distribution of wealth in a society, but as a contextually justified and as an always subjected to revision satisfaction of primary freedoms in view of the exercise of purposive action in general.[19]

Freedom concerns here not the status of the subject, but rather its action presuppositions. Freedom is a presupposition to action when the agent is capable of having at her disposal such preconditions for action during her engagement into purposive agency. And yet, to have something at one's disposal means never being capable of fulfilling the status of freedom as a condition of possession. Agents "assume" that such a condition of presupposition is to be postulated as an unavoidable element for the practical engagement in the realization of their goods, that is, as an *un-rejectable* universal condition for purposive agency.[20] Following from such

---

[19] A situated and yet exemplarily valid allocation of resources for the fulfilment of basic well-being sets a contextual non-objective requirement while rejecting arbitrariness. For instance, within a purely objectivist position, Griffin has opposed moral non conventional objectivity to social conventional indeterminacy in the definition of a standard of well-being, as when he writes: "For instance, we can banish the indeterminateness by defining a standard on people's natural expectations in that society; expectations adjust to possibilities, and a standard of minimum acceptable level of life, admittedly very rough, will naturally emerge, Although that is true, it is not clear why we should merely detach well-being from objective features of human nature and connect it instead to accidental social changes that have no obvious moral significance" Griffin (1988, 44).

[20] I believe that this understanding of the connection between purposive agency and experience can help to clarify and distinguish my position from that of those, like Honneth, that, starting from

assumption, the revision of one's possible *desiderata* which would contradict those same intersubjective conditions of purposive agency does not collapse into a contingent revision of one's achievable projects in accordance to a specific context. If one were to confound an idealized perspective with an actual one, then the revision of possible projects as according to circumstances would make the same notion of liberty empty. On the contrary, I am here calling for the most extensive protection of anyone's purported projects, so that any contingent restriction in actual situations will amount to a disruption of the fundamental intersubjective relation of recognition grounding the formal system of equal rights among people.

Since an equal system of liberty rights can be drawn from a relation of mutual recognition of otherness as potential participants to communicative actions, then, any experiential violation of the system of liberty rights, does amount to a form of misrecognition of potential agency and therefore to the negation of that ideal community of moral agents which only can grant the legitimacy of any system of law. And yet such an ideal community of moral agents is still a formal category considered as a necessary prerequisite for the validity of speech-acts. The recognition of a generalized other from which the respect of certain coordinating parameters in pursuing one's own purposes can be derived, does not rely on a previously grounded substantive concept of human kind. To rely on a previously established category of humankind would be both to reintroduce an essentialist-metaphysical perspective within a post-metaphysical process of justification, and to provide a recursive argument for mutual recognition. Since no *a priori* concept of human kind can be provided, then, the commitment to the most extensive activity of recognition of otherness cannot but rely on a form of *a quasi-transcendental hypothesis to recognition* of otherness as a potential addressee of the most extensive equal system of freedoms.[21] Lacking a pre-established fixed criterion of human nature, it is on the basis of the attribution, through recognition, of an equal system of liberties that we come to *construct* an idea of humankind as a form of maximally inclusive moral community. The principle of equal liberty that agents reciprocally recognize counterfactually each other as purposive agents, is therefore at the basis of a form of intersubjective autonomy which precedes the individual capability for autonomy of each purposive agent.[22] Potential infringements of such intersubjective recognition constitutes a performative contradiction that bears as a consequence that of rendering irrational all those agents' behaviours refusing to subordinate their own strategic actions to the fulfilment of a coordinating force.

---

similar premises have then insisted upon the normative stand of social suffering and the experiential ground of social injustice, as in Fraser and Honneth (2003, 129–30).

[21] The notion of quasi-transcendentality is here deployed to indicate the entire dialectical process from immediate to negatively mediated recognition.

[22] As far as the function played by the notion of recognition, it can be said that: "In contrast to Rawls, the idea of the good on which a recognition-theoretical conception of justice is based is tailored from the start to the intersubjective character of human relations. For it assumes that the subjects for whose sake just social relations are to be established are aware that their autonomy depends on the autonomy of their partners in interaction" Fraser and Honneth (2003, 259).

Recognition of otherness plays the role of transition from a purely rational first person perspective into an "us" considered both in terms of the anticipation of an ideal community of fellow human beings to which ascribe a certain number of necessary rights for the actualization of potentialities, and once undergone into dialectical mediation, as a political self-determining community, as a concrete universal.

Once, identity is initially constructed through immediate recognition in terms of a moral community deserving the maximization of liberty satisfaction, then along the dialectical process of recognition, the judgmental activity engaged into the contextual political specification of fundamental rights, will orient the formulation of reflective judgments to the construction of a political community. The moral premises of a constructed human community are completed by the political development of human rights formulations. Viewed in terms of fully-fledged formulated rights, liberty-rights have to await the deliberative activity of a political community which would shift from the attribution of a formal system of rights to a moral community of humankind, to the formulation of substantive rights in view of a political self-determining community. With respect to a specific political community, recognition of otherness, when raised by an exemplar human rights formulation, constitutes unavoidable premises. To see how the normativity of equal freedoms as ideal conditions of purposive agency might cope with the realization of the political autonomy of self-determining bodies, one needs to find an explicatory model capable of combining, in a creative and dynamic way, the validity of a system of freedoms with the search of a form of contextual political validity on the basis of a deliberating activity. This is what will be considered next as the role that reflective judgment – as a meta-judgement springing from illocutionary speech-acts – plays in the political formulation of human rights.

3.3 The Exemplar Validity of Human Rights

In the foregoing sections, I attempted to outline a justification of human rights by claiming that, from the perspective of a reformulated theory of communicative action, one can derive necessary background conditions for the normative validity of speech-acts by referring to the fundamental conditions of recognition of a generalized otherness. It has been said that in order to achieve normative rightness, illocutive speech-acts must respect, first, the intersubjective condition of recognition. For the sake of clarification, one might distinguish between a metalinguistic function of speech acts and a properly linguistic function, and state that the political activity of human rights discourses represents a linguistic activity oriented to a metalinguistic reflection upon those same normative validity conditions of our speech-acts. The discursive "filtering" function of a formal system of recognized liberties is reformulated and enriched by community-situated discourses of human rights producing the backward effect of resetting those same metalinguistic rules of our political grammar.

In the following section I will canvass upon the second-mentioned validity claim raised by illocutionary speech-acts, that is, the claim of exemplar validity raised once a formal compliance to an intersubjective dimension of recognition is fulfilled. In particular, I will explain how the formal system of liberty rights can be related to the notion of "judgment" according to Kantian premises, and how reflective judgment can explain the construction of specific human rights legal provisions from within socio-political contexts.

The transition from human rights as conditions of purposive agency to the exemplar validity of reflective judgments does establish the transition from a formal system of freedoms to a substantive one. Indeed if, on the one hand, the presupposition of mutual recognition fixes the conditions of formal liberties for the individuals, on the other hand, their specific configurations and situated validity achievable through the use of the reflective judgments, translate such formal constraints into substantive political principles capable of providing motivation to action for socially and politically embedded subjects.

From this it follows that through reflection on the necessary implied conditions for the realization of purposive agency – understood as elements of a coherent life plan – the agent becomes the depository of a sphere of liberties as political necessary conditions for realization of reasonable plans of life. Inasmuch as these requirements represent *political enabling* conditions for purposive agency, the so-called liberties of the ancients and those of the moderns become concurrent elements, and not competing candidates, of one single system of rights.

This position cuts across the two extremes represented by those communitarians and liberals who oppose, reciprocally and respectively, the rights of the community as enforceable against the individual, and the notion of methodological individualism as a way of deducing the rights of the individual against the community. Defenders of the so-called "adversarial conception" of rights and community[23] maintain not simply that, on a liberal basis, community rights could be a threat to the enforcement of individual rights but also that, on a communitarian basis, the recognition of individual rights as rights might undermine the solidarity character of a community which becomes thus atomized and disaggregated by the individual rights whose enforcement is claimed.

Turning to the specific contribution afforded by the reflective judgment, one can claim, in general, that all judgments, according to Kant are dependent on both the conditions posed by the determinant and by the reflective judgment – without (at least in theory) this entailing the impossibility of distinguishing between a pure determinant and a pure reflective judgment.[24] If determinant judgment, given the transcendental laws of the intellect, subsumes the particular within an already given universal category,[25] reflective judgment must supply itself with a principle for

---

[23] This position is extensively criticised in Gewirth (1996, 1–105).

[24] According to Kant, there are two categories of purely reflective judgments – aesthetic judgments (the judgment of taste and the judgment of the sublime) – and teleological judgment.

[25] Kant (1953 [1790], Section 4).

functioning as a judgment and this operation is assisted by an *a priori* principle represented by the regulative idea of the finality or purposiveness of nature.[26] That this represents, for Kant, a *functional* and not a *structural* distinction can be understood by reference to the three-fold partition of judgments into the categories *a priori*, *a posteriori*, the analytic and the synthetic distinctions.[27]

Analytic judgments, inasmuch as they do not need to find a law for themselves, are *a priori* judgments, which belong to the domain of the determinant judgment. Nevertheless, they are not typical determinant judgments since, for analytic judgments, the problem of the subsumption of the particular to a universal is easily solved by the fact that the particular already contains the universal within itself, so that the process is that of manifesting their mutual relationship, rather than of subsuming one within the other. But whereas synthetic *a priori* judgments must also be linked to the function played by determinant judgment – since, in their case, a universal is given and is *a priori* – in the case of *a posteriori* judgments, one must recognize a connection to the activity of reflective judgment. For *a posteriori* judgments, indeed, a particular is given but a universal concept under which the particular is to be subsumed still needs to be found.[28] It is precisely the *a posteriori* judgments that, for Kant, possess the status of judgments of knowledge, both in their more empirical-descriptive version, as in the case of the judgment of experience, and in their more paradigmatic versions, such as in the case of scientific-normative judgments constructed on synthetic *a priori* judgments.

Scientific judgments are not, therefore, constituted only by synthetic *a priori* conditions, since the latter provide simply the *a priori* conditions for those judgments. Synthetic *a posteriori* judgments on the other hand, require the functional conditions provided by the reflective judgment and thus a specific principle, that of the finality of nature, subsuming the particular under the universal.

Proceeding from such Kantian premises, my analysis here seeks to extend Kantian epistemological observations to the practical domain of human rights judgments, through deduction of a guiding principle which can mediate between the

---

[26] "Kant indicates the true nature and function of this principle [the principle of the finality of nature] when he claims that through it, 'judgment prescribes, not to nature (which would be autonomy) but to *itself* [my emphasis] (which is heautonomy), a law for the specification of nature' (KU 5: 185–6; 25). Thus, even though the principle concerns nature as the *object* of investigation, its prescriptive force is directed back to judgment itself. In order to emphasize the purely reflexive, self-referential nature of this principle, Kant coins the term 'heautonomy'. To claim that judgment is 'heautonomous' in its reflection is just to say that it is both *source* and *referent* of its own normativity. In fact, this is what distinguishes judgment's a priori principle, from those of the understanding, which legislates transcendental law to nature, and of (practical) reason, which prescribes the objectively necessary laws of a free will" Allison (2001, 41).

[27] The notion of structural and functional distinction among judgments is defended by Garroni (1976) who also saw a connection with the functional activity of reflective judgment within synthetic *a posteriori* judgments.

[28] This does not rule out that the possibility that *a posteriori* synthetic judgments are connected *also* to determinant judgment, since the condition for their possibility implies that they contain a synthetic *a priori* judgment, as for instance, in the case of experiential judgment.

particular and the formal system of human rights. This principle is what can be defined as the principle of "finality of rights" which, by anticipating the consensus of a universal community, allows reflective judgment to find a form of exemplar universality. The principle of "finality of rights" provides reflective judgment with a regulative idea which is logically antecedent to reflective judgment (in our case, specifically the reflective composite judgment), and which orients it to the construction of a frame which would maximally extend rights internal balancing.

Reflective judgments, starting from the assumption of a formal system of liberty, interpret the latter in a context where the universal rule is not given but still to be found. And inasmuch as reflective judgments play a role, according to their functionality, within *a posteriori* judgments, the notion of exemplar universality takes the form of a universality which can be reviewed and reformulated with reference to different contexts. Distinctly from synthetic *a priori* judgments, which can derive the particular from the universal *independently* of any situated horizon of understanding, *a posteriori* judgments are always constructed on the basis of a contingent frame of informational data which prompt a search for universal criteria of validity.[29]

The constructive function of the reflective judgment, thus, takes its move from the unrejectable presuppositions of purposive agency in terms of constitutive rules of a game, and it works reflectively by constructing within the open space of "grammatical" possibility left open by such constitutive rules, its exemplar forms of rights-judgements. But reflectivity is not only involved in the construction of such principles through the interpretive activity of the reflective judgments of the background conditions of purposive action. Reflectivity is also involved in the application of such rights particularly when there are conflicts of rights, as it will be later discussed.

Since the notion of universal validity of reflective judgment is sensitive to its capacity of expressing a criterion of normative validity particular to a specific context, the same form of universality formulated through the orienting principle of the "finality of rights"[30] must be sensitive to the specific cultural and situational conditions for which it aims to be valid. This amounts to saying that the *a posteriori* status of human rights judgments advances a model whose universal validity, while trespassing on context, is measured against the temporally and experientially determined *locus* of reflection. This does not rule out the possibility that while the

---

[29] Even without drawing all the necessary implications, Habermas seems to recognize the limits of abstract universalism when he writes: "The application of norms calls for argumentative clarification in its own right. In this case, impartiality of judgment cannot again be secured through a principle of universalization; rather, in addressing questions of context-sensitive application, practical reason must be informed by a principle of appropriateness (*Angemessenheit*). What must be determined here is which of the norms already accepted as valid is appropriate in a given case in the light of all the relevant features of the situation conceived as exhaustively as possible". Habermas (1993, 13ff).

[30] The notion of "finality of rights" will be later used in the idea of deontological goal-oriented theory.

normativity of reflective judgment rests upon the *a priori* principle of the "finality of rights", as a synthetic judgment it must be validated from *within* a given experience where the particular can either prompt or impede a feeling of "furthering life".[31] While the accord between the particular and the universal is guided by an *a priori* principle, the judgment is situated within *a posteriori* conditions of reflection.

Of central significance, here, is the idea that there is no rule which tells us how to apply the use of reflective judgement to the substantivisation of the formal system of liberties in any objective way within a specific context. If this were not so, it would be necessary to supply a description of grounds on which it would be possible to introduce an interpretive rule requiring, in turn, a further rule providing an objective interpretation of the rule itself, in infinite regress. In particular, the principle of "finality of rights" plays the same role, within the practical ethical-political domain, as Kant's principle for the finality of nature stated in section 11 of *The Critique of Judgment*. Paraphrasing Kant, one could say that the principle of "finality of rights" is bound, subjectively, to the representation of a socio-political construction – embedding a system of human rights legal provisions – which provides, through a universally communicable sentiment, *sensus communis*, a pleasure, a motivation for judgment.

In Kantian terms, that the universality of a pure judgment of taste rests on a notion of *sensus communis* means that what can be universally communicated presupposes the possibility of a "sense" shareable by all human beings. Such a "sense", in order to be normatively cogent, must lie between a naturalistic reduction, on one hand, and a complete cultural embedding of our possibilities. According to this reading, when engaged in the activity of reflection, the faculty of judgment presupposes *a priori* the modalities of representation of all others. The notion of "common sense", as applied to the notion of aesthetic anticipation and accordance between imagination and intellect, can therefore be explained as an *a priori* delimitation of the horizon within which any possible problem of specification of human rights provisions, either at the national or at the regional and international level, can be validly postulated.

This notion of exemplar validity of human rights judgments brings with it an element of "exemplar necessity", meaning here the necessity of agreement of all with a judgment considered as the rule of a universal principle which cannot be provided as something already given, but as something still to be constructed.[32] The "example" becomes thus the only possible representation of the rule itself, allowing, on one hand, the "exhibition" of empirical concepts showing their closeness to empirical

---

[31] On the purposive active character of this notion and its link with the notion of pleasure, Allison observes: "Underlying this characterization is the definition of life given in the Critique of Practical Reason as 'the faculty of a being by which it acts according to the faculty of desire,' with the latter being the 'faculty such a being has of causing, through its ideas, the reality of the object of these ideas.' In the same context, he defines pleasure as 'the idea of the agreement of an object or an action with the subjective conditions of life' (Kp V 5: 9n; 9–10)" Allison (2001, 69).

[32] Kant (1953 [1790], Sec. 18).

judgments, and on the other, representing the "rule" itself by showing, in this case, its closeness to the pure judgment of knowledge.[33]

Finally, according to the perspective defended here, the principle of "finality of rights" guides and orients the principles of human rights in the creative construction of an exemplar universal model, through the construction and the evaluation of the experience on the basis of an endless interpretive effort and from within a contextualized point of observation.

Interconnected to this point is the concern of this theory on how, through the use of reflective judgments, it is possible to close the gap between, on the one hand, state-evaluation independent of rights proper of the so-called "welfarist instrumentalists" who see rights in terms of their consequences for *right-independent* goals and, on the other hand, the so-called "constraint-based deontologists" who assign relevance to rights without taking into consideration any *consequential justification* as a possible constraint on action.[34] A deontological-goal conception of rights, as the one here defended, distinguishes unjustified violations of rights from their legitimate restriction, with the latter occurring in the course of prevention of infringement of a different fundamental right (inter-rights conflicts) or of prevention of the infringement of a right of the same kind (intra-right conflicts).

This position can be defended by allowing, for a restricted number of basic rights, equal relevance and mutual interdependence, so that restriction of one right (in terms of its generated duties) can be justified if this is to the advantage either of the extensional promotion of the same right in the near future or to the promotion of an higher number of core rights whose enforcement would otherwise have been nullified in default of any right-restriction. But as introduced above, any legitimate restriction of rights amounts, at the end, to a legitimate suspension of some of the duties attached to the referred right. While this view rejects the possibility of a hierarchy of fundamental rights, assigning to each the same value, on the pain of losing the qualitative relevance of each defended right, it admits the possibility of a hierarchical ordering for the relevance of the duties attached to each right. For instance, it might be recognized that, with reference to the right of free speech, while the duty of non interference with someone else liberty is itself a condition for the guarantee of the referred right, on the other hand, the duty to punish those who infringe the right to free speech is only indirectly attached to the sustenance of the right itself, resulting rather as connected to the duty of non infringement of the defended right. In this case, then, were we to support the right to free speech through political actions, we would have to orient our strategies to the positive and negative conditions favoring the duty of non-interference, rather than sacrificing such duty to the advantage of extended punishing measures.

---

[33] See Kant (1953 [1790], Sec. 59). This point helps clarify why Kant sometimes uses the term "objective" when referring to the role that the presupposition of common sense brings to the subjective necessity of the judgment of taste, for example, in Sec. 22 (Kant, 1953, [1790]).

[34] For the gap left unsolved by both approaches see Sen (1988, 190).

Whenever a conflict of rights is to be resolved through the deontological-goal oriented activity of the judgment, then what is actually to be assessed is the weight of each connected duty and to its possible suspension in relation to another duty, either internally connected to the same right (in the case of infra-conflicts of rights), or related to a different right (in the case of inter-conflicts of rights). The least one duty connected to a right is crucial for the enforcement of that same right, the more it can be legitimately suspended in the case of conflict.

But let us suppose that there is at least one case of infra-rights conflict where, due to the non-compossibility of two simultaneous duties, a subject A is prevented from satisfying both B's and C's right and has to decide which of the two has to be obeyed. In such a case one cannot claim that A has violated the deontological constraint by trading off one right with an other. Such instance, indeed, remains a case of practical difficulty which does not question the normative point defended by the present theory; it can at most force an articulation and an enforcement of a more extensive number of positive measures for the prevention of similar cases in the future and thus it connects to an idea of functional differentiation and of a division of labour for the protection of rights. This indicates also which is the interconnection and development from a subject-related, individually-based theory of rights and an institutionalized theory of human rights, where practical impossibilities on the side of the individual are resolved through the intervention of state-action.

In this scenario, the notion of holism, as a general theoretical approach to the concurrent validity of human rights, is maintained as a background condition, while mutual weighing and progressive enforcement of rights is at the same time promoted. Holism is interpreted as a regulative idea, representing the ultimate goal towards which any system of rights and obligations should conform.

So, similarly, if rights conflicts (stemming from conflicting duties) prevent the global satisfaction of individuals' rights, then evaluation of the overall consequences on a global system of rights may more adequately justify the temporary weakening of a right (in terms of its connected non-primary duties), if supported by clear evidence of extent and severity than inaction consequent on inability to defend both at the same time. This paves the way for an idea of the finality of rights within a deontological argument and activates the notion of situated judgment as something capable of assessing those circumstances and solutions which better advance overall protection of human rights. General human rights principles, cannot determine by themselves their most appropriate specifications for any possible situation. They can only attempt to do this through an aesthetic understanding of the specific experiences at stake on the basis of imaginative projections of possible consequences brought forth by different options. This means that human rights principles, in order to be translated into specific political decisions, in terms of both constitutional articles and of the balancing of right-configurations along judicial sentences, need the support of a situated judgment which, through imaginative thinking, evaluates and derives specific human rights provisions from general moral constraints. Due to the plurality of configurations of valid judgments satisfying the general commitments of agency, I would define this approach as a form of *pluralistic universalism.*[35] Such form of pluralistic universalism embraces two different levels of reflection which articulate the activity of the reflective judgment both to its *external function*, that is, the hermeneutic interpretation of the transcendental conditions of liberty which, through the reflective judgment does establish the political formulation of constitutional principles, and its *internal* function, that is, the reflective activity of the judgment deployed *case by case* through the judicial activity of the courts. If in the first case, the reflective judgment confronts moral transcendental liberty rights with juridical-political principles autonomously deliberated by and for a community of political beings, in the latter case the terms of confrontation concern the juridical-political relevance of social facts as such. It is precisely in accordance to its *internal function* that reflective judgments do explicate the function of providing exemplarily justified thresholds of quantitative allocation of basic goods in order to satisfy, on social basis, the right to basic well-being, and with this, the possibility of individuals to accede to civil and political freedoms. The so-called "liberty from hunger", "deprivation", "illness" etc. while formally established through a formal system of liberties can receive an adequate fulfilment and proportionate allocation of required services and goods, only when conceived from a situated point of reflection.

3.4 Deliberative Constraints and Pluralistic Universalism

In this section I will canvass upon some implications of the model of rights sketched so far with reference to the functioning of the public sphere. This will provide an explanation of how a *dialectically mediated form of recognition* can be achieved within the context of exemplar pluralism. Indeed, from a reinterpretation of the Rousseauian model of a "general will" which, from the above analysis, has turned into a form of a "pluralized reasonable will" exhibiting conformity to liberty-rights, I have sketched a deliberative model which is in competition with a Benthamite conception of political deliberation.[36] Indeed, the fulfilment of a system of fundamental rights exhibited by speech-acts formal constituents represents, rather, a specific enabling condition for the emergence of valid claims. Even if, for any public discourse, no direct link can be established between the capacity to provide an answer to human rights claims and the validity as a public justification, one can still maintain that it is

---

[35] It must be observed that within such supra-ordinate frames of pluralistic configurations of right balancing and principles a large plurality of moral normative standards are allowed, in such a way that moral reasonable dissent is temporally recomposed at the rights level. On the relation between contrasting moral standards and fundamental rights, see Waldron (1993, 63–87).

[36] As opposed to my conception, in the latter case self-interested deliberations is counterbalanced by an external justification of rights aimed at protecting possible side-effects of the majority over the minority, so that rights are simply conceived in terms of limiting conditions rather then as enabling conditions for the political will formation.

only from those discourses subordinated to the respect of a system of human rights, that some sort of public validity can be reasonably *expected*.[37]

More specifically, human rights do raise conceptual issues which involve a relation of multiple implication between constraining principles of the kind P1, P2, etc. and a relation of implication with reflective judgments of the kind: $P1 > R1, R1.1,$ $R1.1.1$ etc. The conditions of human rights can thus be viewed as the grammar of the practice of reflective judgments which rather than closing up possible moves to future generations, open up a variety of exemplarily valid interpretations within a rule-constrained game. This point is strictly linked to what Benhabib, quoting Derrida, defines as *democratic iterations* for the jurisgenerative processes of law production:

> The rights claims that frame democratic politics, on the one hand, must be viewed as transcending the specific enactments of democratic majorities under specific circumstances; on the other hand, such democratic majorities *reiterate* these principles and incorporate them into democratic will-formation processes through argument, contestation, revision, and rejection. Since they are dependent on contingent processes of democratic will-formation, not all jurisgenerative politics yields positive results [. . .] productive or creative jurisgenerative politics results in *the augmentation of the meaning of rights claims* and in *the growth of the political authorship of political actors*, who make these rights their own by democratically deploying them. Benhabib (2004, 140).

A further condition under which pluralism can be analysed concerns both its synchronic and diachronic point of observation. Indeed, the relation among the formal system of human rights and the judgments of human rights gives place to a form of pluralism both in terms of a the temporal axis and, synchronically, in terms of pluralism of justified perspectives. In the first case, as a background condition, a form of synchronic unity which changes over time must be assumed, whereas in the second case a criterion must be adopted that rejoins the plurality of morally valid contrasting points of observation through what it can be named as a *second-order reflective judgment*. Precommitment to human rights categories, thus, cannot by itself solve persistent disagreement between two or more well-grounded and yet

---

[37] The dispute over the apparent contradiction between democratic self-determination and constitutional precommittments is very old indeed and cannot be fully dealt with here. Holmes (1997) offers an interesting presentation of the most prominent historical contributors to the discussion; he rightly recognizes the enabling capacities of the "constitutional essentials": "Paine and Jefferson shuddered at the idea of binding the future because they could not conceive of 'binding' in a positive, emancipatory or freedom-enhancing way. Their blind-spot was due partly to a belief in progress. But it also resulted from their overly conservative conceptions of how constitutions function. The metaphors of checking, blocking, limiting and restraining all suggest that constitutions are principally negative devices used to prevent the abuse of power. But rules are also creative. They organize new practices and generate new possibilities which would not otherwise exist. Constitutions may be usefully compared to the rules of a game or even to the rules of grammar. While *regulative* rules (e.g., 'no smoking') govern pre-existent activities, *constitutive* rules (e.g., 'bishops move diagonally') make a practice possible for the first time [. . .] In general, constitutional rules are enabling, not disabling; and it is therefore unsatisfactory to identify constitutionalism exclusively with limitations on power" Holmes (1997, 226–227).

opposing positions in the public arena. Pluralism of perspectives and views is radically inevitable in modern societies and constitutes the essential core of vibrant democratic discourse. The point of pluralist variation does not concern simply the variation of the different circumstances of given data for the exercise of judgment and, thus, the variation of the balancing of rights provided by the judgment in relation to the change of the circumstances. Pluralism is instead concerned with the idea that the relevance of the considered data is dependent upon the cultural images that each interpretive domain has in its own context, so that judgmental pluralism is always mediated by the pre-cultural understanding of the evidences to be submitted to balancing and to their same optimal balancing itself.

One important implication of the deliberative right-based process here defended, indeed, is that a "radial" pervasiveness of human rights, as well as of their extensive application for the achievement of a normatively justified process of political decision making, is a crucial element. Public statements must always be legitimated, at least indirectly, on the basis of the effects human rights bring forth for a proposed public plan. Taking into account the interests of all the affected that are put at stake by a governmental action, contrasting views can be assessed and evaluated for compliance with fundamental interests. Indeed, dialectical mediation can occur between conflicting parties only within an institutional framework that guarantees the reasonableness of political outcomes which, when so constrained, can deliver results acceptable to all parties on the basis of the guarantee of the non-infringement of the conditions of purposive agency.[38] Institutional designs strictly affect the democratic interplay among parties and the possibility that they reach an agreement within a morally justified frame: while precluding *a priori* predictability of the results themselves, fundamental rights nevertheless configure essential guarantees for the expectation of the reasonable outcomes that do not infringe those same basic interests of the competing parties.[39]

---

[38] As recently observed: "[...] No compromise could ever be purely substantive: some institutions exist even if they are not the object of negotiations. The model of 'substantive' compromise is based on the assumption that no decisions have been yet made about the institutional framework or that the institutions are such that the probability of a substantive compromise holding is quite low [...] democracy can be established only if there exist institutions that would make it unlikely that the competitive political process would result in outcomes highly adverse to anyone's interests given the distribution of economic, ideological, organizational and other relevant resources" Przeworski (1997, 66).

[39] At this regard, Habermas writes: "In contrast to the ethical constriction of political discourse, the concept of deliberative politics acquires empirical reference only when we take account of the multiplicity of communicative forms of rational political will-formation. It is not discourse of an ethical type that could grant on its own the democratic genesis of law. Instead, deliberative politics should be conceived as a syndrome that depends on a network of fairly regulated bargaining processes and of various forms of argumentation, including pragmatic, ethical and moral discourses, each of which relies on different communicative presuppositions and procedures. In legislative politics *the supply of information and the rational choice of strategies are interwoven with the balancing of interests, with the achievement of ethical self-understanding and the articulation of strong preferences, with moral justification and tests of legal coherence. Thus 'dialogical' and 'instrumental' politics, the two ideal-types which Frank Michelman has opposed in a polarizing*

In the two-step argument for human rights which I have so far presented, I proposed an understanding of the use of the reflective judgment as subordinated to certain inescapable formal conditions derived from the notion of mutual recognition. In so doing, the creative use of the reflective judgment has been normatively constrained to invariable performative conditions for the production of both publicly valid claims and specific articulations of human rights principles. This point has implicitly advanced the idea that claims, in general, can gain access to the public sphere only when they don't infringe, even indirectly, the formal system of purposive liberties. From such view it follows that the same notion of public reason can be pluralized and viewed as fragmenting itself into competing positions, which are in turn submitted to the scrutiny of the public opinion itself. In order to achieve public agreement, we do not need to search for a general support springing from the dividing and incommensurable views of the goods characterizing modern pluralistic societies. We must, instead, look for a *second-order judgmental construction* of an internally articulated reflective judgment that, from the plurality of those views passing the test of performative contradiction posed by the formal conditions of action, overcome interpretive conflicts and mis-recognitions through the construction of a yet new exemplar universal configuration as a result of a *dialectically mediated form of recognition* among the reasonable position of the concurring parties. The use of a second-order reflective judgment in the public sphere can indeed favour creative solutions capable of mediating between those public statements showing faithfulness to the conditions of agency.[40] The normatively constrained use of the reflective judgment can indeed reformulate yet new paradigms of universal forms, and be capable of including the plurality of publicly admissible, but adversarial, views in a never accomplished attempt of revision of the common standards for a political community. Once admitted such a relation between the constructivist universality of a system of formal liberties and reflective judgments, then, the same process of judicial review by constitutional courts is saved due to the extra burden that courts have in evaluating conformity to a given constitutional text, and more importantly, checking the validity of an hypothetical constitutional innovation in relation to the possible configurations that the formal systems of which human rights give place. A constitutional innovation, indeed, places itself in between the abstract universality of the principles of human rights and the legal crystallization of such principles into an adopted constitution, forcing the constitutional courts to interpret social change in view of the moral and legally accepted imperatives of a community. Synchronically, such a process of never ending self-reflection can advance precisely when new insights in the public sphere are introduced by scientists and social critics,

---

fashion, do in fact interpenetrate in the medium of deliberations of various kind [emphasis added]" Habermas (2006a, 282–283).

[40] The present notion of the public sphere, while being indebted to the negative constraint advanced by Bohman (1996), reinterprets the validity of public claims as precommitted to the conditions of purposive agency, and the notion of moral mediation as constrained by a creative agreement advanced by the reflective use of judgment.

in general, on the basis of yet new experiential considerations bearing direct effects upon the exemplarily agreed standard. The introduction of new epistemic-cognitive elements can re-open the debate over apparently publicly settled issues, and foster the formation of new deliberative groups confronting each other within a revised framework of deliberation.

Chapter 4
The Legal Dimensions of Human Rights

In this final chapter I will canvass upon the legal model which my proposed view points to, as well as some practical implications in international relations. As far as the first point is concerned, I discuss different approaches to the relationship between law and morality, and advance a view which reformulates Hart's notion of "recognition" as a social practice. The result of my reformulation consists in introducing the constraint of a maximally inclusive notion of recognition within a cooperative enterprise oriented toward social coordination. One necessary but not sufficient criterion for the validity of law consists in the fulfilment of such a refor-mulated condition of recognition so that, as opposed to Hart, the relation between law and morality is not simply contingent, but necessary. This condition does not exhaust all the properties that valid law is called to exhibit and, in this sense, I consider that the legal framing of human rights is a fundamental component for social coordination of complex societies. A second point which I touch on concerns the legal dimension of human rights. It reconstructs the theoretical structure that the dynamics between rights and duties gives place to. I suggest that a correlative relation between rights and duties underpins the kind of structure which I have in mind, and that human rights can be defined also in relation to their possibility of fulfilling such structure. In order to clarify this point I reconsider the polyvalent functionalities played by a system of liberty-rights, and in particular the general Hohfeldian distinction between claim rights, liberty rights, power rights and im-munities. What I criticize in the Hohfeldian scheme is the clear-cut distinction he proposes of negative restrictions and positive duties associated respectively with immunity rights and liberty-rights. The formal system of basic liberties which I defend combines both a negative approach of duties conferral with a consideration of positive conditions of self-determination.

In the remaining two paragraphs, I investigate upon the possibility of human rights transplantability and upon the consistency and plausibility of the democratic peace argument. In many ways such two arguments are interrelated, since if it is true, as democratic peace theorists claim, that a condition of international stability can be achieved only once all countries turn into democratic institutions, then it is true that part of such stability depends upon a uniform regime of human rights implementation. The way in which I address such two interconnected issues is

C. Corradetti, *Relativism and Human Rights*, DOI 10.1007/978-1-4020-9986-1_4,
© Springer Science+Business Media B.V. 2009

the following one: while I consider that human rights transplantability as such is implausible and normatively wrong, I also reject the empirical-normative model advanced by democratic peace theorists. There are, indeed, contradictory data –to say the least– running counter the hypothesis that democracies do not fight each other, as well as vague criteria adopted for the definition of what has to count as a democratic arrangement and as to how war can be defined. Modern techniques of economical and technological power control cannot be dismissed from a refined consideration of war scenarios. My understanding is that, for how desirable a people's democratic enjoyment of rights can be, it is normatively wrong and pragmatically counterproducting to orient democratic (western) states foreign policy to a global process of democratization. The suggestion is thus that of advancing a process of juridification of international relations through the creation of binding legal mechanisms of control and sanction of states behaviours. This point is merely sketched and a full development would require a more articulated enquiry. The idea is that as within state borders, also in the international realm a sort of division of labour between international institutions must be recognized and that clear-cut limits on interventions as based upon precise minimal criteria of states' decency must be set and agreed. As limited in its articulation as this view might be, it runs certainly counter to recent practices of (some) western states for "wars for democracy".

4.1 The Source and the Content Validity of Law

Thus far while providing the philosophical groundwork for a post-metaphysical understanding of human rights principles, I have not yet explained the role that is to be assigned to human rights as legal provisions and their role as regulating principles among states. These two domains are strictly interconnected considering that if the function of law completed by moral-political constraints can be proved, then the same inter-state relations in the global dimension become subordinated to the fulfilment of certain normative-legal conditions of validity.

Let's address each issue in turn. I will start with an explanation of the position I defend for the validity of law and then direct my enquiry to the more applicative extensions of such form of validity across interstate interactions.

In the attempt to provide a critical classification of the models of law, a first general distinction can be drawn between those theories testing the validity of law according to its source, and those theories conferring validity on the basis of the law's substantive moral merit. Doctrines following the first line of argumentation are positive law doctrines, whereas those following the second line are natural or alternatively critical morality law doctrines.[1] Within the first subdivision, for example, H.L.A. Hart's inclusive legal positivism claims that, albeit there is no necessary

---

[1] For reasons of completeness it must be said that there are also law doctrines seeing a necessary connection between law and positive morality. While this subcategory is relevant for reasons of classification, it looks quite uninteresting in its philosophical merits.

implication between law and substantive moral claims, it is still possible for a system to introduce, *conventionally*, moral criteria establishing conditions of validity within the specific legal system itself. The point, though, is that even in cases of this kind the ultimate check for the validity of law remains a social practice – the rule of recognition – which may not give weight to moral considerations. Exclusive legal positivism, in its turn, defends a strong version of the "separability thesis", according to which there are neither necessary nor sufficient implications between law and morality. Law is a purely social and conventional fact whose validity turns on the role of the authority which provides reasons for action to the governed (Raz, 1985).

In this paragraph I will suggest an overall assessment of the relation between law and morality. I will investigate and classify law theories with reference to four criteria: internal-conventional, external-conventional, internal-normative (natural/critical), external-normative (natural/critical). The above-mentioned mutually exclusive criteria, while representing an idealized index, do not exhaust the spectrum of possible classifications and at least some of the doctrines considered can be interpreted as grounded on multiple foundations. Hobbes's theory of political obligation, for instance, can be classified as a mixed theory, grounded on both an external-natural and an internal-natural criterion, which converge towards an external/conventional authority – the Leviathan. Before proposing my reading of Hobbes, I will first present some of the central cases fitting into the scheme generated by the above-mentioned opposing criteria.

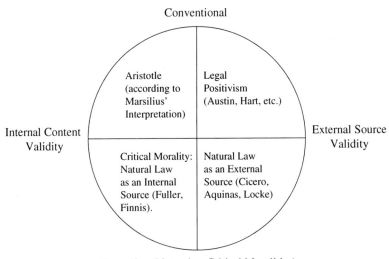

Instances of the combination of an internal and a conventional criterion for the underpinning of a specific model of law theory might be thought hard to find and, in fact, it must be observed that very few philosophers have explicitly recognized this combination as fruitful. Nevertheless, Aristotle can be seen as one of the few figures who have brilliantly developed a notion of natural law as compatible and not opposed to the conventional and mutable exigencies of political society.

According to Aristotle, it is somehow foul to think of a total transcendence of law regarding the inherent political nature of men and the practical needs of a political society, as apparently expressed in Plato's idea of the Republic. Aristotle's claim in the *Nichomachean Ethics* is that natural law is an essential part of political justice, pertaining to the *polis* and that natural justice overall is not to be understood as something fixed and given once and for all.[2]

It might seem that this position reduces the external character of natural law to the internal-conventional process of law production arising from political deliberation. However, such a reading is precluded by Aristotle's recognition that there is a distinction between, on the one hand, conventional laws arising from popular deliberation and binding only the deliberative body from whence they spring and, on the other hand, natural law relations among individuals that are not part of the same *polis*. Hence, it seems that the problem becomes that of finding a balance between the internal character of natural law and the conventionality and mutability of political law. The problem for Aristotle, however, is that he admits that natural law itself is mutable, thus introducing further complication into the understanding of its meaning. Here, an interesting interpretation is found in Marsilius of Padua, who states that, for Aristotle, natural law is to be taken as grounded upon human conventions, but distinguishes itself from mere positive law because

---

[2] "Of political justice part is natural, part legal, natural, that which everywhere has the same force and does not exist by people's thinking this or that; legal, that which is originally indifferent, but when it has been laid down is not indifferent, e.g. that a prisoner's ransom shall be a mina, or that a goat and not two sheep shall be sacrificed, and again all the laws that are passed for particular cases, e.g. that sacrifice shall be made in honour of Brasidas, and the provisions of decrees. Now some think that all justice is of this sort, because that which is by nature is unchangeable and has everywhere the same force (as fire burns both here and in Persia), while they see change in the things recognized as just. This, however, is not true in this unqualified way, but is true in a sense; or rather, with the gods it is perhaps not true at all, while with us there is something that is just even by nature, yet all of it is changeable; but still some is by nature, some not by nature. It is evident which sort of thing, among things capable of being otherwise, is by nature, and which is not but is legal and conventional, assuming that both are equally changeable. And in all other things the same distinction will apply; by nature the right hand is stronger, yet it is possible that all men should come to be ambidextrous. The things which are just by virtue of convention and expediency are like measures; for wine and corn measures are not everywhere equal, but larger in wholesale and smaller in retail markets. Similarly, the things which are just not by nature but by human enactment are not everywhere the same, since constitutions also are not the same, though there is but one which is everywhere by nature the best. Of things just and lawful each is related as the universal to its particulars; for the things that are done are many, but of them each is one, since it is universal. There is a difference between the act of injustice and what is unjust, and between the act of justice and what is just; for a thing is unjust by nature or by enactment; and this very thing, when it has been done, is an act of injustice, but before it is done is not yet that but is unjust. So, too, with an act of justice (though the general term is rather 'just action', and 'act of justice' is applied to the correction of the act of injustice). Each of these must later be examined separately with regard to the nature and number of its species and the nature of the things with which it is concerned" Aristotle (Book 5, para. 7).

it relies on conventions that are universally valid. It differs from pure natural law because there can be specific political instances in which it is necessary to contravene such laws, as for instance, when the survival of that same political society is at risk. Thus, under this interpretation, Aristotle's natural law is a conventional notion. As suggested by Strauss (1957, 161), one could even interpret the Aristotelian notion of natural law as not referring primarily to general principles of law, but rather to concrete decisions, so that natural law does not reside in general principles, but in specific deliberations. Generality can prevent the possibility of taking a just decision in a specific instance and natural law, so understood, requires the examination of all empirical evidence and circumstances in order to indicate what is just. If natural law is apprehended in this way, generality is implied within concrete judgments, and a degree of conventionality and mutability can be admitted within natural law theory as a form of justified exception to what Aristotle believes to be the general aim characterizing justice: the determination of the common good.

The school of legal positivism, instead, originates in part in the work of J. Austin and Bentham. Bentham, for instance, in the attempt of rejecting any pretence of validity to natural law principles, defines natural rights as "nonsense upon stilts" (Bentham, 1987, 53). According to Bentham, the significance of the legal terms of human rights, as natural and imprescriptible rights of men, manifests simply a form of rhetorical emptiness, a deprivation of meaning, since no experiential reference can be assigned to them. With reference to such weaknesses, the method of "paraphrasis", elaborated by Bentham, consists in assigning significance only to those terms which can be explained through their reiterated occurrence within simpler propositional constructions. In simpler propositional constructions, each word bears significance only in terms of its syntagmatic relations. It is possible to explain the significance of more complex sentences in terms of those sentences which have a wording more directly attached to experiential evidences. However, there are no positive juridical texts nor parallel experiential contexts in which natural rights can be paraphrased in this manner. As clearly labelled by Bentham: "right and law are correlative terms: as much so as son and father. A natural right is a son that never had a father" (Bentham, 1987, 73). But to claim that natural law expressions are without meaning does not mean that they have no linguistic use, nor that they cannot play any function even if limited to a form of pure subjectivist or expressivist appreciation. The possibility of expressing appreciation, even if limited to a form of subjectivism, can then bear important interconnections with the possibility of expressing a moral evaluation to natural rights themselves.

On the other hand, J. Austin, in *The Province of Jurisprudence Determined* (1995, [1832]), explores the way law can be defined without reverting to natural law principles as necessary and sufficient conditions for its validity. J. Austin further proposes that the definitional criteria of legality, while not grounded on the moral value of law, can be grounded on its source: that is, the proclamation made by the sovereign. Law and legality in general, are dependent on a specific authority which transfers validity to the proffered norm. But since it is not possible to move from this fact to its normative value, J. Austin attributes normativity to the punishments attached to violations of law.[3] Agents are bound to comply with law on pain of sanction, implying that commands unaccompanied by sanctions cease to be law at all. Evidently, J. Austin's normativity relies on "prudential reasons", which are based on the fear of incurring sanction. This fear leads citizens to comply with the obligations imposed by law.

There are elements in J. Austin that were later incorporated as some of the central tenets of modern positivism, particularly its specific view of the radical conventionality of law as necessarily distinct from morality. In his *Fifth Lecture*, J. Austin discusses what is taken to be the tendency of confusing what law "is" with what law "ought" to be. His target here is Blackstone's assertion that positive law is valid only if it conforms to natural law. J. Austin replies to Blackstone that laws contravening the law of God "have been and are continually enforced as laws by judicial tribunals" J. Austin (1995, [1832], 158). Since overlap between moral principles and law is an empirically fortunate coincidence, positivists rejects the idea that morality is a *necessary* prerequisite of legal validity: " 'Legal validity' is the term we use to refer to *whatever* is conventionally recognized as binding; to say that all the officials could be wrong about what is legally valid is close to nonsense" Bix (2002, 73). From J. Austin onwards, and even for the later Hart and the internalist-positivists, the fundamental notion of the conventionality of law rests on a clear-cut separation between the legal status of a law and the possibility that it provides a rational standard for action: "The existence of law is one thing; its merit or demerit is another" J. Austin (1995, [1832], 157).

Hart also maintained a strict separation between the existence of law as law, and its conformity to a moral standard of validity (Hart, 1961). Notwithstanding certain continuities between their views, Hart's criticism of J. Austin and his innovations inside the parameters of the positivist model remain extremely relevant.

Essentially, Hart objects that J. Austin's notion of normativity and his typology of laws are simplistic: "On this simple account of the matter, which we shall later have to examine critically, there must, wherever there is a legal system, be some persons or body of persons issuing general orders backed by threats which are generally obeyed, and it must be generally believed that these threats are likely to be implemented in the event of disobedience. This person or body must be internally supreme and externally independent. If, following J. Austin, we call such a supreme and independent person or body of persons the sovereign, the laws of any country will be the general orders backed by threats which are issued either by the sovereign or subordinates in obedience to the sovereign" Hart (1961, 25). Against J. Austin's, Hart poses his own notion of normativity, which rests on a pure act of the sovereign as a source of law and on prudential reasons which bind agents to comply with law for the fear of punishment. Hart then adds further sophistication to the normative

---

[3] "Law is a command which obliges a person or persons [...]. Laws and other commands are said to proceed from *superiors*, and to bind or oblige *inferiors* [...]. But, taken with the meaning wherein I here understand it, the term *superiority* signifies *might*: the power of affecting others with evil or pain, and of forcing them, through fear of that evil, to fashion their conduct to one's wishes" J. Austin (1995, 29–30).

monotonic picture presented by J. Austin by recognizing two fundamental different types of rules – primary and secondary rules – where primary rules aim either at limiting or extending individual liberties, and secondary rules confer powers for the issuing of primary rules (power of legislation and power of adjudication), with the exception of the rule of recognition which fixes the conditions of validity for primary rules, consequently playing the role of a meta-rule.[4] Identifying secondary rules as power-conferring rules is also deployed by Hart in order to tackle the issue of the normative source of law, seen by J. Austin as springing from the will of the sovereign. If the authority of the sovereign derives from certain power conferring rules of succession and legitimation ("the first male son" etc.), then the normative source of law is not dependent on an empirical individual which might determine the collapse of law with his death. Rather, it relies on secondary rules conferring normative power on a specific subclass of human beings, according to the content expressed. If this is true, then the meta-juridical rule of recognition serves the task of validating the entire process of conferring rules and primary rules in general. The existence of secondary rules breaks the symmetric structure between rules and associated punishments proposed by J. Austin. No punishments are associated with secondary rules, but this does not mean that such rules are deprived of legal value. Therefore, normativity cannot be understood in terms of punishments, since secondary rules also have a normative force despite not being coupled to threats.

Within the class of secondary rules, the rule of recognition establishes the normative conditions for the validity of rules in general. For Hart, in contrast to J. Austin, rules maintain a social dimension of legitimation, and provide agents with reasons for complying with the law by adding to the mere fact or habit of obedience also a reason. The rule of recognition operates within the social space, allowing for *internal* acceptance by officials (that is, judges and not the sovereign) of further new rules. The validity of rules is thus subordinated to their acceptance under the constraint posed by the rule of recognition, transferring authority to the new rules whose validity is fixed by their remaining valid under the rule of recognition.

---

[4] One interesting criticism of Hart's distinction between primary and secondary rules, and in particular of the function of the rule of recognition, is advanced by Fuller: "If one is intent on preserving a sharp distinction between rules imposing duties and rules conferring powers, there are reasons for being unhappy about any suggestion that it may be possible to withdraw the lawmaking authority once it has been conferred by the rule of recognition. If Rex [fictional sovereign deployed as a subject in Fuller's mental experiment] began to keep his laws secret from those legally bound to obey them, and had his crown taken away from him for doing so, it would certainly seem foolish to ask whether he was deposed because he violated an implied duty or because, by exceeding the tacit limits of his power, he had worked an automatic forfeiture of his office and thus became subject to 'the sanction of nullity'. In other words, a rule that confers a power and provides, expressly or by implication, that this power may be revoked for abuses, presents in its proviso a stipulation that straddles ambiguously the distinction between duty-imposing rules and those that grant powers" Fuller (1969, 138). However, as noted by Fuller, within the category of secondary rules, Hart distinguishes secondary power-conferring rules from the rule of recognition, the latter imposing the duty on judges of respecting rules that satisfy criteria of validity (on this point, see Mac Cormick, 1981, 21).

There are two points to be noted here, the first concerning the social character of the rule, and the second concerning the notion of normativity. That only the rule of recognition, and not all rules, is a necessarily special social rule, is a point that Hart clarifies progressively within his work *The Concept of Law* (1961). Here he observes that, in many cases, legal rules lack a corresponding social practice, whereas some legal rules are introduced to substitute a given practice with a new one, or to mediate between incommensurable social practices. Furthermore, if one provisionally concedes that the normative character of rules placed within the validity function of the rule of recognition is limited to officials, and does not extend to a process of internal recognition by the constituent body in general, then the possibility of providing reasons for rule-following is limited only to a restricted group of people. And if agents, with the exception of officials, are not motivated by an internal process of recognition of the validity of rules, then normativity takes the form of a *de facto* convergent behaviour exhibited by the majority.[5] But to follow the majority's conduct is not to be internally motivated by rules; it relies, at most, on a prudential judgment about following suit with what it is generally believed as valid. If one extends this line of reasoning also to those who apply the internal process of recognition, such as officials, then the problem of taking for normativity what is in fact behaviour based on prudential reasons remains unchanged. Unless it is demonstrated which moral reasons a rule of recognition is to be built on, in order to be authority transferring, the mere fact of conformist behaviour of judges towards certain standards does not in and of itself indicate their following of a normative criterion. Strictly speaking, as Dworkin notes, Hart considers that rules can be binding according to two different criteria: "[. . .] because that group through its practices *accepts* the rule as a standard for its conduct" and because a rule is "[. . .] enacted in conformity with some *secondary* rule that stipulates that rules so enacted shall be binding" Dworkin (1977b, 41). As a result, it is necessary to evaluate on which basis a secondary rule can grasp its validity, if this does not turn merely on the convergent behaviour on which it is constructed. Hence, the two criteria of nor-

---

[5] Serious criticisms can be advanced against this view of legal authority and validity that the rule of recognition is supposed to have: "There are two problems with this account of legal authority. Even if we accept that the rule of recognition is authoritative in virtue of its being a social rule, it does not follow that rules valid under the rule of recognition are authoritative in virtue of their validity under the rule of recognition. The rule of recognition applies only to the behaviour of relevant officials. It provides officials with very narrowly defined reasons for acting – that is, grounds for applying certain criteria as standards for assessing the validity of other 'legal' actions. These reasons simply have nothing to do with the reasons legal rules in general might be said to provide ordinary citizens. Whereas the validity relationship is truth preserving, it is not authority transferring. Second, the authority of the rule of recognition does not derive from its being a social rule, that is, its being accepted from an internal point of view. Acceptance from an internal point of view is expressed through the behaviour/of appealing to the rule as grounds of criticism and justification. The claim that the authority of a social rule derives from the internal point of view thus amounts to the view that what makes a norm reason giving is the fact that the majority of individuals treat it as such. But the authority of a rule (its reason-giving capacity) cannot be grounded in the mere fact that individuals treat it as reason giving" Coleman and Leiter (1996, 247).

mativity can be reduced to one. The moral character of law is thus what positivism has to recognize as the normative source of law. Here, however, Hart would reply that positivism can be an inclusivist theory: that is, it can include moral principles as rules, without being forced to include them, thus maintaining the *separability* thesis. In other words, moral principles can be admitted as parts of the validity conditions for a legal system without being explicative of the multiple functions played by morality itself. The distinction between exclusivist legal positivism and inclusivist legal positivism would be precisely attached to the relation of implication between law and morality. In the case exclusivist legal positivism morality would be *necessarily* unconnected to law, whereas in the case of inclusivist positivism, granting respect to the separability thesis, law is not necessarily connected to morality. This saves the distinction between law and morality, while recognizing moral principles as an external element of law whose validity is implicitly presupposed by the rule of recognition itself. To this one can reply that the evaluative dimension of judgmental activity cannot be clearly separated from the judgmental activity itself, and that the recourse to normative moral principles is, since the beginning, part of ordinary, first-order legal arguments.[6] According to this line of reasoning, it is rather difficult to isolate a neutral second-order methodology, as Hart would claim, and to approach the problem of the validity of law from a merely descriptive perspective. I believe these are crucial points positivism has to answer, even if they do not suffice by themselves to show that legal normative approaches are right. The point I will make, therefore, concerns whether the requirement of moral normativity is a necessarily embedded element of the rule of recognition, and how, if this is the case, one can conceive of a rule of recognition which is both normative and social: that is, a social practice normatively constrained.

Thus, with this in mind we can turn to the understanding of the specificities of what I have named as normative critical moral theories of law defending an internal link between law and morality. Several authors can be considered as defending this view, but my purpose here is to show how and why my position gives a specific contribution in this sense. In the foregoing sections, indeed, I have attempted to justify a view of human rights which considers the validity of law as in constant normative tension with the principles of morality, the latter imposing a regulative ideal from which law operates. What I have termed as the "discursive dialectic of recognition", while embedded within a social practice, introduces a moral normative constraint for the validation of human rights discourses. In this sense, legal reasoning must not simply mirror already fixed moral contents, but it is bound to shape and specify constructive experiential constraints through the activity of the reflective judgement: it is neither a matter of translating into law already fixed moral norms, nor to construct from scratch such juridical constraints. It is rather a productive activity carried on by the reflective judgement which works constructively by simply assuming – through the use of a pragmatic attitude to recognition of a generalized other – that there are some generally inviolable conditions for purposive agency which must be specified

---

[6] See Dworkin (2006, 140ff).

into legal terms. The productive activity of the reflective judgement, then, is that of advancing articulated exemplar judgments balancing internal tensions of human rights principles, while determining in so doing the legal specific configurations of such general principles through the construction of exemplar judgments. The reflective and principled-constrained activity of the judgment places itself in between the externality of such formal system of liberty enabling purposive action and the contingency of a *de facto sensus communis*. Within my defended view law, while non infringing on morality, it exhibits integrative functions regarding the moral discourse, as in the cognitive, motivational and organizational functions. It is precisely for these reasons that it can never be completely identified with morality. While an internal relationship between law and morality is thus recognised, the spheres of their functions still differ quite broadly. Let's further specify this point.

According to general formal terms, in order to provide decisive reasons agents should conform to, law must be capable of exhibiting four necessary and mutually sufficient conditions of functioning; that is, it must exhibit the properties of a *characteristic activity*, of *goal productivity*, of *teleology*, and of *value*. If a system of law does not exhibit these four elements fully, this does not imply that it is not to be considered as a system of law at all; rather, it means that its function as law is deficient and only approximates to the proper legal standard. Within this picture, legal recognition of basic human rights grounds the necessary, but not sufficient, conditions for the rational functioning of a system of law. In turn, individuals not conforming to legally recognized human rights principles would be defective rational agents who, were they functioning on the basis of relevant reasons, would conform to the dictates of a fully functioning law. Nickel (1987, 29–35), has distinguished between "entitlement theories", which conceive rights as goals without any need to specify duty holders and "entitlements-plus theories", which take the correlative thesis seriously, but fail to draw a distinction between moral rights, legal rights, and "legally implemented entitlements theories", which conceive of rights strictly as positive laws. In contrast with these distinctions, the theory advanced here considers human rights as universally valid formal presuppositions exhibiting, a structure of entitlements and duty assignments which ought then to be interpreted discoursively. Human rights as conditions of purposive agency, are presuppositions of a legal discursive processes based upon a social and moral embedded rule of recognition. This process gives place to a pluralist form of human rights judgments whose second-order judgmental recomposition is delegated to public officials. Beyond the categories presented by Nickel, then, a fourth model can be advanced, combining elements of both "entitlements-plus theories" and of "legally implemented entitlements theories". According to this reading, substantive fundamental principles of human rights comprise inevitable conditions for the realization of law's binding force.

Turning to the proposed classification, non-conventional natural law theories address precisely the point of convergence between law and morality, and the idea of a necessary interlinking with morality which implies that wherever law fails to meet a moral standard it can be considered either as defective law (weak-naturalist thesis) or as not law at all (strong naturalist thesis). If natural law positions were all reducible to the strong naturalist thesis, there would be no scope for their compatibility with inclusive positivism. However, as already mentioned, there is another version of naturalism which does not consider legal codes as completely conditional upon morality. This is the view advanced by weak naturalists. According to weak naturalism, a legal code failing to comply with moral principles can still be defined as law, albeit in an imperfect way and therefore weak naturalism does allow an interesting connection with the form of revised inclusive positivism presented above.

Following from the distinctions between internal-external and conventional-normative theories, one can distinguish theories that view the normativity of law as springing from an external source and those that instead conceive normativity as springing from an internal source. In the first case, one is committed to a metaphysical view which conceives of a specific ontological being as the source of legitimacy of morality and of law, whereas in the second, one may justify the morality of law on the basis of procedural principles, or alternatively on the basis of substantive principles.[7]

Fuller can be seen as the most interesting representative of natural-internal proceduralism. Central to his view is the assertion of law as a "purposive activity", as "the enterprise of subjecting human conduct to the governance of rules" Fuller (1969, 106). But such rules, "have nothing to do with any 'brooding omnipresence in the skies' [...] They remain entirely terrestrial in origin and application". The natural morality of law is thus internal and procedural, the latter meaning that "a system of rules for governing human conduct must be constructed and administered if it is to be efficacious and at the same time remain what it purports to be". Procedurality means that law, in order to advance moral claims, must conform to certain standards, that is to say, to "ways in which a system of rules for governing human conduct must be constructed and administered if it is to be efficacious and at the same time remain what it purports to be" Fuller (1969, 96–97). This point underscores an interesting feature of Fuller's view of morality, which is that a "morality of aspiration" is distinguished from a simple "morality of duty". In so far as the inner procedurality of law is concerned, its claims aspire to more than merely establishing negative claims of forbearance towards others; instead, they aspire to fixing positive formal goals that law must achieve in order to be morally justified. If law's morality were concerned only with negative duties, it would fail to specify the degree of non-fulfilment of such duties. Thus, for instance, says Fuller, if law were couched only in negative terms in the interests of clarity, the possibility of realizing this goal would rest with the intention of the legislator: "But this only postpones the difficulty, for in some situations nothing can be more baffling than to attempt to measure how vigorously a man intended to do that which he has failed to do" Fuller (1969, 43).

Law as a "purposive activity" can thus be thought of as achieving its functionalist goal only if positive standards guiding the production of law are respected. Fuller

---

[7] Concerning "self-evident principles", this expression refers to their non-deducibility from any other principle, as well as to their non syllogistic demonstrability, see Bix (1996, 229).

considers eight procedural principles whose respect guarantees the success of the law production enterprise. He introduces such constraints by narrating a fictional story where a king, Rex, attempting to behave wisely by introducing reforms, completely fails to create a system of law. A system of law can be so defined only if all such conditions are respected, whereas a system ceases to be a system of law if only one principle is omitted. This does not prevent a system of law from conforming "more or less well" to a standard of well-formedness; there might, indeed, be degrees of well-formedness to a supposedly perfect legal enterprise respecting all eight criteria. To the charge that a legal system cannot "half exist", Fuller replies that "both rules of law and legal systems can and do half exist. This condition results when the purposive effort necessary to bring them into full being has been, as it were, only half successful. The truth that there are degrees of success in this effort is obscured by the conventions of ordinary language [. . .] It is probably well that our legal vocabulary treats a judge as a judge, though of some particular holder of the judicial office I may quite truthfully say to a fellow lawyer, 'He's no judge' " Fuller (1969, 122).

Fuller lists eight pitfalls to be avoided by any system of law: "The first and most obvious lies in a failure to achieve rules at all, so that every issue must be decided on an *ad hoc* basis. The other routes are: (1) a failure to publicize, or at least to make available to the affected party, the rules he is expected to observe; (2) the abuse of retroactive legislation, which not only cannot itself guide action, but undercuts the integrity of rules prospective in effect, since it puts them under the threat of retrospective change; (3) a failure to make rules understandable; (4) the enactment of contradictory rules or (5) rules that require conduct beyond the powers of the affected party; (6) introducing such frequent changes in the rules that the subject cannot orient his action by them; and, finally, (7) a failure of congruence between the rules as announced and their actual administration" Fuller (1969, 39).

Compliance with law, defined according to the avoidance of these pitfalls, cannot be reduced simply to obedience of authority. While authority can be obeyed without being constrained by motivating reasons, "fidelity to law" requires that rule-following is motivated by the procedural principles defining morality: "A mere respect for constituted authority must not be confused with fidelity to law. Rex's subjects, for example, remained faithful to him as king throughout his long and inept reign. They were not faithful to his law, for he never made any" Fuller (1969, 41).

One interesting additional aspect is that the *holistic* validity of such constraints is in many respects *contingent* on the modification of empirical circumstances. While, taken globally, they are "means toward a single end", if circumstances change, "the optimum marshalling of these means may change" Fuller (1969, 104) so that "adjustments" between the different "*desiderata*" might lead to compensating solutions between different weights and extensions that procedural principles assume on each occasion. What law is bound to serve is the realization of a "purposive activity", but the content of its purpose is left open by Fuller to representation of "the legal expression of the political national state" Fuller (1969, 110). Now, adopting whichever objective the political will of a state may express as a valid purposeful action for the determination of what counts as law would appear to be a weak criterion for fixing the normative substantive standard that law as morality must respect. Indeed, if Fuller's analysis halted at this point, his theory would be openly flawed. However, Fuller goes on to claim that the natural relation between law and procedural moral principles, while being a necessary condition, is not yet sufficient for the definition of morality of law in general: " [. . .] I have attempted to show that the internal morality of law does indeed deserve to be called a 'morality'. I hope I have demonstrated that an acceptance of this morality is a necessary, though not a sufficient condition for the realization of justice, that this morality is itself violated when an attempt is made to express blind hatreds through legal rules, and that, finally, the specific morality of law articulates and holds before us a view of man's nature that is indispensable to law and morality alike" Fuller (1969, 168).

But how can "blind hatreds" be distinguished from "justified punishments", if no substantive moral goal is assumed as driving the purposive activity of law? Fuller seems to imply, in several passages, that there is one further constraint leading to acceptable results: the notion of reciprocity and self-determination, which implies the submission of the same governors to the rules they promulgate, and which can be taken as a complementary criterion constraining law-making towards morally satisfactory results and posing, therefore, a sufficient condition of validity.

I doubt, however, that this condition is sufficient to achieve what Fuller wishes. One can imagine a perverse but very charismatic sovereign who decides upon the extinction of his community, including himself and his family, and who leads all his followers happily to death. On the basis of Fuller's criticism of Hart's supposedly " 'central indisputable element' in human striving" namely the wish for survival, it is observed that this possibility is not to be denied in principle (Fuller, 1969, 185). But Fuller's reply to this criticism is not too convincing. His notion of the morality of law, while purporting to be neutral regarding divergent moral theories, clearly seeks to exclude at least some substantive aims: "But a recognition that the internal morality of law may support and give efficacy to a wide variety of substantive aims should not mislead us into believing that *any* substantive aim may be adopted without compromise of legality" Fuller (1969, 153). Notwithstanding this reasonable desire, the only reply offered by Fuller to the case of the malign monarch mentioned above is that it has never occurred in history that faith in law has accompanied total disinterest in human welfare. But this *de facto* answer does not show the impossibility in principle of pursuing both goals. Further, there *is* perhaps some empirical evidence of what Fuller wishes to deny, for instance, in the cases of suicide by fanatic communities who choose death in exchange for salvation. In other words, procedural constraints, as those conceived by Fuller, do not seem neither *necessary* nor *sufficient* to guarantee a good system of law.

A further line of attack against Fuller's internal proceduralism pursued by Hart's concerns the limits of the eight principles in underpinning morality: "Poisoning is no doubt a purposive activity, and reflections on its purpose may show that it has its internal principles. ('Avoid poisons however lethal if they cause the victim to vomit'. . . .) But to call these principles of the poisoner's art 'the morality of poisoning' would simply blur the distinction between the notion of efficiency for a purpose and those final judgments about activities and purposes with which morality in its various forms is concerned" Hart (1965, 1285–86). This seems to confirm that Fuller's internal procedural principles, while necessary conditions of the morality of law, cannot yet be taken as sufficient conditions. The morality of law, for Fuller, rests only on such constraints while aiming to remain neutral between the different goals each moral view might pursue. Even with the introduction of the concepts of reciprocity and self-determination, two unfortunate conclusions can be drawn: first, the validity of the theory cannot be accepted as remaining on a purely formal level; second, admitting the hypothetical case of a malign charismatic ruler, the eight principles do not suffice to guarantee morally constrained purposive activity.

Within what I have defined as the internal-normative naturalist paradigm, a substantive view of the morality of law is taken by Finnis (1980). According to Finnis, inquiry into the necessary and sufficient conditions for what counts as law is not relevant; more fruitful is establishing paradigmatic cases of what defines law as morally justified. Substantive natural law principles explain "the obligatory force (in the fullest sense of 'obligation') of positive laws, even when those laws cannot be deduced from those principles" Finnis (1980, 23–24). This means that, in the case that a law disrespects such principles, according to Finnis, it can be still considered a valid law, but insofar as it fails to be law in its fullest sense, it can neither ground individual moral obligation nor justify enforcement by the state.[8]

Let us try to disentangle this view by reconsidering definitions. One can distinguish between strong and weak criteria of natural law with reference to two different interpretations of the following statement: "Necessarily, law is a rational standard for conduct". This claim can be interpreted either as meaning "necessarily, two plus two is equal four", or as "necessarily, cars have four wheels".[9] If the first interpretation refers to an all or nothing fulfillment of the definitional criterion, the second interpretation can admit the existence of imperfect cars which, while not being four-wheeled still fall, nonetheless, within the category of cars. Finnis's view of law falls within this second reading. He sees law as a multi-property category, whose validity is detached from substantive motivating reasons law might provide to agents. Once the paradigmatic case of law as endowed with morally convincing reasons is underpinned, imperfect law can be still thought of as valid, even if not as an adequate motivating standard for action. In order for law to be an adequate motivating standard for action, it has to be adequate in the eyes of an hypothetical fully reasonable citizen. With this move, however, Finnis risks defending something

---

[8] Finnis maintains that law has a coordinating role in adjudicating allocation of basic goods (i.e. life, friendship, religion etc.), leading towards the achievement of common good: "['Law' is to be understood] primarily to rules made, in accordance with regulative legal rules, by a determinate and effective authority (itself identified and, standardly, constituted as an institution by legal rules) for a 'complete' community, and buttressed by sanctions in accordance with the rule-guided stipulations of adjudicative institutions, this ensemble of rules and institutions being directed to reasonably resolving any of the community's co-ordination problems (and to ratifying, tolerating, regulating, or overriding co-ordination solutions from any other institutions or sources of norms) for the common good of that community" Finnis (1980, 276).

[9] On this point see Murphy (2005, 21).

similar to "the uninteresting Moral Reading, leaving his critics to wonder what all the fuss was about natural law theory" Murphy (2005, 24–25).

A completely different route of justification is advanced by what I have called external naturalism. Several varieties of this theory can be listed, some of which extend beyond the strictly philosophical domain to occupy also the religious and theological domains.

Within the classical philosophical tradition, the most interesting instances are those represented by Cicero, Aquinas and Locke. This represents only a small indicative option for the many scholars who have advanced a theory of obligation on the basis of a classical theory of natural law. According to Cicero, for instance, the enquiry upon what is the significance of natural law is strictly entrenched in the understanding of the significance of justice. To provide an answer to the content of natural law implies to understand to what civil law and a legitimate government must be subordinated to (Cicero, 2001, 35). By starting from the assumption that reason is the most "superior attribute" present both in men and God and that there is no people so savage not to be acquainted with the law of God, then, reason as a rule of the celestial body, is the normative source of natural law. But once reconstructed through inferential reasoning, then the relation between natural reason and its attainment through the cultivation of men's virtues can be reverted, so to state that: "[...] Nature created all mankind to share and enjoy the same sense of right of which I may speak is derived from Nature [...] if wise men, prompted by Nature, would agree with the poets that whatever touches humanity concerns them too, then everyone would cultivate justice. For all to whom Nature gave the power of reasoning have received from her also the ability to reason correctly. Thus has arisen law, which is right reason as expressed in commands and prohibitions; and from law has come justice" Cicero (2001, 38). There are at least three distinct definitions of natural law springing from such passage: (a) natural law as just or "right" reason; (b) natural law as an essence of things; (c) natural law as a law of God.

While under (a) a state of affairs can be assessed as "right" if it accords with nature, the law of nature, in turn, is the product of God's will, so that agreement with natural essences *a fortiori* constitutes concordance with the law of God. Compliance with law is compliance with the law of God and not with the written law of nations very often based upon a criterion of utility. Were utility to be the criterion for the production of laws, then not only instability would be derived according to Cicero, due to ever changing perspectives on the maximization of utility but, most importantly, compliance to law as utility would not lead to the fulfillment of the criteria of justice.

Similarly, for Aquinas, the conception of natural law theory is constructed around two basic properties: God as the source of natural law, and natural law as an evaluative standard for assessing the reasonableness of human action (Aquinas, 1991, *Question* 94 *Prima Secundae*). From these two premises, it follows that compliance with natural law draws human beings into participation in God's eternal law (Aquinas, 1991, IaIIae 91, 2), that is, into the rational plan God has foreseen for his creatures as a design of providence to which men can freely adhere. Natural law principles, springing from the benevolence of God, are both universally binding (Aquinas, 1991, IaIIae 94, 4) and universally knowable by nature (Aquinas, 1991, IaIIae 94, 4). Upon rational reflection over what is good to do they are freed from evil sentiment and desires (Aquinas, 1991, IaIIae 94, 6). In these two authors it is possible to find the central elements that mark the focus of the classical paradigm for natural law, as developed from the Stoic-Scholastic tradition onward, and grounded upon the notion of *partecipatio* (participation) of human reason into the divine *lex aeterna*. The Stoic notion of *logos* as a cosmic form of rationality is thus reinterpreted in terms of the *lex aeterna* (eternal law) by the medieval tradition and part of the divine reason (*ratio divina*). As defined by Aquinas, the elements of the *lex aeterna* regarding men are then properly defined in terms of natural law (Aquinas, 1991, chap. 3 n. 1, Ia IIae, quaest.91, art.2).

Within the paradigm of natural law as an external standard of validity, one of the most relevant elements marking Locke's modernity, is precisely his distancing from the notion of *lex aeterna* and therefore from the notion of a human participation into the rationality of the universe. Such reinterpretation of the relation between human and cosmic/divine rationality bears extremely relevant consequences within the theory of obligation by natural law. By abandoning the notion of participation, Locke dismisses also the idea of innate seeds of natural justice and of a natural tendency and transparent knowledge of men of the divine will. Men are left by themselves in finding, starting from their individual inclinations and knowledge acquisitions, their routes to the interpretation of the natural law which still remains in Locke, a partition of the divine law. Differently from the classical model of natural law theory, though, within the modern system at least two crucial problems arise: on one hand, the gnoseological problem concerning how natural law can be known, given that men are no longer participating in a rational cosmic system and thus do not possess any innate ideas of such a law, and, on the other hand and as a consequence, a further sub-fracture must be reconciled: that of a theory of motivation with a theory of obligation by natural law.

In his first essay on natural law (1954 [1660–64]), Locke criticises the classical justifications advanced for the knowledge of the natural law. Those are generally recapitulated into three forms: *inscriptio, traditio* and *consensus* (inscription, tradition and consensus). If, as far as the first justification is concerned, the law of nature were inscribed in all hearts of humanity, then it would be easy to find a general agreement upon its content. But since there is no such agreement, it seems unlikely that men possess innately such commandments. As later clarified in the work *An Essay concerning Human Understanding* (1975 [1690]), for Locke the mind is a *tabula rasa* and all cognitive elements are acquired from experience. I will return to this point, since it represents Locke's starting point for the gnoseological explanation of how natural law is acquired. Concerning the two others sources of knowledge – tradition and consensus – Locke claims that were tradition the standard, then the problem of justification would simply be postponed, since there must have been someone who initiated a tradition, that either had such knowledge inside or acquired it somehow. Finally, regarding consensus, Locke claims that a formal and binding consensus, that is a contract, concerns only the stipulation of positive laws and not of natural laws and that, were a natural consensus upon natural law possible, then at least a general uniformity of costumes would be required. Since there are all sorts of diverging habits and intolerable practices among peoples, then it is not possible to claim that natural law is the result of a natural consensus among peoples themselves. From the critical exclusion of three such classical justificatory patterns, Locke advances his theory of the soul as a *tabula rasa* and his theory of the acquisition of the natural law precepts on the basis of the senses. The mutual activity carried out by the senses and reason is to produce the contents of the conscience as "complex ideas" (Locke, 1975 [1690]), where such ideas represent the human gnoseological pattern tending toward the acquisition of the law of nature. And yet, the fracture between the law of nature and human epistemology remains unfulfilled if not supplemented by some further elements of connection.

Such unfulfilled epistemological connection between the two, receives a practical solution when one turns to the assessment of Locke's theory of motivation and obligation. To suggest such a practical solution of the dichotomy between human understanding and divine law is to underscore also one further point of distinction between the classical view of natural law as based upon the recognition of the just contents in the commands of God, from the modern solution oriented toward compliance for the fear of God's sanctions. Obligation to God is due both to the fear of punishment and to an innate motivation for happiness and self-conservation –not justice! But between the two a precise relation must be understood: compliance to natural law as a divine obligation is motivated on the basis of the fulfilment of an innate tendency to happiness and self-conservation (Locke, 1954 [1660–64], 73ff). Whereas the foundation of the moral obligation remains upon God's formulation of the natural law, motivation to compliance to the moral law is not a recognition of the just content of such laws, but rather the realization of one's happiness through obedience of such moral commands. Violating natural law precepts, indeed, would mean to incur God's punishments, thus nullifying the possibility of achieving happiness. The relevance that natural law and rights assume in relation to political power, represents then only a further step in the legitimation of the action conducted by a collective political body.[10]

---

[10] "11. From these *two distinct rights*, the one of *punishing* the crime *for restraint*, and preventing the like offence, which right of punishing is in everybody; the other of taking *reparation*, which belongs only to the injured party, comes it to pass that the magistrate, who by being magistrate hath the common right of punishing put into his hands, can often, where the public good demands not the execution of the law, *remit* the punishment of criminal offences by his own authority, but yet cannot *remit* the satisfaction due to any private man, for the damage he has received. That, he who has suffered the damage has a right to demand in his own name, and he alone can *remit*: The damnified person has this power of appropriating to himself the goods or service of the offender, by *right of self-preservation*, as every man has a power to punish the crime, to prevent its being committed again, *by the right he has of preserving all mankind*, and doing all reasonable things he can in order to that end: And thus it is, that every man, in the state of nature, has a power to kill a murderer, both to deter others from doing the like injury, which no reparation can compensate, by the example of the punishment that attends it from every body, and also *to secure* men from the attempts of a criminal, who having renounced reason, the common rule and measure God hath

Generally, external naturalism promotes an ordered view of beings, placing the source of truth at the top of a hypothetical hierarchy. And even when not committed to a metaphysical-ontological ordering of beings, external naturalism maintains a metaphysical view according to which "truth is something out there", waiting to be apprehended by the individual subject; in other words, it is something objectively and realistically knowable. But the problem with objectivism and realism is precisely that they mistake an *epistemological* problem for an *ontological* one. Let us suppose that realism and objectivism are correct that there are "true facts out there". Does this compel each and every one of us to reach a precise, unanimous conclusion once our judgment is exercised? One might claim that this would indeed be so, "if rational moral judgment were exercised in the right way". But how do we assess which way is the correct way, if not through an argumentative discussion in which the best and most convincing explanation prevails? So, if the problem becomes that of making the best argumentative presentation of our thesis, in order to convince our counterparts of its plausibility, the fact that there is an objective truth out there, to be grasped, becomes irrelevant. The confrontation remains one between different opinions, tested in terms of which best explains the matter in question. If this is so, then the argument remains within the confines of moral and semantic epistemology, and does not touch questions of metaphysics.

As stated at the beginning of this section, there may be cases escaping classification here proposed. Indeed, Hobbes's view can be understood as a mixed theory, combining an external/natural and an internal/natural criterion, within an external/conventional perspective represented by the law of the Leviathan. Concerning the role of natural law principles, one can further distinguish between a *system of obligations*, culminating in obligations of obedience to the law of nature as a divine command, and a *system of motivations*, culminating in the subjective desire of the individual to ensure her own self-preservation. Consideration of only one of the two normative sources precludes full understanding of the complexity of Hobbes's views.

In terms of the theory of obligation, it can be observed that covenants can also be established in the state of nature and not only within civil society. The difference between the two pertains only to the *circumstances* within which covenants are concluded, and not to the nature of the moral principles involved. This point bears relevance in explaining how it is possible to move from the first to the second condition.

If the law of nature and, in particular, its first article concerned with the promotion of peace, obligates only in *foro interno*, the sovereign, while himself obliged to *foro interno* by the law of nature, obliges also *foro externo* since the laws of nature are taken minimal negative constraints of his rule. The obligation towards

---

given to mankind, hath by the unjust violence and slaughter he hath committed upon one, declared war against all mankind, and therefore may be destroyed as a *lion* or a *tiger*, one of those wild savage beasts, with whom men can have no society nor security: and upon this is grounded that great law of nature [...]" Locke (1982 [1689], 6–7).

the sovereign is valid until the condition of security is guaranteed. The foundation of political obligation is thus the role that the notion of natural law plays within Hobbes's theory. Laws of nature in the state of nature are only theorems and abstract rational principles, but not yet laws in themselves. In order to become duty-bearing, and thus laws, they must be considered commands springing from a normative source, namely God, and subsequently the civil sovereign. Thus the foundation of political obligation is found in God and not in the rational aspect of law. The reason one must obey natural law principles is because they represent God's rule. If the duties of men (that is, to promote peace and respect covenants) are founded on the law of nature, the political covenant has the advantage of making them even more specific.

So far, only part of Hobbes's theory of political obligation has been reconstructed, by indicating the external and natural criterion of normativity springing from God. The other part, which situates Hobbes in the realm of modernity concerns his notion of political motivation as deriving from an internal source. Hobbes's modernity consists exactly in his deduction of compliance with natural law from individual desire driven by the motive of self-preservation. Probably, Hobbes recognized that it is only if natural law can be supported by agents' internal motivation that compliance with it might be secured. Natural law is thus supported by humankind's most forceful passion, fear of death – and not of natural death, but of violent death, that is, the result of intentional action. But then, if natural law is to be externally validated, it is the validity of that same desire that comprises the basis of any natural configuration of justice. Duties, thus, are constituted by what is in some ways a conceptual *prius*, that is, the fundamental right to self-preservation. Only a right of this sort is unconditional and absolute, since there are no other similarly binding duties that are not generated by this primary right. In nature then, there is only a perfect right and not a perfect duty – a perfect right springing from a natural condition where, *contra* the conventionalists, such a right is identified in terms of the most elementary human needs. If this is so, then, absoluteness of the right implies the priority of the individual to society, and the latter only inherits rights derived from the individual and her preservation (*Leviathan*, chaps. XVIII and XXVIII). In Hobbes, in contrast to the positions borne by classical thinkers, everyone is judge of her own means for survival and self-preservation; knowledge plays no overriding role over consensus. But consensus, as noted in Strauss's analysis of Hobbes (1957), is not enough, if it is not subject to the sovereign. Thus, the sovereign is such, not because of rational deliberation, nor because she is endowed with knowledge, but only because she results from a fundamental covenant that attributes to her a legitimate authority. Sovereign commands are not necessarily reasonable, that is, they need not all be action motivating. The minimal requirement springing from this reconstruction imposes the sovereign to respect a negative requirement of non-infringement of the internal natural principles of law. This implies that, while a sovereign command, by necessity, must not violate natural law principles, this is not a sufficient condition for its being a fully reasonable command providing positive reasons for action. Hence, if the command of the sovereign is taken as valid and obeyed, this is because of the authority the sovereign has received through the covenant.

This long excursus on the specific properties and models representing different views on the validity of law was necessary for the clarification of the picture which emerges from the paradigm of law that I have advanced. As indicated in the discussion, my position reinterprets the notion of recognition as a form of quasi-transcendental mechanism for the validation of positive rights. This pattern of production of morally valid legal norms does not exhaust the significance of law within socio-political bodies since, once that a mechanism of validity has been established, what is required is a reconstruction of the functional roles that codes play in creating a system of individual's rights and duties bearers. In the course of the next paragraph I will therefore explain in detail the structure and the function that human rights in particular do indeed exhibit, so that doubts concerning what counts as human rights can receive full elucidation.

4.2 The Structure and Function of Human Rights

As has emerged in the preceding section, a formal system of liberty-rights generates a system of human rights grounding the validity of purposive action in general. Human rights constitute the ethically argued domain of freedoms to agency; they protect the coordinating preconditions to purposive agency in respect to which one can claim to have a right. To obtain something as a right is therefore different from obtaining it through a permission or privilege. Having a right is to have a convincing justification for acting purposively while remaining faithful to the respect of certain constraints.[11] The exercise of one's right is something that gives a much stronger assurance of immunity from criticism than acting only according to permission. Since human rights define spheres of liberties on the basis of their protection, they also define the number and range of social expectations.[12] As Buchanan has recently argued, the violation of human rights does not simply imply violating an obligation, but rather wronging someone; if this is the case, then, in a relevant way for our previous considerations it follows that: "If your obligation regarding how I am to be treated is merely an obligation, not the correlative of my right, then there is a sense in which your acknowledgement of your obligation regarding me does nothing, in itself, to recognize me as a rational agent [...] The notion of human rights, so far as it gives prominence to rights that can be 'wielded', is peculiarly appropriate for expressing both the shift to a subject-centered conception of justice and the realization

---

[11] On the recurrence to reasons grounding moral rights Feinberg writes: "[...] To have a right is to have a claim against someone whose recognition as valid is called for by some set of governing rules or moral principles. To have a *claim* in turn, is to have a case meriting consideration, that is, to have reasons or grounds that put one in a position to engage in performative and propositional claiming. The activity of claiming, finally, as much as any other thing, makes for self-respect and respect for others [...]" (2001, 185).

[12] On some of the properties exhibited by rights, see Wassertrom (1964).

that a central feature of the subject that grounds her primary moral status is her capacity for rational agency" (2006, 20).

In view of the polyvalent functionalities played by a system of liberty-rights the general Hohfeldian distinction between claim rights, liberty rights, power rights and immunities is reinterpreted (Hohfeld, 1919). Indeed, to defend a three-place notion of liberty, means not only that a claim right is advanced as a sphere of protected interactions (liberty-rights *stricto sensu*) which places the others under correlative duties, but it means also to exercise a power, to have a right to certain immunities against the possible influences of other subjects. Each category is paralleled by specific forms of obligations since, for instance, while for a claim-right there is a corresponding duty, for an immunity-right there is a disability. And yet, for instance, to reduce immunity rights to disabilities appears an oversimplification. What is unacceptable of the Hohfeldian scheme is the clear-cut distinction of, on the one hand, claim-rights and immunity rights as implying simply negative restrictions and, on the other hand, that of liberty-rights and power-rights as implying positive duties. From the previously argued thesis, the formal system of liberties here defended combines both a negative approach of duties conferral as in terms of "refraining from intervention" with a consideration of liberties as positive conditions of self-determination. This point will be addressed more specifically hereafter.

That the right to liberty as specified above is a basic right is due to the fact that no other moral right or no purpose can be enjoyed without having this granted in advance as a human right. With this, it does not follow that the rights springing from liberty are to be seen as simply instrumental to the enjoyment of one's preferred purposes or to the enjoyment of other non fundamental rights. Indeed, it is only once the practical enjoyment of a purpose is realized that the condition of freedom also comes to be satisfied so that, reversely, the satisfaction of such conditions of purposive action do allow for the realization of one's desired goods. Such a relation of symmetrical implication between fundamental rights and purposes is further complicated when delimited only to the relation of reciprocity between rights among themselves. Indeed, in this case it has been claimed that if the satisfaction of all basic rights to basic well-being are necessary to the realization of liberty rights, no every right to liberty is essential to the fulfillment of the rights to basic well-being. It seems that there is here an asymmetrical relation and that the right to participation is to be taken as having a priority over all other liberty rights.[13]

Seen in terms of their structural properties, human rights do imply that, for any subject, to be recognized implies to have a human right to x and this in its turn is to be free to enjoy x. If A has x without having a right to x, then A might be justified, on several grounds, to x, without however having secured her capacity to access x. Indeed, the formal minimal structure defined by this interrelationship can be described in the following way: if "A has a right to x (respect to B)", then

---

[13] This is the position defended for instance by Shue (1980, 74ff).

this relationship specifies the right-holder (A), the object of the right (x), and the duty-bearer (B). It also describes the relationship in which they stand with respect to one another. Namely, A is capable of exercising x (respect to B) and B stands under correlative obligations to A (respect to x). Rights establish, therefore, interactions centered on the right-holder and, consequently, burdens can be derived only from recognized rights without the possibility of playing no role beyond this correlation. If this is true, then, it follows that the entire category of the supererogatory or of the imperfect duties, such as the duty of being charitable, must be considered only as a derivative category as regards the right-theory to purposive-agency. In such case, indeed, one has a *moral obligation* (an ought) without such obligation being generated by a right, and since the obligation to be charitable is not a condition generated by a moral right, then one remains under a persisting moral obligation of fulfilment without *also being obliged* to a specific behaviour (being under a specific situational duty). From this, it does not follow that the whole moral life is exhausted by a system of right-duties relations. On the contrary, while insisting on the specificities of a right-based morality, the possibility is left open for appreciation of moral obligations or ethical virtues which are not right-generated but instead are notwithstanding relevant complementary measures for civic coexistence.

The correlation of rights and duties, within the perspective of the agency theory, thus constitutes the core theory of rights here defended, maintaining any perspective of imperfect duties only as a derivative perspective in respect to such a framework. To claim that it is derivative, means that imperfect duties cannot ground autonomously the possibility for a theory of human rights due to the unfulfillment of the principle of recognition, and thus to the unspecified characterization of the actors involved. Such qualification for non paralleled duties which do not conform to the principle of correlativity of rights and duties, is not simply a matter of logical completeness but rather an issue connected, in many respects, to the generative function that freedoms protected by rights play in creating a set of corresponding duties for their fulfilment. In other words, the thesis of correlativity between rights and duties as considered in this section is a result of the principle of recognition grouping in its turn the duty generative force that rights play as universal conditions for communicative agency; it appeals to a strong notion of correlativity, since it claims that rights, in terms of human rights, must always be paralleled by duties.

As far as the relevance that right-contents assume in respect to the normative binding placed upon the duty-holder, one important implication of the correlativity of rights and duties raised by the principle of recognition consists in the light it sheds upon the notion of beneficiary respect to the notion of promise. In the case of basic rights, indeed, duties are not advanced in terms of promises as they might be in the case of moral rights which are *not* fundamental rights. In the latter case, in fact, one might state that: "if I promise someone I will take care of her mother, I generate a situation where it is the promisee who holds the right, whereas her mother is the beneficiary of my promise" (see Hart, 1982, 187ff), but according to a human rights theory like that sketched above, a formal frame of intersubjective interdependences is generated only on the basis of a counterfactual scenario where communicative agents must recognize, on the pain of performative contradiction, the reciprocal attribution of rights. This means that my having a right to something is independent from the promise of a third-party even if I remain in control, as a right-holder, of its fulfillment.[14]

In what follows, I consider how the protection of the rights for agency determines the construction of an intersubjective interaction which at the end calls for the justification of a functional differentiation for the protection of duties as well as to an institutional model for the protection of the guaranteed rights. That the protection of recognized rights leads to a form of functional and institutional division of labour owes to a variety of reasons some of which are grounded, in the best case, in the overwhelming burdens that their fulfillment would place on the subjects themselves and, in the worst case, in the impossibility for the same subject to come up with a solution in the case of infra-conflicting rights, or, in other words, in the case of a lack of compossibility of two or more duties. The case of infra-rights and of inter-rights conflicts will be addressed more extensively later, and therefore it suffices here to point to the relevance it assumes as a reason for a social division of labor place both on the shoulders of individuals and of institutions in the case of right-enforcements. In general, the discussion of rights conflicts is a way of taking the distances from any absolute theory of human rights and of allowing for a criterion of legitimate balancing of rights. Once an absolute theory of human rights is dismissed, then human rights, inasmuch as they can be overridden by other right-based considerations, gain the status of *prima facie* rights. But according to the present theory, differently from the utilitarian theory of *prima facie* rights which argues that rights themselves can be overridden by considerations over the good of some consequences, a perspective of *prima facie duties* is defended, where human rights duties can be temporally suspended only because of other human rights' duties and not in view of other values or considerations which would take into account the best possible consequences, in terms of utility, which can be produced.[15]

Having recognized a right due to its same generative process of duties creation, it results that an entire category of duty-bearers is constituted for the respect of the recognized right. This creates a system of reciprocal rights and obligations which in turn generates a community of subjects connected by rights. This element concerning the necessarily active interrelationship between individuals in the enforcement and protection of human rights can also provide an indication according to which the classical distinction between negative and positive rights is inadequate. Indeed, it is quite clear that rights are not simply guaranteed by "refraining from" an intervention into the private individual sphere. On the contrary, they require the active involvement of the community in the positive and negative *duties* required for the fulfillment of a right. Notwithstanding such an overlap between positive and negative duties, one should not forget that, positive constraints fulfill, for instance, the

---

[14] "[...] When we attribute a right to the promisee in a third-party-beneficiary contract, we should do so not because of his power to enforce or waive his claim against the promisor, but because of the interest-protecting claim itself" Kramer (1998, 80).

[15] See McCloskey (1985, 133ff).

function of guaranteeing the general negative right of the subject not to be interfered with in her sphere of private liberty and self-determination. While a rigid separation between positive and negative freedoms is still to be rejected (since, in both cases, according to the particular circumstances, a complementary function might be required) an ideal characterization of either negative or positive enjoyment of a right can be maintained. This is to say that, for instance, while freedom, in order to be enjoyed as a necessary prerequisite for purposeful action, is to be protected on the basis of several positive guarantees for the agent, once these positive requirements are satisfied, freedom as the right not to have one's action interfered with, can be defended in purely negative terms. The same complementary relationship also holds in the case of positive rights. This "complementary" view of positive and negative rights, besides not considering as valid a clear-cut typological distinction between the two, does not support for instance the three-way partition of the kind provided by Gewirth (1996, 35–36) according to which, for example, the right to education is seen as purely positive. That the right to education involves positive action is beyond doubt; but that, in order to favour this right, the state and the community are restricted to positive action only, is doubtful. Indeed, in order to fulfil the right to education, several negative requirements, or non-infringements of cultural and individual liberties must be secured – without cancelling out all the previous theoretical points which aimed at distinguishing the positive or negative brand into which each right can ultimately and consistently be said to fall. Overall, one might wonder whether those specific negative and positive duties attached to a right can be taken as universal duties belonging to a universal system of human rights, or if instead they represent the legal-cultural instantiations of a system of universal rights. It seems that a degree of variation of appropriateness can be detected at this level, and that therefore one can separate the universal validity of a set of fundamental rights from those legally national specific provisions that are required for their fulfilment.

If this is correct, then the role of the duty-holder is certainly an active one. This means that, in a theory of human rights centered on the right-holder, in the case A has a right, x, and B and C have a correlative duty toward A, whenever B, for whatever reason, does not intend to respect A's right to x, C must prevent B from violating A's right. The reason for this obligation on C is grounded in the relevance of the right protected, on the basis of which the perspective of a self-interested agent is combined with that of a reasonable agent.[16] A's right to x (e.g. liberty from threat)

---

[16] The development of third-party duties for the enforcement of someone's right is one of the most striking advantages of Interest Theory over Will Theory: "To know whether someone such as X's mother has a claim or not, we should merely ascertain whether or not the person has a power of enforcing and waiving the claim. The answer to the latter inquiry would settle the answer to the former inquiry. Hence, unless X's mother has a power of enforcing/waiving X's duty to provide her with sustenance, she has no claim to his provision of the sustenance – not even a claim which she is unable to enforce or waive [. . .] According to this latest manoeuvre by the Will Theorists, there is simply no such thing as a claim that is unenforceable or unwaivable by its holder; and there is likewise no such thing as a power of enforcement/waiver that is held by someone other than the person whose claim is to be enforced or waived" Kramer (1998, 100). Will Theory, without an adequate reformulation in terms of experiential conditions, would not be able to

is not only relevant to herself, but to all of us as agents, and hence it mediates the self-interest of A's right not to be killed with the reasonableness of a community of individuals compelled to act in the defense of that right.[17] This point attempts at addressing at least one form of criticism that can be moved to a theory of rights, that is, the charge of egoism and self-interest supposedly exhibited by any form of rights exercise.[18] This is also interestingly connected to the intrinsic limits that a purely individualistic theory of rights would face when the enforcement of such rights were required by the active involvement of a community. But let's see first some further development of this argument.

Jones has recently observed that: "If A is B's creditor, A has a right to be repaid by B and B has a correlative duty to repay A. A's right may be a good reason for requiring C (typically a government) to ensure that B performs his duty to A. But that is what it is: a good reason. A's having a right to be repaid does not, of itself, *entail* that some third party is obligated to ensure that he is repaid; rather, whether A's right provides adequate reason for some third party's being held duty-bound to intervene to protect that right remains to be argued" (1994, 43). If this were true, then, the kinds of relations which rights would give place to, remain simply within the constraints of bilateral relations, without moving towards the construction of multilateral intersubjective sets of right-duties relations. But according to what has been claimed so far, the violation of human rights by itself provides a sufficient reason also for third parties to intervene in favour of its protection.

As I have shown, duties are not simply correlates of rights; they are rather generated by rights on the basis of the reasons rights advance for their protection, so that duties are necessarily linked to rights as conceptual correlates. With this generative process, the correlativity of rights and duties does not simply connect ordered sets of persons (right-holders vs. duty-bearers) but generates the actors and the content of the duties in relation to the recognized right. As far as the subject-generative role that rights perform in order to fulfill their function as rights, at this point it is possible to frame a formal triple set of duties which, for example, the right to liberty could give place to:

(a) The fulfillment of the right to liberty is dependent upon the fulfillment of three generated duties[19]:

(a.1) a negative duty to avoid deprivation of liberty by individuals and institutions

(a.2) a positive duty to protect and secure from deprivation of liberty:

---

include in a system of rights either children's rights or the rights of people with mental or physical disabilities!

[17] In legal theory this feature is described according to the distinction between "rights in personam" and "rights in rem", where the first implies duties to be followed in respect of specific individuals, whereas the second implies duties to be obeyed as regards everyone, by virtue of the content of the right itself.

[18] For a reply to such charge see also Waldron (1987, 191ff).

[19] The framework presented below presents a modified case of the tripartite distinction of duties as the one presented by Shue (1980, 52–53 and 60ff).

(a.2.1) through the enforcement of (a.1) by the individuals and by the creation of institutional mechanisms oriented to rights protection

(a.3) a positive duty to aid the deprived subjects of liberty through the institutional allocation or the reallocation of the required conditions for its enforcement due to failures of fulfillment of (a.1) and (a.2).

This tripartite framework of duty allocations can be conceived as being complete, meaning that all typologies of duties generated by fundamental rights are considered. But at this regard it is interesting to see how three such typologies are interconnected in a relation of lexical priority. As a matter of fact, were the duty to avoid deprivation of liberty fulfilled, one would be exempted from the duty to secure such right and, in its turn, were the duty to protect one's right fulfilled, there would not be the necessity of enforcing the positive duty of aid through the reallocation of the necessary conditions for the enjoyment of one's liberty. An objection might be raised in the case of an unintentional loss of liberty due, for instance to unforeseeable unintended consequences of an intentional action or simply as a consequence of an unintentional natural disaster. Even in such cases of unintentional deprivation of rights, my understanding is that the same possibility of exercising the negative duty to refrain from depriving someone of her liberties rests upon the condition of being enabled to exercise her own liberty, and therefore leads to the requirement of having the conditions of liberty enjoyment being fulfilled. Were one to pretend to exercise her own duty not to deprive someone else liberty without any guarantee for this other to be in the condition of exercising such liberty, then the duty of avoidance of deprivation would simply remain empty and without any content-substance to defend. Indeed, if I am deprived of my liberty due to unforeseeable and unintentional consequences, there cannot be a legitimate system of rights enforcements which could be discharged from the duty of stopping the perpetuation of my liberty deprivation. A society governed by a system of rights, can perpetuate its condition of enforcement of the rule of law only if it is kept responsible for the exercise of rights by its members. An unfortunate circumstance provoking the temporary loss of capability to exercise of one's rights must be remedied by a right-based society precisely because it is in the interest of the perpetuation of the right-system itself that society members do enjoy a regime of rights enforcements. To this it is connected the idea that the lexical priority of the duties (a.1)–(a.3) relies somehow upon a circular relation of mutual implication which, once allowed for an effective exercise of the duty (a.1), leads to the fulfillment of all the others.

If all this explicatory strategy were fully satisfactory, then, it would suffice not only to establish common inter-subjective duties to be respected by B, C and so on, but it would also subordinate such duties to the justifications of A's right. In other words, this explanation would be capable of bridging subjective with intersubjective reasons.[20] My duty to respect A's right, thus, depends upon the undesirability of a

---

[20] In many respects, this approach tries to bridge the gap between the welfarist and deontologist positions by providing a theory which is both deontological and goal-oriented. That there is a need for a theory attempting to close this gap is observed by Sen, when he notes: "Their ways

possible state of affairs where the relevance of the right in question were rejected. But this kind of explanation for the reasons that human rights should have regarding a community of people for whom they are to exhibit a normative guidance, if not integrated by the relevance of the notion of exemplarity and of judgmental activity discussed before, would reproduce an abstract form of justification as the one just rejected. As a matter of fact, the consideration of the principles of human rights in terms of a formal system of human rights categories rests incapable to provide motivations to action. It is from such difficulties, indeed, that the relevance of the reflective judgment in its political productive engagement appears as the most capable justificatory tool for bridging the abstract universality of a moral system of human rights categories with the contextually exemplar force of human rights as laws. It is this point, therefore, that should be taken as the background condition for the explanation of human rights functionalities.

4.3 Transplantability and Legal Commensurability

In order to formulate an answer to the question of human rights transplantability, it is essential to refer, first, to the previously argued thesis for the idea of a conceptual-legal status of human rights, and then to provide an understanding of the notion of transplantability itself. These points can be validly argued only if a general precondition is first satisfied: general comparability among systems of rights. Indeed, it is only if the possibility of general comparability among legal systems can be admitted that might arise the moral and political obligation to expand, through legal transplantability, the system of protected liberties and fundamental rights.

Now, as within one single system of fundamental rights there seem to arise several difficulties in commensurating between individual rights themselves, in the same way, between different right-systems there seems to be little utility in looking for a common neutral ground of commensuration assessing whether one exemplar liberty in a legal system S1 is better formulated than an analogous liberty exemplarily formulated in a legal system S2. And yet, a form of partial commensurability among different systems of liberty-rights can be conceived as taking the form of a *general balance* of satisfied freedoms. While exemplar rights *per se* remain reciprocally incommensurable, both at an infra-system level and at an inter-system level, in relation to general balance of guaranteed freedoms it is still possible to provide a general assessment confronting the overall fulfilment of freedoms among different legal systems.[21]

---

part there [the welfarist and the deontologist positions], however, with the welfarist instrumentalist viewing rights in terms of their consequences for right-independent goals and the constraint-based deontologist reflecting rights without consequential justification as constraints on actions. State-evaluation independent of rights leaves a gap that cannot be adequately closed by either of these approaches" Sen (1988, 190).

[21] At such regard, for instance, Feinberg claims that: "[...] Freedom of expression times freedom of movement yields nothing comparable. If these areas of freedom are called 'dimensions', they must also be labelled 'incommensurable'. Still, limited comparisons even of incommensurabilities

A further reason for a preliminary clarification of the concepts at stake is that the correlation between rights and transplantability leads to apparently counterintuitive conclusions. Indeed, if the theory of legal transplants points to the transfer of legal norms from one legal system to another – a horizontal relation between two states' legal systems – its application to human rights seems rather to involve a vertical relation between an international system of human rights protections and its reception within national boundaries. This would be true even in the case of an apparent horizontal, state-to-state, transfer of an internationally recognized human right norm, where the trans-national element of bilateral advocacy is functional to the incorporation of a supra-ordinate norm for both systems. An additional difficulty connected to the first point, would relate the dynamics of legal transplants to the evaluative aspect of transplantation and address the socio-cultural impacts that human rights transplants would produce together with the desiderability of the produced effects. But before entering into these problems, let's discuss first some different approaches to the concept of law and its socio-cultural interconnections, and then evaluate how, from a multilayered concept of human rights, it is possible to reformulate the constrained plausibility of a notion of human rights transplantability.

I will consider three possible approaches to law which respond in different ways to the problem of transplantability: the first considers law as an autonomous domain and it represents the best candidate for a pure theory of legal transplants; the second conceives of law as a domain strictly embedded into and dependent upon society, thus rejecting any legitimate form of legal transplantability; finally, the third model represents an intermediate paradigm in between autonomy and autochthony, conceiving of the possibility of legal transplants as an option subordinated to certain specific constraints.

The first position is the one clearly defended by Watson (1993) who claimed, on the basis of his investigations into the effects of Roman law into civil and common systems of law, that changes occur on the basis of "legal borrowing", or "transplantation", due to the prestige and authority that certain laws assume towards other legal systems. His thesis is that legal change is independent from the mirroring of cultural beliefs specific to a local context, and that changes and borrowings occur in a way that is autonomous from the non legal, cultural domain from which they originate. It might seem that, in so doing, Watson defends a completely anti-sociological thesis of law, but this is not quite so. Indeed, he conceives of law as exhibiting both a general function of purposiveness, such as social integration and conflict resolution, and an element of content validity. While keeping these two properties as completely independent variables, he runs counter to totally social dependent theories of legal change.

The dependence of law upon context is assumed by Watson in terms of its dependence *upon a legal culture* and not of a culture in general. The autonomy of

---

are possible. If the average American has greater freedom in *every* dimension than his Ruritarian counterpart, it makes sense to say that he has greater freedom on balance" (1973, 19).

legal change and transplantation is thus conceived of as an autonomy of the specific dynamic followed by law through the operational activity of *lawyers* and *legislators* taking part in the local legal culture. The borrowing activity, thus, is possible on the basis of the empirical appreciation by the legal culture, that is, at the level of legal concepts of the authority and prestige of an external norm, so that the activity of "transplantation" becomes a process restricted to the cooperation between two autonomous legal spheres. Indeed, the legal sphere is not subordinated, according to Watson, to the cultural sphere in general. That legal spheres can reciprocally communicate and be contaminated is, for Watson, due to the specific conception he holds for the structure of law in analogy with a structuralist conception of language. Watson's project is that of reconstructing an invariable structure of law starting from historical patterns of law-change from an original "mother" language (Roman law). All or almost all systems of law do have historical traces of this past, and through their reconstruction within each law system it is possible to explain, in comparative ways, any type of legal development.

Watson's theory has been criticized by classical comparative lawyers, as for instance Zekoll (1996) who asserts that the thesis of "legal transplants" as strictly limited to legal borrowing cannot explain reforms of domestic law through international treaties. In this case, indeed, modifications at the domestic level do occur on the basis of commonly agreed premises by all signatories. I have already canvassed upon this point which leads to a different source of normativity hanging on domestic and international legal codes that is a morally shareable point of view seen in terms of an open attitude towards recognition of otherness grounding common premises.

Let's turn, therefore, to the second explicatory model, the one conceiving of law as something inherently embedded into culture and context. According to this approach, and in particular according to the criticism of Abel to Watson's theory (Abel, 1982), the central tenet is that the dis-functionalities and the divergences between law and society pointed out by Watson are not a sign of the independence of law from society, but that they express instead a multiplicity of functions that law has towards society, that is, the function of legitimation, expression and mystification. This means that it is precisely for this reason that the study of a legal system must be holistic, relating each single law to the entirety of the legal system, which in its turn must be connected then to the totality of society.

Any possible difference between legal systems cannot be taken in isolation from the entire system itself, so that even small divergences between systems must be always taken as referred to a totality of divergence between the considered legal systems themselves. Since laws cannot be separated by the interpretative activities accompanying them and involving both intra-legal systemic and extra-legal societal interpretations, it becomes illusory to try to explain legal change simply by looking at the "black-letter rules", as thought by Watson. This means that one cannot proceed without any consideration of the interpretive presuppositions underlying the understanding of a legal code, thus making of the meaning of such a code something inherently interwoven within the local cultural *Weltanschauung*. If law is understood as a tool for the self-understanding of society in its totality, then, not much space is left for legal transplants, since the transferring of even a small element of law from one system to another not only implies a differently incommensurable perspective upon the world springing from the target domain, but it is also a sign of an unjustified hegemony of one legal culture over another.

This argument is based upon purely relativistic assumptions which I will criticize hereafter at least in their cultural-normative version.

Indeed, if one were to promote a fully relativist thesis, for the sake of coherence, a precise view of the notion of truth as something strictly dependent upon cultural determination, would also have to be endorsed, leading us into what can be defined as a truth-paradox:

(I) "Truth is culture-bound" is true'
Either 'I' is itself culture-bound or it is not.
(a) If 'I' is culture-bound, that is if it is true, there will be some cultural settings in which it is false, or in which it cannot be formulated at all.
(b) If 'I' is not culture-bound, that is if it is false, then it will be true in all cultures.
Therefore, if 'I' is true it is false, and if it is false it is true.

                                                                            Harré and Krausz (1996, 28)

And yet, even if truth-claims not falling into such paradox must be capable of showing a form of universal necessity beyond their specific context of origination, this does not imply that they have necessarily to be context-free or spring from the so-called "view from nowhere". On the contrary, my suggestion is that, within a paradigm of judgment, it is still possible to propose a constrained-constructivist notion of validity as springing precisely from a context and also as capable of trespassing it.

As far as the third paradigm is concerned, then, a mediation between the absolute autonomy of law and its holistic socially embedded counterpart is defended by the work of Teubner (1998) with particular reference to a non-holistic relationship between law and society, a process of "selective connectivity" with social sub-systems. Teubner claims that the subsystem of law is specifically linked with the subsystem of politics and that specifically in post-modern societies and globalization we assist a pluralization of subsystem connectivities linking law to a plurality of different social subsystems and discourses. This is what Teubner defines as the Janus-face of binding agreements, that is while having at the same time a legal and a social aspect, and thus a reciprocal exchange of inputs and structural compatibility, each element maintains relative autonomy (Teubner, 1992). Within this picture every small change in one domain can "perturb" and provoke "irritations" in all the others. In the case of legal transplants, the introduced innovation "irritates" the connected social discourses, provoking a readjustment and a reformulation of the newly introduced rule and consequently, on the side of the legal domain, of the way of incorporating the rule itself.

Thus, according to Teubner, while a legal transplant cannot occur in the way Watson has explained, it can nevertheless be conceived of as something possible once multiple "irritants" pertaining to the social-sub-field are also taken into account. The result is that the rule to be transplanted is substantially reformulated by the target subsystems, and with it, its specific functioning assumes a completely different form and modality. According to this position, while law maintains an autonomous functioning and logic, it remains connected also to a multitude of social-subsystems which "irritates" whenever legal transplants and innovations take place in any system of law.

I believe Teubner is right in pointing out such dynamics and interrelations between law and the other social sub-systems. In what follows I will explain why the descriptive reconstruction of Teubner intermediary model is adequate also from the point of view of the notion of pluralistic universalism, here defended in terms of a human rights theory.

Human rights, indeed, intuitively seem to contain both subjective and universalist elements, that is, a pretence of universal validity as attached to a first-person perspective. Once such a double characterization is taken seriously, it leads to a sort of conceptual entrapment assuming the form of a neither/nor constraint. One can neither defend a basic right without thinking, first, that it requires a subjective endorsement and entitlement – this is my right! – nor by thinking that its validity can be limited in scope – I'm entitled to the right to free speech, but you are not!

The combination of subjectivism and universalism seems therefore to constitute the most relevant characterization for an intuitive understanding of human rights. But in order to prove the validity and the possibility of reciprocal approximation of the two above-mentioned properties, a reference to a precise justificatory model is to be made, in terms of all those necessary conditions at the basis of principle-constrained human rights reflective judgments as the two-step theory developed before has aimed at defending.

Once such a normative theory of human rights has been provided, how can one respond to the possibility of human rights transplants?

I believe that, first of all, a justified possibility of human rights transplants can take primarily the form of a top-down direction. That is, by assuming the normative constraints as reformulated within a model of communicative action, one must cultivate the reasonable hope that fundamental rights will constitute the moral premises of those judgmental activities characterizing the constitutional constructions of societies. From within such a common framework, then, further internal and reciprocal pluralisations and differentiations, will be reflected in the national and regional constitutional debates and legislations in terms of comparative legal partial commensurability.

This point implies that the reception of international treaties into local contexts is to be taken as sensitive to the local culture itself, so that a clear distinction between different "conceptions" of human rights realized through the activity of reflective judgment, will support the same sorts of "concepts" of human rights, that is, would reinterpret a common formal system of human rights into exemplarily valid mutually distinct local constitutional norms. Once such differences remain within the boundaries set by morally and internationally agreed human rights principles, constitutional differences will become perfectly acceptable, since they will accommodate universal principles to the socio-cultural exemplar validity of local contexts.

Thus, according to the presently defended view, human rights transplantability can become a justified thesis only when it follows essentially two mutually dependent constraints:

(1) a top-down process of legal/cultural interpretation of universally justified human rights formal categories which prevent a horizontal projection of idiosyncratic interpretations from one country to another.
(2) the activation of "legal irritants", that is according to Teubner, the activation of several social-subsystems which react and reinterpret international norms according to contextual patterns of interpretation and incorporation of the rule.

This means that a mechanical transferring of one legal element from one country to another, as that described by Watson, is not only very unlikely to happen when human rights are at stake but, more importantly, is also normatively unjustified. Further, mechanical transferring seems also descriptively wrong, since one might want to allow for a *de facto* existence of an international system of human rights protections, characterized by a large number of states signatories, even if this, according to my interpretation, cannot suffice to assign its self-legitimation.

If the current framework of international protection of human rights reflects such lack of empirical legitimation, it follows that priority must be given to the fostering of international and regional councils and convention through the construction of culturally pluralist frameworks of deliberation from which deliberative human rights legal provisions would be agreed upon on the basis of a precommitted judgmental activity presupposing, as normative constraints, the universal conditions of equal freedoms.

From such outcomes, then, one might proceed to the local legal specification of formal universal principles into legal framings, which would then be open to a bi-univocal horizontal legal comparative discussion and possible revision by different, and yet partially commensurable, sub-systems of human rights codifications. This understanding of human rights transplantability can be successful only upon the condition that certain prerequisites of public reasonability and institutional structuring are met by all those who are in charge for the drafting of a regional or international system of human rights provisions. Though, the more challenging and difficult question to answer is that concerning those more frequent cases in which institutional arrangements of democratic legitimacy are not fulfilled in the international sphere. How should western democracies behave in such cases? Is it possible to hope for an international order showing stability even if non-democratic states are included?

As is evident from contemporary developments in international politics, it seems that the strategy pursued has been that of basing international stability upon the wide spread imposition of a liberal *ethos* originating from a specific cultural and political context. Indeed, some western scholars have considered that international peace can be achieved only once all institutional frames of national governments take a democratic twist and start promoting a form of liberal attitude. For this reason, human rights transplantability has been used beyond the search of a socio-political consensus of the countries involved and a specific political strategy for the achievement of international stability has been developed in order to address the issue of international political peace. This strategy is based upon what is known as the "democratic peace theory" and in what follows, I will criticize some of the elements upon which this view is based. While I maintain that democratic arrangements are desirable ideal solutions for the legitimacy of self-determining political bodies, I reject the view that there is strong empirical evidence in support of the democratic peace theory. I save therefore democratic arrangements only as desirable goals for the achievement of a status of internal justice, but I reject the idea that they can provide evidence for international peace. I will suggest, instead, that a more promising solution comes from what could be a process of progressive legalization of international relations, which would include both democracies and non democracies, and which would be oriented toward the flourishing of a plurality of perspectives organized within international and functionally differentiated systems of checks and balances of powers.

4.4   What is Wrong in the Democratic Peace Theory? A Defence of International Legal Pluralism

I will conclude this work by considering some practical implications for policy making which derive directly from my defended notion of pluralistic universalism and from the multiplicity that reasonable perspectives assume within the public domain. Analogously with the domestic public sphere, it is here sustained that also the international realm must grant those basic conditions for the flourishing of a multiplicity of culturally-based legitimate practices, and that relations among states should not follow an idea of justice as the "advantage of the strongest".

Indeed, the field of international relations since the times of Thucydides has been interpreted as a regime of anarchy where states have been able to operate legitimately as self-interested entities and where peace has always resulted from a temporary equilibrium of forces. As Hobbes has observed (1998 [1651], chap. XXXI, 30), while individuals can transfer their sovereignty to the Leviathan, states are prevented from doing so due to the lack of a supra-ordered entity to which it is possible to transfer their power. Therefore, even if there are for Hobbes natural law principles grounding a theory of obligation within the sphere of international relations, they are not morally compelling due to the lack of reciprocal expectation of compliance. Without an institutionalized system of adjudication and sanctioning, compliance to international natural law principles can be advanced *in foro interno* but not *in foro externo*. For this reason, even if it is a mistake to think that for realists states are a-moral entities,[22] it is certainly true that within such interpretive frame, it is state self-interest to base ethical considerations towards other states as part of the *calculi* of foreign politics. In other words, Hobbesian realists claim that within the anarchical scenario of international relations, the only ethically justified state behaviour relies in the advancement and defence of its self-interest: to act morally is to act in the defence of one's self-advantage.

---

[22] For instance Morgenthau (1951) thought that if politics had taken on an altruistic form, forgetting national interests, they would not have behaved in a moral way.

The defended dis-analogy of realists between the domestic and the international sphere has appeared to some international normativists as absolutely wrong. For instance Beitz (1999, 36ff [1979]) claims that there are four necessary and sufficient conditions which must be maintained in order to defend a form of Hobbesian international scepticism equating the international scenario to the state of nature. Such conditions are: the view that only states are the subjects of the international scenario, that they have equal power, that they are mutually independent in terms of their organization of the internal affairs, and finally that, in the absence of a supra-national organization enforcing international principles, there is no mutual expectation of compliance with rules. Since there are counter-evidences to each of such claims, then the analogy does not hold. For instance, according to Beitz, coalitions or secondary associations do indeed play an international role in minimizing conflicts and particularly today, trans-national associations do exert pressures for cooperation among states. All this empirical evidence amounts to the understanding that states are not simply subjects acting within the international dimension, and that a plurality of subjects representing a variety of interests do indeed advance claims of international politics. As far as the second Hobbesian claim is concerned, the one regarding an equal balance of power of states within the state of nature, Beitz upholds the view that the element of non-dominance among states is functional to the elimination of a possible moral responsibility by the strongest to make international order to comply with natural law principles. If states are equal in terms of power, then it is irrational of anyone to try to behave and convince other states to behave in accordance to international principles. And yet, we know that this is not the present condition for the distribution of power in the international realm and that, according to this reasoning, strongest states are morally compelled to observe and make the others observe the international principles of morality.

The confutation of the third condition, then, which connects strictly to the arguments that will be later developed, maintains that states' internal affairs cannot be organized independently from the specific internal organizational configurations of other states. Since, as mentioned, there are trans-national economic and political lobbies pressing for the fulfilment of common interstate interests, and since even pursuance of any idiosyncratic state interest might require cooperation by the others, then configurations of internal politics cannot be shaped independently. Finally, the criticism of the fourth condition maintained by realists is that there can not be compliance to international moral rules even in the absence of a supra-state institution capable of enforcing international moral principles. The international remedies adopted nowadays show that there are several instruments, such as sanctions and political and economic isolation for forcing outlaw states into compliance to international norms. And yet, one might add, if violations of moral norms are made by the most powerful states, those international institutions acting on the basis of laws and sanctions, rather than on a liberal *ethos*, would be preferable for the guarantee of success of an international project of justice.

The critical rejections of at least one of such four principles is sufficient to reject the Hobbesian thesis of a structural disanalogy between the domestic and the international dimension. And thus, if this disanalogy does not hold, then it follows that international behaviour by states must be coherent with those precepts which would be morally justified within an internal sphere of application. The discrepancy on this point leads to further debate between normativists and realists.

According to international normative theories, indeed, if states are governed, internally, by specific political principles, then their external behaviour must be equally determined by those same political principles. For realists, on the contrary, proximity, the *status* of power, alliance, militarization, economic development and differences in capacity, are only some of the fundamental factors that determine the conflict between states. Both realists and normativists maintain that crucial factors at a sub-national level determine state's behaviour in foreign policy, including governmental variables such as the type of political system, the distribution of influence within the regime, bureaucratic characteristics, the organizational process and electoral cycles affecting the position of each state on the international scene. One could even concede to realists that, in most cases, proximity is the most important factor regarding the probability of war. At the same time, however, liberals suggest that the absence of democracy is an equally salient element that serves as a sufficient condition. This means that liberal normative theories acknowledge that other factors can, in fact, play a role in the deterrence of war. Moreover, of considerable importance are international economic ties, perhaps leading a state to be more reticent in declaring war against another state in which it has invested. This idea is supported by those scholars, who cite the many direct and indirect alliances formed in the aftermath of the Second World War.

Some international normative theorists have sustained that there is a generally peaceful tendency between democracies. Since in democratic contexts citizens are subjected to principles guaranteeing fundamental rights, these same principles are applied analogously also at the international level towards other liberal democracies. The main goal of statistical research, for those normative scholars who believe in peaceful relations among democracies is to demonstrate that the pacific attitude of democracies towards other democracies operates independently from other dyadic attributes such as wealth, economic growth, contiguity and so on (Maoz and Russet, 1993, 627). This parallelism between the internal and external behaviour of liberal democracies redirects *ceteris paribus* towards peaceful relations among democracies and ensures that the only law of international politics is that of democratic peace.

In an article published in 1983, Doyle redirected the attention of scholars to the topic of Kantian *Perpetual Peace* (1970a, [1795]), seen in terms of an empirical-normative theory. Following this pioneering study, several other quantitative studies have since concentrated on regime characterization as a necessary and sufficient condition for the determination of democratic peace, by developing generally dyadic terms of comparison between democracies and non-democracies.[23] Even if deep disagreement persists over which key statistical variables are to be taken into consideration, common to all of these studies is that peace, as opposed to the

---

[23] For a presentation of numerous quantitative analyses see Chan (1997).

multi-causal explanation of Kant, is the product of a mono-causal hypothesis. The defenders of the democratic peace argument claim that liberal democracies, due to their uniform nature (i.e. their internal division of powers and respect for fundamental rights), inherently behave peacefully towards other democracies. The basic tenet of all democratic peace arguments agree with the following central assumption:

General Assumption

Due to liberal cultural constraints and to the institutional separation of powers, democracies never, or very rarely, declare war to each other

Democratic peace scholars, therefore, are divided in those who claim that democracies *never* go to war with each other, and those who claim that democracies only *rarely* enter into reciprocal conflict, these latter admitting the possibility of exceptional circumstances conducing even democracies to enter into violent resolution of conflict. This whole picture seems to be supported by a robust series of empirical data that demonstrate how since the beginning of the XIX century, according to the specific key variables adopted, there have been only few cases, tending to zero, of wars between democracies.[24] Whereas most of the contemporary studies in international relations have aimed at expanding the statistical evidence of the supported thesis, very few have attempted to elaborate a more articulated definition of at least two of the central concepts deployed by the democratic peace theory: the definition of war and that of democracy. In the following sections I will provide but a few insights into the definitional problems without attempting at constructing fully-fledged alternative concepts. According to democratic peace theorists, war is generally defined in terms of 1000 deaths during the conflict, according to the criteria adopted by the Correlates of War (COW). Some of the problems with such a criterion are that extremely relevant conflicts from the political international point of view, not falling within the number of 1000 deaths, do not count as wars, and wars that have from 1000 to 1 million of deaths count in the statistics as a single war. If the criterion becomes proportional to the number of deaths and to the political international relevance of the crises, the First World War could count as a considerable counter to the theory of democratic peace, since Germany was perceived until a certain moment as a democracy by the other states. There are further problems with such definition, concerning for example whether war be defined only in a mono-directional way. By this I mean whether war signifies solely a militarized conflict. Indeed, if one considers the damages of a conflict in terms of the *effects* of international politics towards the general impoverishment of a population, then, the definition of war can be multiplied into different domains of possible intervention. It seems, then, that there are theoretical problems with such a notion due to its unsatisfactory socio-political elaboration. Indeed, when confronted with other intuitive definitions, one can observe that the concept of war, when strictly understood

---

[24] Even if supported by an impressive amount of empirical data, the supporters of democratic peace theory must demonstrate that the dyads of the democratic states would have gone to war, had they not been democracies.

in relation to its violent consequences, results as being quite naïve respect to what can be properly understood as war. It is noteworthy that even in an ancient Chinese text of the IV century B.C., *The Art of War*, attributed to the school of Sun Tzu ([IV BC] 1963), it is recognized that the best result that can be obtained in war is not the victory of one-hundred battles over one-hundred, but rather the defeat of the enemies without the recurrence to any battle in the traditional sense. The concept of war and of the forms in which it can be fought, must be extended beyond physical battle.

If one turns then to the notion of democracy, it must be recognized that the adopted definition of what is a democracy among democratic peace theorists, is quite variegated, to say the least. Some consider the structural separation of powers, a system of representation, and a liberal *ethos* for the respect of fundamental rights; others analyze the representative body and separation of powers. In still others there is a tendency to define a state as democratic only after a third round of elections. These variations are crucial for the considerations of the data within statistical analysis since, for instance, the behaviour of newly established democracies is not at all less aggressive than that of authoritarian regimes. In some cases, there is instead a tendency to consider contested exceptions of wars between democracies as justified upon the "perception" of one state over the non democratic character of the other. But if the definition of democracy remains sensitive upon a contingent perception, then statistical correlations become biased. For instance, as in the case of the previously mentioned example, Germany, at the end of the nineteenth century was perceived as a democracy, and only before the deterioration of its relations with the USA, England and France, it became perceived as a non democracy. If one remains within weak definitions of what counts as a democracy, then Germany might have been considered as a democracy and the First World War as counting as a counter-example to the democratic peace theory. On the contrary, though, if the notion of what it counts as a democracy is reinforced, then one might end up at restricting enormously the amount of empirical data in favour of the democratic peace theory.

Scholars who favour the theory of democratic peace derive their conclusions essentially from two characteristics of democracies: the cultural-normative constraints of a democratic nature and the structural constraints of a democratic order. The first type of explanation calls the political culture of a democratic state into question, whereas the second concentrates on the democratic political structure (i.e. the *decision-making* constraints). The perspective offered by the first kind of explanation, according to the normative school, is that decisions of a democratic political community are obtained through consensus and compromise. This argument is constantly accompanied by another normative assumption which establishes that in the anarchic nature of international politics, when there is a clash between democratic norms and non-democratic norms, the latter prevail (Maoz and Russet, 1993, 625). This means that contrary to what happens in contexts of disagreement between democracies, when a non democracy is involved in the dyad, political competition gives way to a zero sum game, where the winner takes all through violent and coercive means.

The second justification, based on structural or institutional factors, claims that the pressure of various groups on the government, together with the division of power and consequent checks and balances, impose specific restrictions on a democratic government and its involvement in war. This model relies on the assumption that political leaders must receive domestic support in order to obtain legitimation for international challenges. Such characteristics would render liberal democracies less inclined to go to war than non-democratic regimes. According to Kant, for instance, the sovereign of a Republic, as opposed to a despot, cannot push his country to war and be confident that the negative consequences on the everyday life resulting from such situation will leave him unscathed. But such conclusions seem in some cases to be falsified, as recent events have demonstrated, by the increase in popular support which political leaders have obtained precisely through declaring war. For instance, Margaret Thatcher was recognized as a true political leader only after the Falklands conflict in 1982, and George W. Bush, who won the presidential elections of the United States with a thin majority, increased his popularity and was re-elected thanks to his aggressive foreign politics. Notwithstanding, a general criticism of the theory of democratic peace can be articulated with reference to the asymmetric relations between states. What does it mean for democratic states, characterized by institutional structures embodying the separation of powers and liberal principles, to be bound to an external politics of peace only in cases in which they are confronted with other democracies?

If institutional structures regulated by the separation of powers and respect for human rights subordinate the politics of a liberal state to international binding norms, then the state should not adapt its own political behaviour according to the whether it is confronted with a democratic state or not. Following the same argumentative strategy, if liberal normative principles produce external constraints, then since citizens of a national state are normatively bound, internally, to the principle of equality and non discrimination, they should also feel bound not to discriminate, externally, between democratic and non-democratic peoples. Thus the foreign policy of states should be coordinated on the basis of their internal deontological principles.

A legitimate exception to this view would be the case in which security and personal integrity of the state's own citizens were directly put at risk. But since the thesis of democratic peace seems to concede involuntarily that democracies may maintain aggressive behaviour towards non-democracies even in the absence of imminent danger, the perspective defended is not purely based on respect for liberal normative principles, but seems to conceal a realist strategy. This means that the normative-cultural constraints give added effect to the rational egoistic calculus without, however, acting as discriminating reasons, since they are added only *ex post*. At any rate, if the institutional structures and the normative principles produce effects other than the realist calculus, defenders of the theory of democratic peace fall into deep incoherence if they concede in one case legitimacy to the functioning of normative and structural principles, whereas in other particular cases they legitimate the suspension of such criteria. Additionally, if one considers the normative-cultural constraint as represented by the respect of fundamental rights in the case of the democratic dyads, then what type of reasoning is involved here? In other words, what type of reasoning justifies the non-aggressiveness of democratic states towards like-minded others, once the analogy of shared liberal principles is admitted, but simultaneously guarantees their aggressiveness towards non-democratic states?

If such behaviour can be granted as empirically true, then democratic states are not simply externally bounded by the need to remain faithful to their own liberal democratic principles and defence of human rights, but rather by their self perceptual identification with other liberal democracies, which implies in turn that reciprocal agreement over liberal principles is sufficient to rule out a possible war. But then, if this is so, the theory of democratic peace relies on an unstable notion of democratic perception of the other entity, since this remains a relatively subjective notion, hypothetically modifiable *ad hoc* and based on contingent types of interests which have nothing to do with the evaluation of liberal principles. This means that the perception and definition of the notion of democracy is subjected to other types of interests, and that it cannot therefore be taken as a fundamental element in enumeration of the reasons against going to war. Drawing from the above observations it is possible to draw a first provisional conclusion:

Provisional Conclusion I

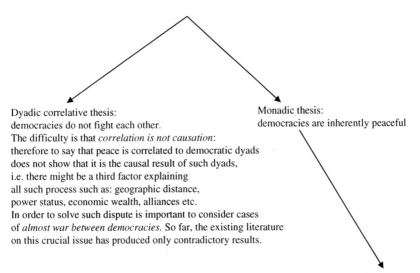

If the definitions of war and democracy are thickened, then the empirical correlations for democratic peace become less significant both because the number of what counts as wars grow and because the number of what counts as a democracies diminishes.

Dyadic correlative thesis:
democracies do not fight each other.
The difficulty is that *correlation is not causation*:
therefore to say that peace is correlated to democratic dyads
does not show that it is the causal result of such dyads,
i.e. there might be a third factor explaining
all such process such as: geographic distance,
power status, economic wealth, alliances etc.
In order to solve such dispute is important to consider cases
of *almost war between democracies.* So far, the existing literature
on this crucial issue has produced only contradictory results.

Monadic thesis:
democracies are inherently peaceful

History dismisses the inherent peaceful character of the monadic thesis: democracies have demonstrated to be very belligerent towards non democracies, i.e. wars of colonization.

If one remains only within the dyadic thesis, then what sense can we make of the normative aspect of the democratic peace theory? That is its cultural liberal *ethos pro* human rights and its institutional separation of powers favouring rational political outputs? A non aggressive behaviour should be maintained by democracies, also when facing cases of non democratic states (with the only exceptions of demonstrated potential attacks by non democracies towards democracies and with the exception of mass murdering and genocide of local population).

The democratic asymmetry of behaviour, towards democracies and non-democracies, respectively, is a counter-argument to the over simplistic theory of the democratic peace. Democratic states must be faithful to the respect of their internal normative criteria even in their relations towards non-democracies. This latter point leads to a further criticism of the theory of democratic peace, that is to the evaluation of liberal principles as non-sufficient conditions for not entering into war. From this, one might claim that the reciprocal identification between different states as states guided by liberal principles is simply an *additional element* among others. While such principles maintain a *relative*, though not *decisive, weight* in any overall evaluation of the possible convenience of entering or not entering into war.

The democratic peace argument could enlarge the spectrum of the elements that democratic states take into consideration, but the normative and institutional elements have not shown to be, *by themselves*, sufficient conditions for abstaining from initiating wars of aggression. If liberal principles must have a role in international relations, then they must render external relations coherent with internal ones (Archibugi, 1997), which means that they must promote an international system of law based on human rights.

Peace cannot be understood simply as the absence of war, like the defenders of the democratic peace theory pretend, but must be understood, instead, in terms of the promotion of international justice according to the standard of promotion of peoples' self-determination. As a matter of fact, if the absence of war were normatively the most relevant criterion in the moral orientation of international relations, then one would simply be satisfied with a world deprived of massacres beyond 1000 deaths, this being the minimal standard agreed internationally in order to define violent conflicts. Further, one would unjustifiably abstain from criticizing the absence in such concept of peace of economic cooperation on the side of the richest countries towards the poorest ones or even systematic cases of injustice towards individuals and ethic groups (the Rawlsian peoples) that are beyond the minimal proposed standard. The lack of acceptance of such a restricted vision of the notion of peace implies that a world without peace (in the sense of a world in which war is absent, in terms of minimal standards of deaths) is not the desired goal. Most importantly, though, it implies that an *unjust* world, deriving from non ethical international relations, produced both by democracies and by non democratic systems, is not desirable.

From all of these remarks one can formulate a second provisional conclusion which integrates the cultural-institutional considerations of democratic peace theorists with further elements already introduced by Kant's *Perpetual Peace*:

Provisional Conclusion II

Beyond Kant's First Definitive Article – a republican nature of political power-, the demo-cratic peace theory must integrate also the Second Definitive Article, the creation of a con-federation of republican states for the protection of peace within their boundaries and the Third Definitive Article, the advancement of a cosmopolitan condition.

This point has been curiously addressed only by the renovator of Kant's view, M. Doyle (1983), while it has been dismissed by subsequent scholars. Neverthe-less, Doyle's notion of the democratic peace theory, as well as his interpretation of Kant bears several limitations. First of all, an aggressive behaviour by democracies towards non democracies cannot be justified by claiming that this is due to the lack of a liberal *ethos* by non democratic states. It is conceptually self-contradictory to pretend to advance human rights internally by disrespecting them externally (dif-ferent is the case of intervention when exterminations or genocides are occurring in third countries). Secondly, Doyle considers Kant's *Third Definitive Article* simply as based upon the right to international commerce, but Kant's cosmopolitan condition includes also the progressive creation of a world public sphere (as when he claims that a violation of a right done somewhere is felt everywhere else in the world), as initial seeds of a yet to come cosmopolitan condition.

If the activities of states are evaluated according to these parameters, then the empirical evidence according to which democracies do not, or rarely, declare war against each other, becomes irrelevant. Examples of deep incoherencies between internal and external politics clearly characterize the behaviour of democratic states at the international level and thus substantially different causes could explain the statistical evidence.[25] The lack of recognition of this point amounts to an attempt to conceal the evidence showing that the same democracies have often been respon-sible for wars of colonization, as well as for unjustified wars of aggression against other non democratic states. General conditions of international peace cannot be considered as relying only on the normative or institutional bounds of democratic states. Instead, a multi-causal understanding of the sources of political stability on the international scene should be adopted, where in addition to the liberal demo-cratic structure and respect for fundamental rights, economic interdependence and the international web of bilateral and multilateral treaties are included as binding states together. These two further elements introduce, in fact, mechanisms of ra-tionalization of states' preferences by rendering inconvenient, in the first case, the declaration of war in territories where strong financial investments subsist, and in the second case by subordinating state interests to the general interest of the regional and international community. Such a triadic model of international peace does not have to be considered as representing necessary and sufficient conditions that, once satis-fied, guarantee *tout court* the conditions of peace and stability. Instead, they should

---

[25] Archibugi claims that additional criteria should be adopted in order to evaluate whether a state exhibits coherence between its internal and external policies, such as an evaluation of the amount of the Gross Domestic Product allocated by a state to military expenses, or the state's support of the activities of the United Nations and so on (1997, 382).

be considered as orienting a historical progression towards peace within a transcultural and trans-political process of learning. In fact, if states' preferences are fully rationalized and the borders of international peace extended,[26] then, democracies can become capable of admitting within their *foedus pacificum* examples of decent Rawlsian states.[27] There is not, in fact, any counter-evidence concerning the dyads of non-democratic states and whether they are excluded from the historical process of learning which leads to peace, even if purely on the basis of a *modus vivendi* and not traceable to just principles.[28]

This last remarks lead to the stipulation of a final conclusion, which can be formulated in terms of an indication of the lines to be pursued for future research:

Final conclusion and guidelines for future research

Kant's alternative between a World Republic and a League of liberal States must be reinterpreted in terms of a liberal *phoedus pacificum* which rationalizes democracies' and non democracies' external action "as if within a world republic" considered as a normative ideal

A move of this sort would advance a progressive juridification of international relations among both democratic and non democratic regimes. This will foster the full realization of a cosmopolitan condition as a form of "concrete universal", as Hegel would call it, in line with the overall sketch drawn recently by Habermas (2004), who considers the control of individual and state rights through the activity of functionally specialized agencies such as a reformed UN agency and the trans-national activity of global players. But within the internationalist picture proposed by Habermas, I would emphasize, rather, the change of function which a centralized agency as the UN should play in terms of international arbitration aimed at guaranteeing, through the entrustment of formal categories of human rights, both the authentic reiteration of jurisgenerative processes of law production by regional human rights charters of decentralized local communities, and the fostering of a *process of legal pluralism and court dialogues* in terms of a multilevel legal pluralism of regional and national courts. This would provide a way of avoiding a form of legal despotism as in the case of the power despotism of a World Republic already foreseen by Kant and to proceed, progressively, into the construction of a *thin* cosmopolitan condition having its roots in local contexts.

---

[26] The reference here is obviously to the *Second Definitive Article* of Kant's *Perpetual Peace*.

[27] Decent states, in Rawls' *The Law of Peoples* (1999), are those states characterized, among other things, by a hierarchical, but decent, constitution that does not amount yet to being governed by the principle of "one man one vote".

[28] See Cederman, Tab. 2 (2001, 20).

Bibliography

Arendt, H. (1982), *Lectures on Kant's Political Philosophy*, Beiner, R. (ed.), University of Chicago Press, Chicago IL.

Abel, R. (1982), "Law as lag: inertia as a social theory of law", in, *Michigan Law Review*, 80, 785–809.

Adorno, T.W. (1994), *Hegel. Three Studies*, trans. Weber Nicholsen S., The MIT Press, Cambridge MA.

Albert, H. (1985, [1968]), *Treatise on Critical Reason*, Princeton University Press, Princeton, NJ.

Allison, H.E. (2001), *Kant's Theory of Taste. A Reading of the Critique of Aesthetic Judgment*, Cambridge University Press, Cambridge, MA.

Apel, K.O. (1973), "Das Apriori der Kommunikationsgemeinschaft und die Grundlagen der Ethik. Zum Problem einer rationalen Begründung der Ethik im Zeitalter der Wissenschaft", in *Transformation der Philosophie*, Suhrkamp, Frankfurt am Main, 358–435.

Apel, K.O. (1988), *Diskurs und Verantwortung. Das Problem des Übergangs zur postkonventionellen Moral*, Suhrkamp, Frankfurt am Main.

Apel, K.O. (1990), "Faktische Anerkennung oder einsehbar notwendige Anerkennung? Beruht der Ansatz der transzendentalpragmatischen Diskursethik auf einen intellektualistischen Fehlschluß?", in, Apel, K.O. and Pozzo, R. (eds.), *Zur Rekonstruktion der praktischen Philosophie. Gedenkschrift für Karl-Heinz Ilting*, Frommann-Holzboog, Stuttgart-Bad Cannstatt, 67–123.

Aquinas, T. (1991), *Summa Theologiae*, Mcdermott, T. (ed.), Thomas More Publishing, Allen Texas.

Archibugi, D. (1997), "So what if democracies don't fight each other?", in, *Peace Review*, Carfax Publishing Ltd, London, 9, 379–384.

Arendt, H. (1958), *The Human Condition*, Chicago University Press, Chicago.

Aristotele (1963), *De Anima*, Hamlyn, D.W. (ed.), Oxford University Press, Oxford.

Aristotele (1965), *Poetics*, Kassel R. (ed.), Oxford University Press, Oxford.

Aristotele (1998), *Nicomachean Ethics*, Ackrill, J.L., Ross, D.W., Urmson, J.O. (eds. and trans.), Oxford University Press, Oxford.

Austin, J. (1995 [1832]), *The Province of Jurisprudence Determined*, Cambridge University Press, Cambridge MA.

Austin, J.L. (1975), *How to Do Things with Words*, Harvard University Press, Cambridge MA.

Avineri, S. (1972), *Hegel's Theory of the Modern State*, Cambridge University Press, Cambridge MA.

Bach, E. (1968), "Nouns and Noun Phrases", in, Bach, E. and Harms, R. (eds.), *Universals in Linguistic Theory*, Holt Rinehart and Winston, New York NY, 90–122.

Beitz, C.R. (1999 [1979]), *Political Theory and International Relations*, Princeton University Press, Princeton NJ.

Beitz, C.R. (2001), "Human Rights as a Common Concern", in, *The American Political Science Review*, 95, 269–282.

Bell, L.S., Nathan, A.J. and Peleg, I. (eds.), (2001), *Negotiating Culture and Human Rights*, Columbia University Press, New York NY.

Bellamy, R. (2004), "The Normality of the Constitutional Politics: An Analysis of the Drafting of the EU Charter of Fundamental Rights", in, *Constellations*, 11, 412–433.

Bellamy, R. (2006), "The European Constitution is Dead, Long Live European Constitutionalism", in *Constellations*, Blackwell, Oxford, 13, 181–189.

Benhabib S. (2004, 15–19 March), "Reclaiming Universalism: Negotiating Republican Self-Determination and Cosmopolitan Norms", in, *The Tanner Lectures on Human Values*, University of California, Berkeley, 113–166.

Bentham, J. [1843], *Anarchical Fallacies. Text*, in, Waldron, J., (ed.), (1987), *'Nonsense upon Stilts'. Bentham, Burke and Marx on the Rights of Man*, Methuen, London, 46–76.

Berlin, B. (1968), *Tzeltal Numeral Classifiers*, The Hague Mouton, Paris.

Berlin, B. and Kay, P. (1969), *Basic Colour Terms: their Universality and Evolution*, University of California Press, Berkeley.

Berlin, B., Breedlove, D.E. and Raven, P.H. (1974), *Principles of Tzeltal Plant Classification*, Academic Press, New York NY.

Bernstein, R.J. (1983), *Beyond Objectivism and Relativism: Science, Hermeneutics, and Praxis*, Basil Blackwell, Oxford.

Bix, B. (1996), "Natural Law Theory", in Patterson D. (ed.), *A Companion to Philosophy of Law and Legal Theory*, Blackwell Publishers, Oxford, 223–240.

Bix, B. (2002), "Natural law theory: the Modern Tradition", in Coleman J. and Shapiro S. (eds.), *Oxford Handbook of Jurisprudence and Philosophy of Law*, Oxford University Press, Oxford, 61–103.

Black, M. (1955), "Metaphor", in, *Proceedings of the Aristotelian Society*, 55, Blackwell Publishing, Oxford, 273–294.

Black, M. (1962), *Models and Metaphors, Studies in Language and Philosophy*, Cornell University Press, Ithaca.

Black, M. (1993), "More about metaphors", in, Ortony, A., (ed.) *Metaphor and Thought*, Cambridge University Press, Cambridge MA, 19–43.

Boers, F. and Demecheleer, M. (1995), "A Few Metaphorical Models in (Western) Economic Discourse", in, *Discourse and Perspective in Cognitive Linguistics*, Benjamins, Amsterdam, 115–129.

Bohman, J. (1996), *Public Deliberation: Pluralism, Complexity, and Democracy*, The MIT Press, Cambridge MA.

Bolinger, D. (1965), "The Atomization of Meaning", in, *Language*, 41, Cambridge University Press, Cambridge MA, 555–573.

Brandt, R. (1959), *Ethical Theory*, Prentice Hall, Englewood Cliffs, NJ.

Brandt, R. (1979), *A Theory of the Good and the Right*, Oxford University Press, Oxford.

Brandt, R. (1996), *Facts, Values, and Morality*, Cambridge University Press, Cambridge MA.

Brugman, C. (1990), "What is the Invariance Hypothesis?", in, *Cognitive Linguistics*, 1, 247–266.

Brugman, C. and Lakoff, G. (1988), "Cognitive Topology and Lexical Networks", in, Cottrell, G., Small, C., Tannenhaus, M. (eds.), *Lexical Ambiguity Resolution*, Morgan Kaufmann, San Francisco CA, 477–507.

Brunkhorst, H. (2005), *Solidarity: from Civic Friendship to a Global Legal Community*, The MIT Press, Cambridge, MA.

Brunkhorst, H. (2006), "The Legitimation Crisis of the European Union", in *Constellations*, 13, Blackwell, Oxford, 175–177.

Buchanan, N. (2006), *Moral Progress and Human Rights*, on-line paper http://www.ethics.utoronto.ca/pdf/events/Paper-AllenBuchanan.pdf

Butterworth, B. (1975), "Hesitation and Semantic Planning in Speech", in, *Journal of Psycholinguistic Research*, 4, Springer, Netherlands, 75–87.

Bybee, J. and Fleischman, S. (eds.), (1995), *Modality in Grammar and Discourse*, Benjamins, Amsterdam.

Campbell, T.D. (1996), *The Legal Theory of Ethical Positivism*, Darthmouth, Aldershot.

Caney, S. and Jones, P. (eds.), (2001), *Human Rights and Global Diversity*, Frank Cass Publishers, London.

Cardona, G.R. (1985), *I sei lati del mondo, linguaggio ed esperienza*, Laterza, Roma-Bari.

Carson, T.L. and Moser, P.K. (2001), "Relativism and Normative Nonrealism: Basing Morality on Rationality", in Moser P. K. and Carson L. (eds.), *Moral Relativism. A Reader*, Oxford University Press, New York NY, 287–304.

Cederman, L.-E. (2001), "Back to Kant: Reinterpreting the Democratic Peace as a Macrohistorical Learning Process", in, *American Political Science Review*, 95, 15–31.

Chan, S. (1997), "In Search of Democratic Peace: Problems and Promise", in, *Mershon International Studies Review*, 41, 59–91.

Chang, R. (ed.), (1997), *Incommensurability, Incomparability, and Practical Reason*, Harvard University Press, Cambridge MA.

Chapanis, A. (1965), "Color Names for Color Space", in, *American Scientist*, 53, 327–346.

Chomsky, N. (1957), *Syntactic Structures*, Mouton, Paris-Aja.

Chomsky, N. (1965), *Aspects of the Theory of Syntax*, The MIT Press, Cambridge MA.

Chomsky, N. (1972), "Some Empirical Issues in the Theory of Transformational Grammar", in, Peters, S. (ed.), *Goals of Linguistic Theory*, Prentice Hall, Englewood Cliffs, NJ, 63–130.

Chomsky, N. (1991), *Language and Problems of Knowledge. The Managua Lectures*, The MIT Press, Cambridge MA.

Chomsky, N. (2003 [1966]), *Cartesian Linguistics: A Charter in the History of Rationalist Thought*, Cyber editions Corporation, New Zealand.

Cicero, (2001), "On the Laws. Book I", in, Hayden, P. (ed.), *The Philosophy of Human Rights*, Paragon House, St.Paul.

Clark, H.H (1996), *Using Language*, Cambridge University Press, Cambridge MA.

Clark, H.H. (1973), "Space, Time, Semantics, and the Child", in, Moore, T.E. (ed.), *Cognitive Development and the Acquisition of Language*, Academic Press, New York NY, 27–63.

Clark, H.H. (1992), *Arenas of Language Use*, University of Chicago Press, Chicago IL.

Coates, J. (1983), *The Semantics of the Modal Auxiliaries*, Croom Helm, London.

Coates, J. (1995), "The Expression of Root and Epistemic Possibility in English", in, Bybee J. and Fleischman S. (eds.), *Modality in Grammar and Discourse*, Benjamins, Amsterdam.

Cohen, J. (2004), 'Minimalism About Human Rights: The Most We Can Hope For?', in *The Journal of Political Philosophy*, 12, 190–213.

Coleman, J.L and Leiter, B. (1996), "Legal Positivism", in Patterson, D. (ed.), *A Companion to Philosophy of Law and Legal Theory*, Blackwell, Oxford, 241–260.

Copestake, A. and Briscoe, T. (1995), "Semi-productive Polysemy and Sense Extension", in, *Journal of Semantics*, 12, 15–67.

Cowan and Rakušan (1985), *Source Book for Linguistics*, Benjamins, Amsterdam.

Cowan, J.K., Dembour, M.-B. and Wilson, R.A. (eds.), (2001), *Culture and Rights*, Cambridge University Press, Cambridge MA.

Cranston, M. (1973), *What are Human Rights*, The Bodley Head Ltd, London.

Dahl, R. (1997), *Democracy and its Critics*, Yale University Press, New Haven CT.

Damasio, A. (1994), *Descartes' Error: Emotion, Reason, and the Human Brain*, Grosset/Putnam, New-York NY.

Daniels, N. (1996), *Justice and Justification: Reflective Equilibrium in Theory and Practice*, Cambridge University Press, Cambridge MA.

Davidoff, J. (1997), "The Neuropsychology of Color", in, *Color Categories in Thought and Language*, Hardin, C.L. and Maffi, L. (eds.), Cambridge University Press, Cambridge MA, 118–133.

Davidson, D. (1982), "Expressing Evaluations," *The Lindley Lecture*, University of Kansas, Lawrence, KS.

Davidson, D. (1984), "On the Very Idea of a Conceptual Scheme", in, Davidson, D., *Inquiries into Truth and Interpretation*, Clarendon Press, Oxford, 183–198.

Davidson, D. (2001), *Subjective, Intersubjective, Objective*, Oxford University Press, Oxford.

De Mauro, T. (1982), *Minisemantica*, Laterza, Roma-Bari.

De Saussurre, F. (1967 [1922]), *Corso di linguistica generale*, De Mauro, T. (ed.), Laterza, Roma-Bari.

Deng, F.M. (ed), (1990), *Human Rights in Africa: Cross-Cultural Perspectives*, The Brookings Institution,Washington DC.

Dennet, D. (1991), *Consciousness Explained*, Little Brown and Co., Boston MA.

Dershowitz, A. (2004), *Rights from Wrongs. A Secular Theory of the Origins of Rights*, Basic Books, New York NY.

Dewey, J. (1958), *Experience and Nature*, Dover Publications Inc., New York NY.

Dewey, J. (1963), "The Construction of Good", in, Alston, W.P. and Nakhnikian, G. (eds.), *Readings in Twentieth-Century Philosophy*, The Free Press of Glencoe, New York NY, 194–295.

Diamond, J.L., Linz, J.J., and Lipset, S.M. (eds), (1995), *Politics in Developing Countries: Comparing Experiences with Democracy*, Lynne Rienner Publishers, Boulder.

Donnelly, J. (2003), *Universal Human Rights in Theory and Practice*, Cornell University Press, Ithaca NY.

Downs, A. (1957), *An Economic Theory of Democracy*, Harper and Row, New York NY.

Doyle, M. ([1983] 1996), "Kant, liberal legacies, and foreign affairs", in, Brown, M.E., Lynn-Jones, S.M. and Miller, S.E. (eds.), Debating the Democratic Peace, The MIT Press, Cambridge MA, 3–57.

Duncker, K. (1939), "Ethical Relativity? (An Inquiry into the Psychology of Ethics)", in *Mind*, 48, 39–57.

Durkheim, E. (1933), *The Division of Labor in Society*, The Free Press, New York NY.

Dworkin, R.M. (1977a), *Taking Rights Seriously*, Harvard University Press, Cambridge MA.

Dworkin, R.M. (1977b), "Is Law a System of Rules?", in Dworkin, R.M. (ed.), *The Philosophy of Law*, Oxford University Press, Oxford, 38–65.

Dworkin, R.M. (1986a), *Law's Empire*, Fontana Press, London.

Dworkin, R.M. (1986b), *A Matter of Principle*, Clarendon Press, Oxford.

Dworkin, R.M. (2006), *Justice in Robes*, The Belknap Press of Harvard University Press, Cambridge MA.

Eco, U. (1980), entry *"Metafora"*, in, *Enciclopedia Einaudi*, IX, Einaudi, Torino.

Edelman, G. (1993), *Sulla materia della mente*, Adelphi, Milano.

Elster. J. and Slagstad, R. (eds.), (1988), *Constitutionalism and Democracy*, Cambridge University Press, Cambridge MA.

Eriksen, E.O. and Weigård, J. (2003), *Understanding Habermas. Communicating Action and Deliberative Democracy*, Continuum, London-New York.

Fauconnier, G. (1985), *Mental Spaces: Roles and Strategies*, The MIT Press, Cambridge MA.

Feinberg, J. (1973), *Social Philosophy*, Prentice-Hall, Englewood Cliffs, NJ.

Feinberg, J. (2001 [1970]), "The nature and Value of Rights", in, The Journal of Values Enquiry, 4, 1970, 243–257. Reprinted in Hayden, P. (ed), (2001), *The Philosophy of Human Rights*, Paragon House, St.Paul MN, 174–185.

Ferrara, A. (1996), "Passione democratica e routine degli interessi", in *Micromega*, Roma, 21–25.

Ferrara, A. (2000), *Giustizia e Giudizio*, Laterza, Roma-Bari.

Ferrara, A. (2003), "Two Notions of Humanity and the Judgment Argument for Human Rights", in, *Political Theory*, 31, 1–30.

Fichte, G. ([1796/7] 2000), *Grundlage des Naturrechts nach Principien der Wissenschaftslehre*, engl. Trans., *Foundations of Natural Right*, ed. F. Neuhouser, trans. M. Baur, Cambridge University Press, Cambridge MA.

Fillmore, C. (1975), *Santa Cruz Lectures on Deixis*, Indiana University Linguistics Club, Bloomington.

Finnis, J. (1980), *Natural Law and Natural Rights*, Clarendon Press, Oxford.

Fodor, J. (1988), *La mente modulare*, Il Mulino, Bologna.

Foot, P. (2001), "Moral Relativism", in, Moser P. K. and Carson L. (eds.), *Moral Relativism. A Reader*, Oxford University Press, New York NY, 185–198.

Foucault, M. (1969), *L'Archéologie du savoir*, Éditions Gallimard, Paris.

Fraser N. and Honneth A. (2003), *Redistribution or Recognition? A Political-Philosophical Exchange*, Verso, London-New York.

Freeman, M. (2003), *Human Rights. An Interdisciplinary Approach*, Polity Press, Cambridge MA.

Fuller, L. (1969), *The Morality of Law*, Yale University Press, New Haven and London.

Garroni, E. (1976), *Estetica ed Epistemologia. Riflessioni sulla ≪Critica del Giudizio≫*, Bulzoni, Roma.

Garroni, E. (1986), *Senso e paradosso*, Laterza, Roma-Bari.

Gauthier, D. (1986), *Morals by Agreement*, Oxford University Press, Oxford.

Gewirth, A. (1981), "The Basis and Content of Human Rights", in, Pennock, J.R. and Chapman, J.W. (eds.), *Human Rights*, New York University Press, New York NY, 119–147.

Gewirth, A. (1982), *Human Rights. Essays on Justification and Applications*, The University of Chicago Press, Chicago and London.

Gewirth, A. (1984), "The Epistemology of Human Rights", in Frankel, P.E., Miller Jr, F.D. and Jeffrey, P. (eds.), *Human Rights*, Basil Blackwell, Oxford.

Gewirth, A. (1985), "Why There Are Human Rights", in, *Social Theory and Practice*, 11, 235–248.

Gewirth, A. (1986), "Why Rights are Indispensable", in, *Mind*, 95, 329–344.

Gewirth, A. (1996), *The Community of Rights*, The University of Chicago Press, Chicago and London.

Glock, H. J. (1996). A Wittgenstein Dictionary, Blackwell, Oxford, 1996.

Gossens, L. *et alii* (1995), *By Word of Mouth*, Benjamins, Amsterdam.

Graham, G. (2001, [1996]), "Tolerance, Pluralism, and Relativism", in Moser, P.K. and Carson, T.L. (eds.), *Moral Relativism. A Reader*, Oxford University Press, Oxford, 226–240.

Green, G. (1974), *Semantics and Syntactic Regularity*, Indiana University Press, Bloomington IN.

Grice, P. (1989), *Studies in the Way of Words*, Harvard University Press, Cambridge MA.

Griffin, J. (1988), *Well-being. Its meaning, measurement, and moral importance*, Clarendon Press, Oxford.

Gutmann, A. (1994), *Multiculturalism. Examining the Politics of Recognition*, Princeton University Press, Princeton NJ.

Gutmann, A. and Thompson, D. (2000, [1996]), *Democracy and Disagreement*, Harvard University Press, Cambridge MA.

Habermas, J. (1984a), *Vorstudien und Ergänzungen zur Theorie des kommunikativen Handelns*, Suhrkamp, Frankfurt AM.

Habermas, J. (1984b), *The Theory of Communicative Action*, vol. 1 and vol. 2, Beacon Press, Boston.

Habermas, J. (1987), *The philosophical discourse of modernity*, Polity Cambridge MA.

Habermas, J. (1990), "Discourse Ethics: Notes on a Program of Philosophical Justification", in, *Moral Consciousness and Communicative Action*, Polity Press, Cambridge MA, 43–116.

Habermas, J. (1993), "On the Pragmatic, the Ethical, and the Moral Employments of Practical Reason", in, *Justification and Application*, Polity Press, Cambridge MA, 1–17.

Habermas, J. (1994), "Postscript to Faktizität und Geltung", in, *Philosophy & Social Criticism*, 20, 135–150.

Habermas, J. (1996a), *Between facts and norms*, The MIT Press, Cambridge MA.

Habermas, J. (1996b), "Per la critica del liberalismo politico di John Rawls", *MicroMega*, Roma, 26–50.

Habermas, J. (1998a), "Remarks on Legitimation through Human Rights", in, *Philosophy and Social Criticism*, 24, 157–171.

Habermas, J. (1998b), "A Genealogical Analysis of the Cognitive Content of Morality", in, Habermas, J. (1998), *The Inclusion of the Other: Studies in Political Theory*, The MIT Press, Cambridge MA.

Habermas, J. (2003a), "Richard Rorty's Pragmatic Turn", in, Cooke, M. (ed.), *On the Pragmatics of Communication*, Polity Press, Cambridge MA, 243–282.

Habermas, J. (2003b [1996]), "Some further clarifications of the concept of Communicative Rationality", in, Cooke, M. (ed.), *On the Pragmatics of Communication*, Polity Press, Cambridge MA, 307–342.

Habermas, J. (2003c [1976]), "What is Universal Pragmatics?", in, Cooke, M. (ed.), *On the Pragmatics of Communication*, Polity Press, Cambridge MA, 21–104.

Habermas, J. (2003d [1981]), "Social Action, Purposive Activity, and Communication", in, Cooke, M. (ed.), *On the Pragmatics of Communication*, Polity Press, Cambridge MA, 105–182.

Habermas, J. (2003e [1986]), "Communicative Rationality and the Theories of Meaning and Action", in, Cooke, M. (ed.), *On the Pragmatics of Communication*, Polity Press, Cambridge MA, 183–213.

Habermas, J. (2004), *Der gespaltene Westen*, Suhrkamp Verlag, Frankfurt am Main.

Habermas, J. (2006a), "Three Normative Models of Democracy", in, Bellamy, R. (ed.), *Constitutionalism and Democracy*, Ashgate, Dartmouth, 277–286.

Habermas, J. (2006b), "On the Internal Relation between the Rule of Law and Democracy", in, Bellamy, R. (ed.), *Constitutionalism and Democracy*, Ashgate, Dartmouth, 267–275.

Habermas, J. (2007 [2005], "Agire comunicativo e ragione detrascendentalizzata", in, *La condizione intersoggettiva*, Laterza, Roma-Bari, 21–99.

Hacker, P.M.S. (1972), *Insight and Illusion*, Clarendon Press, Oxford.

Haegeman, L. (1983), *The Semantics of Will in Present-Day British English*, Paleis der Academiën, Brussels.

Haiman, J. (1980), "The Iconicity of Grammar: Isomorphism and Motivation", in, *Language*, 56, 515–540.

Hanfling, O. (1989), *Wittgenstein's Later Philosophy*, Macmillan, New York NY.

Hardin, C.L. and Maffi, L. (eds.), (1997), *Color Categories in Thought and Language*, Cambridge University Press, Cambridge MA.

Harman, G. (1977), *The Nature of Morality: An Introduction to Ethics*, Oxford University Press, Oxford.

Harman, G. (1982), "Moral Relativism Defended", in Meiland, J. W. and Krausz, M. (eds.), *Relativism: Cognitive and Moral*, University of Notre Dame Press, Notre Dame, 189–204.

Harman, G. (1996), "Moral Relativism", in Harman G. and Thomson J. J., *Moral Relativism and Moral Objectivity*, Blackwell, Oxford, 1–64.

Harré, R. and Krausz, M. (1996), *Varieties of Relativism*, Blackwell, Oxford.

Harris, Z. (1957), "Co-occurrence and Transformation in Linguistic Structure", in, *Language*, 33, 293–340.

Hart, H.L.A. (1961), *The Concept of Law*, Oxford University Press, Oxford.

Hart, H.L.A. (1963), *Law, Liberty and Morality*, Oxford University Press, Oxford.

Hart, H.L.A. (1965), "Book Review of The Morality of Law", in, *Harvard Law Review*, 78, 1281.

Hart, H.L.A. (1977 [1958]), "Positivism and the separation of law and morals", in Dworkin, R.M. (ed.), *The Philosophy of Law*, Oxford University Press, Oxford, 17–37.

Hart, H.L.A. (1982), *Essays on Bentham*, Clarendon Press, Oxford.

Hayden, P. (ed), (2001), *The Philosophy of Human Rights*, Paragon House, St.Paul MN.

Hegel, G.W.F. (1968 [1802–6]), "Jenaer Systementwürfe (I-II-III)", in, *Gesammelte Werke*, hrsg. Rheinisch-Westphälische Akademie der Wissenschaften, Hamburg.

Hegel, G.W.F. (1969 [1812–16]), *Science of Logic*, Miller A.V. (trans.), Allen and Unwin, London.

Hegel, G.W.F. (1977 [1807]), *Phenomenology of Spirit*, Miller A.V. (trans.), Clarendon Press, Oxford.

Hegel, G.W.F. (2001 [1821]), *Philosophy of Right*, Dyde, S.W. (trans.), Batoche Books, Kitchener.

Herskovits, A. (1987), *Spatial Preposition in English*, Cambridge University Press, Cambridge MA.

Hobbes, T. (1998 [1651]), *Leviathan*, Gaskin, J.C. (ed.), Oxford University Press, Oxford.

Hohfeld, W.N. (1919), *Fundamental Legal Conceptions as Applied in Judicial Reasoning*, Yale University Press, New Haven CT.

Hollis, M. (1982), "The Social Destruction of Reality", in Hollis, M. and Lukes, S. (eds.), *Rationality and Relativism*, The MIT Press, Cambridge MA, 67–86.

Holmes, S. (1997), "Precommitment and the Paradox of Democracy", in, Elster. J. and Slagstad, R. (eds.), (1988), *Constitutionalism and Democracy*, Cambridge University Press, Cambridge MA, 195–240.

Honneth, A. (1995), *The Struggle for Recognition. The Moral Grammar of Social Conflict*, Polity Press, Cambridge MA.

Honneth, A. (2005, March 14–16), *Reification: A Recognition-Theoretical View*, The Tanner Lectures on Human Values, delivered at University of California, Berkeley, on-line paper.

Honneth, A. (2008a), *Preliminary Remarks on Theories of Justice as Analyses of Society*, paper presented at the Colloquium Philosophy and Society, University of Rome II "Tor Vergata"/Centro Studi Americani, Roma.

Honneth, A. (2008b), *Recognition as the Basis of Social Freedom and Justice in Hegel*, paper presented at the Colloquium Philosophy and Society, University of Rome II "Tor Vergata"/Centro Studi Americani, Roma.

Hunn, E.S. (1977), *Tzeltal Folk Zoology: The Classification of Discontinuities in Nature*, Academic Press, New York NY.

Hunter, J.M.F. (1985), *Understanding Wittgenstein*, Edinburgh University Press, Edinburgh.

Huntington, S. P. (1991), *The Third Wave: Democratization in the Late Twentieth Century*, University of Oklahoma Press, Norman.

Ignatieff, M. (2001), *Human Rights as Politics and Idolatry*, Princeton University Press, Princeton NJ, Ignatieff, M. (trans.) (2003), *Una Ragionevole Apologia dei diritti Umani*, Feltrinelli.

Ingram, A. (1994), *A Political Theory of Rights*, Clarendon Press, Oxford.

Johnson, M. (1987), *The Body in the Mind*, Chicago University Press, Chicago.

Johnson, M. (1993), *Moral Imagination. Implications of Cognitive Science for Ethics*, The University of Chicago Press, Chicago and London.

Jones, P. (1994), *Rights*, Palgrave Macmillan, New York NY.

Kahn-Freund, O. (1974), "On uses and misuses of comparative law", in *Modern Law Review*, 371–27.

Kant, I. (1953 [1790]), *The Critique of Judgment*, Meredith, J.C. (trans.), Oxford University Press, Oxford.

Kant, I. (1970a, [1795]), "Perpetual Peace: a Philosophical Sketch", in, Reiss, H. (ed.), *Kant's Political Writings*, Cambridge University Press, Cambridge MA.

Kant, I. (1970b, [1784]), "Idea for a Universal History with a Cosmopolitan Purpose", in, Reiss, H. (ed.), *Kant's Political Writings*, Cambridge University Press, Cambridge MA.

Kant, I. (1983a [1797]), "Metaphysics of Morals", in, *Ethical Philosophy*, Hackett, Indianapolis IN.

Kant, I. (1983b [1785]), "Grounding for the Metaphysics of Morals", in, *Ethical Philosophy*, Hackett, Indianapolis IN.

Kant, I. (1999 [1781]), *Critique of Pure Reason*, Guyer, P. and Wood, A.W. (eds.), Cambridge University Press, Cambridge MA.

Katz, J. and Fodor, J.A. (1963), "The Structure of a Semantic Theory", in, *Language*, 39, 170–210.

Katz, R., S., (1997), *Democracy and Elections*, Oxford University Press, Oxford.

Kay, P., Berlin, B., Maffi, L. Merrifield, W. (1997), "Color Naming Across Languages", in, Hardin, C.L. and Maffi, L. (eds.), *Color Categories in Thought and Language*, Cambridge University Press, Cambridge MA, 21–58.

Koh, H.H., Slye, R.C. (eds.), (1999), *Deliberative Democracy and Human Rights*, Yale University Press, New Haven and London.

Kovecses, Z. (1986), *Metaphors of Anger, Pride and Love: a Lexical Approach to the Structure of Concepts*, Benjamins, Amsterdam.

Kramer, M.H. (1998), "Rights without Trimmings", in, Kramer, M.H., Simmonds, N.E., Steiner, H. (1998), *A Debate Over Rights. Philosophical Enquiries*, Clarendon Press, Oxford, 7–111.

Kramer, M.H., Simmonds, N.E., Steiner, H. (1998), *A Debate Over Rights. Philosophical Enquiries*, Clarendon Press, Oxford.

Kuczaj, S.A. and Daly, M.J. (1979), "The Development of Hypothetical Reference in the Speech of Young Children", in, *Journal of Child Language*, 6, 563–579.

Kymlicka, W. (1999), *La Cittadinanza Multiculturale*, Il Mulino, Bologna.

Lakoff, G. (1966), "Stative Adjectives and Verbs in English", in, Oettinger, A.G. (ed.) *Mathematical linguistics and automatic translation*. Report NSF-17, The Computation Laboratory, Harvard University, Cambridge MA.

Lakoff, G. (1970), *Irregularity in Syntax*, Holt, Rinehart and Winston, New York NY.

Lakoff, G. (1971a), "On Generative Semantics", in, Steinberg, L. and Jakobvits, A. (eds), *Semantics: an Interdisciplinary Reader in Philosophy, Linguistics and Psychology*, Cambridge University Press, Cambridge MA, 232–296.

Lakoff, G. (1971b), "Linguistics and Natural Logic", in, Davidson, D. and Harman, G. (eds.), Semantic of Natural Languages, Reidel, Dordrecht, 545–665.

Lakoff, G. (1972), "Notes Toward a Theory of Global Transderivational Well-formed-ness Grammar", not-published article.

Lakoff, G. (1973), "Fuzzy Grammar and the Performance/Competence terminology Game", in, *Papers from the Nth Regional Meeting, Chicago Linguistic Society*, 9, University of Chicago, Chicago IL., 271–291.

Lakoff, G. (1977), "Linguistic Gestalts", in, *Papers from the Nth Regional Meeting*, 13, Chicago Linguistic Society, Chicago IL, 236–287.

Lakoff, G. (1987), *Women, Fire, and Dangerous Things*, University of Chicago Press, Chicago IL.

Lakoff, G. (1993), "The Contemporary Theory of Metaphors", in, Ortony A. (ed.) *Metaphor and Thought*, Cambridge University Press, Cambridge MA, 202–251.

Lakoff, G. (1996), *Moral Politics*, The University of Chicago Press, Chicago IL.

Lakoff G. and Johnson, M. (1980), *Metaphors We Live By*, The University of Chicago Press, Chicago IL.

Lakoff, G. and Johnson, M (1999), *Philosophy in the Flesh*, Basic Books, New York NY.

Lakoff, G. and Thompson, H. (1975), "Introducing Cognitive Grammar", in, *Proceedings of the Vth Annual Meeting of the Berkeley Linguistics Society*, 1, Berkeley University, California MA, 295–313.

Lakoff, G. and Turner, M. (1989), *More Than Cool Reason*, The University of Chicago Press, Chicago IL.

Langacker, R.W. (1987), *Foundations of Cognitive Grammar*, 1 and 2, Stanford University Press, Stanford CA.

Langacker, R.W. (1995), "Viewing in Cognition and Grammar", in, Davis P.W. (ed.), *Alternative Linguistics: Descriptive and Theoretical Modes*, Benjamins, Amsterdam, 153–212.

Langacker, R.W. (1997), "The Contextual Basis of Cognitive Semantics", in, Nuyts J. and Pederson, E. (eds.), *Language and Conceptualization*, Cambridge University Press, Cambridge MA, 229–252.

Liebert, W.A., Redeker, G. and Waugh, L. (1997), *Discourse and Perspective in Cognitive Linguistics*, Benjamins, Amsterdam.

Lijphart, A. (1977), *Democracy in Plural Societies: A Comparative Exploration*, Yale University Press, New Haven CT.

Lijphart, A. (1999), *Patterns of Democracy*, Yale University Press, New Haven and London.

Locke, J. (1954 [1660–64]), *Essays on the Law of Nature*, Von Leyden, W. (ed.), Oxford University Press, Oxford.

Locke, J. (1975 [1690]), *An Essay concerning Human Understanding*, Nidditch, P.H (ed.), Oxford University Press, Oxford.

Locke, J. (1982 [1689]), *Second Treatise of Government*, Cox R. (ed.), Harlan Davidson Inc., Wheeling IL.

Lomasky, L.E. (1987), *Persons, Rights, and the Moral Community*, Oxford University Press, Oxford.

Lyons, D. (1976), "Ethical Relativism and the Problem of Incoherence", in, *Ethics*, 86, 107–121.

Lyons, J. (1977), *Introduction to Theoretical Linguistics*, 1 and 2, Cambridge University Press, Cambridge MA.

Mac Callum, G.C. (1967), "Negative and Positive Freedom", in, *Philosophical Review*, LXXVI, 312–334.

Mac Cormick, N. (1981), *H.L.A. Hart*, Edward Arnold Ltd., London.

Macintyre (1988), *Whose Justice? Which Rationality?*, University of Notre Dame Press, Notre Dame, Indiana, IN.

Macintyre, A. (1998), "Practical Rationalities as forms of Social Structures", in, *The MacIntyre Reader*, University of Notre Dame Press, Notre Dame Indiana IN.

Maffi, L. and Hardin, C.L. (1997), *Color Categories in Thought and Language*, Cambridge University Press, Cambridge MA.

Maoz, Z. and Russet, B.Z. (1993), "Normative and Structural Causes of Democratic Peace, 1946–1986", in, *The American Political Science Review*, 87, 624–638.

Margolis, J. (1983), "The Nature and Strategies of Relativism", in, *Mind*, 92, 548–567.

Marzocchi, V. (2004), *Le Ragioni dei Diritti Umani*, Liguore Editore, Napoli.

Mccawley, J.D. (1973), *Grammar and Meaning: Papers on Syntactic and Semantic Topics*, Taishukan, Tokyo.

McCloskey, H.J. (1985), "Respect for Human Moral Rights", in, Frey, R.G. (1985), *Utility and Rights*, Basil Blackwell, Oxford, 121–136.

McGinn, M. (1984), *Wittgenstein on Meaning*, Basil Blackwell, Oxford.

McGinn, M. (1997), *Wittgenstein and the Philosophical Investigations*, Routledge, London-New York.

Medin, D.L. and Goldstone, R.L. (1995), "The Predicates of Similarity", in, Cacciari C. (ed.), *Similarity*, Brepols, Turnhout, Belgium, 83–110.

Mill, J.S. (1975 [1858]), "On Liberty", in, *Three Essays*, Oxford University Press, Oxford.

Milner, J. (1976), *Linguistique et logique naturelle*, éditions Klincksieck, Paris.

Moesteller, T (2006), *Relativism in Contemporary American Philosophy*, Continuum, London-New York.

Moody-Adams, M. (2001), "The Empirical Underdetermination of Descriptive Cultural Relativism", in Moser, P. K. and Carson, L. (eds.), *Moral Relativism. A Reader*, Oxford University Press, New York NY, 93–106.

Moravcsik, A. (2002), "In defence of the 'Democratic Deficit': Reassessing Legitimacy in the European Union", *JCMS*, 40, 603–624.

Morgan, J.L. (1968), *Remarks on the Notion "Possible lexical item"*, not published article.

Morgenthau, H. (1951), *In Defence of the National Interest*, Knopf, New York NY.

Murphy, M.C. (2005), "Natural Law Theory", in Golding, M.P. and Edmunson, W.A. (eds.), *The Blackwell Guide to the Philosophy of Law and Legal Theory*, Blackwell Publishing, Oxford.

Nagel, T. (1978), *The Possibility of Altruism*, Princeton University Press, Princeton NJ.

Nagel, T. (1986), *The View from Nowhere*, Oxford University Press, Oxford. It. Trans. *Uno sguardo da nessun luogo*, Il Saggiatore, Milano.

Nagel, T. (1991), *Equality and Partiality*, Oxford University Press, Oxford.

Nagel, T. (1997), *The Last Word*, Oxford University Press, Oxford.

Narveson, J (1981), "Human Rights: Which, If Any, Are There?", in, Pennock, R.J. and Chapman, J.W. (eds.), *Human Rights*, Nomos XXIII, New York University Press, New York NY, 175–197.

Narveson, J. (1985), "Contractarian Rights", in, Frey, R.G., *Utility and Rights*, Basil Blackwell, Oxford, 161–174.

Newton, N. (1996), *Foundations of Understanding*, Benjamins, Amsterdam.

Newton-Smith, W. (1982), "Relativism and the Possibility of Interpretation", in, Hollis, M. and Lukes, S. (eds.), *Rationality and Relativism*, The MIT Press, Cambridge MA, 106–122.

Nickel, J.W. (1987), *Making Sense of Human Rights: Philosophical Reflections on the Universal Declaration of Human Rights*, University of California Press, Berkeley.

Nickel, J.W. (2005), "Poverty and Rights", in, *The Philosophical Quarterly*, 5, 385–402.

Nickel, J.W. and Reidy, D. (2008), "Relativism, Self-determination and Human Rights, in, Chatterjee, D.K (ed.), Democracy in a Global World: Human Rights and Political Participation in the 21st Century, Rowman & Littlefield ld.

Nielsen, K. (1993), "Relativism and Wide Reflective Equilibrium", in, *The Monist*, 76, 316–331.

Nozick, R. (1974), *Anarchy, State, and Utopia*, Basic Books, New York NY.

Nussbaum, M. (1993), "Non-relative Virtues: An Aristotelian Approach", in, Nussbaum, M. and Sen, A. (eds.), *The Quality of Life*, Clarendon Press, Oxford, 242–269.

Oakeshott, M. (1978), *Experience and its Modes*, Cambridge University Press, Cambridge MA.

Ortony, A. (1988), "Are Emotion Metaphors Conceptual or Lexical?", in, *Cognition and Emotion*, 2, 95–103.

Ortony, A. (1993), *Metaphor and Thought*, Cambridge University Press, Cambridge MA.

Owen, N. (ed.), (2003), *Human Rights, Human Wrongs. The Oxford Amnesty Lectures 2001*, Oxford University Press, Oxford.

Palmer, F. (1990), *Modality and the English Modals*, Longman, London.

Peirce, C.S. (1997 [1931]), The *Collected Papers of Charles Sanders Peirce: Principles of Philosophy and Elements of Logic*, Burks, A.W. and Weiss, P. (eds), Thoemmes Continuum, vol. 1. and vol. 2.

Pennock, J.R. and Chapman, J.W. (eds), (1981), *Human Rights*, New York University Press, New York NY.

Perry, M. J. (1998), *The Idea of Human Rights. Four Enquiries*, Oxford University Press, Oxford.

Piaget, J. (1954), *The Construction of Reality in the Child*, Basic Books, New York NY.

Pick, H. and Acredolo, L.P. (1983), *Spatial Orientation: Theory, Research and Application*, Plenum Press, New York NY.

Popper, K. (1994), *Knowledge and the Body-Mind Problem. In Defence of Interaction*, Routledge, London-New York.

Premarck, D. (1983), "The codes of man and beasts", in, *Behavioural and Brain Sciences*, 6, 125–167.

Przeworski, A. (1997), "Democracy as a Contingent Outcome of Conflicts", in, Elster. J. and Slagstad, R. (eds.), (1988), *Constitutionalism and Democracy*, Cambridge University Press, Cambridge MA, 59–80.

Putnam, H. (1975), "The Meaning of Meaning", in, Gunderson, K. (ed.), *Language, Mind, and Knowledge*, Minnesota Studies in the Philosophy of Science, 7, University of Minnesota Press, Minneapolis MN, 131–193.

Putnam, H. (1981a), "Why Reason Can't Be Naturalized", in, *Realism and Reason: Philosophical Papers Volume III*, Cambridge University Press, Cambridge MA.

Putnam, H. (1981b), *Reason, Truth and History*, Cambridge University Press, Cambridge MA.

Putnam, H. (1992), *Renewing Philosophy*, Harvard University Press, Cambridge MA.

Pylyshyn, Z. (1981), "The Imagery Debate: Analogue Media vs. Tacit Knowledge", in, *Psychological Review*, Washington DC, 88, 16–45.

Quine, W.V.O. (1969), *Ontological Relativity and other Essays*, Columbia University Press, New-York and London.

Radford, A. (1983), *La Teoria Trasformazionale della Sintassi*, Il Mulino, Bologna.

Rawls, J. (1971), *A Theory of Justice*, Harvard University Press, Boston MA.

Rawls, J. (1996a [1993]), *Political Liberalism*, Columbia University Press, New York NY.

Rawes, J. (1996b [1995]), "Risposta a Jürgen Habermas", in, *MicroMega*, Roma, 51–106.

Rawls, J. (1999), *The Law of Peoples*, Harvard University Press, Cambridge MA.

Raz, J. (1979), *The Authority of Law. Essays on Law and Morality*, Clarendon Press, Oxford.

Raz, J. (1985), "Authority and Justification", in, *Philosophy and Public Affairs*, 14, 3–29.

Raz, J. (1986), *The Morality of Freedom*, Clarendon Press, Oxford.

Raz, J. (1990a), *Practical Reason and Norms*, Princeton University Press, Princeton NJ.

Raz, J. (1990b), "Facing Diversity: The Case of Epistemic Abstinence", in *Philosophy and Public Affairs*, 19, 3–46.

Raz, J. (1994), *Ethics in the Public Domain. Essays in the Morality of Law and Politics*, Clarendon Press, Oxford.

Raz, J. (2005), *The Practice of Value*, Clarendon Press, Oxford.

Reddy, M. (1993), "The Conduit Metaphor", in, Ortony A. (ed.), *Metaphor and Thought*, Cambridge University Press, Cambridge MA.

Reilly, B. (2001), *Democracy in Divided Societies*, Cambridge University Press, Cambridge MA.

Richards, I.A. (1936), *The Philosophy of Retories*, Oxford University Press, Oxford.

Rorty, R. (1979), *Philosophy and the Mirror of Nature*, Princeton University Press, Princeton NJ.

Rorty, R. (1991), *Objectivity, Relativism and Truth. Philosophical Papers*, 1, Cambridge University Press, Cambridge MA.

Rorty, R. (1993), "Putnam and the Relativist Menace", in, *The Journal of Philosophy*, 90, 443–461.

Rorty, R. (2001, [1993]), "Human Rights, Rationality, and Sentimentality", in, Hayden, P. (ed), *The Philosophy of Human Rights*, Paragon House, St.Paul MN, 241–257.

Rosch, E. (1977), "Human Categorization", in, Warren, N. (ed.), *Studies in Cross-Cultural Psychology*, Academic Press, London, 1–49.

Rosch, E. (1978), "Principles of Categorization", in, Rosch, E. and Lloyd, B. (eds.), *Cognition and Categorization*, Lawrence Erlbaum Associates, Hillsdale NJ, 27–48.

Sarat, A. and Kearns, T.R. (eds.), (1996), *Legal Rights. Historical Perspectives*, The University of Michigan Press, Ann Arbor MI.

Scanlon, T.M. (2001), "Fear of Relativism", in Moser P. K. and Carson L. (eds.), *Moral Relativism. A Reader*, Oxford University Press, New York NY, 142–162.

Schank, R.C. and Abelson, R.P. (1977), *Scripts, Plans, Goals and Understanding*, Lawrence Erlbaum, Hillsdale NJ.

Schmitt, C. (1972), *Le categorie del 'politico'*, Il Mulino, Bologna.

Searle, J. (1969), *Speech Acts*, Cambridge University Press, Cambridge MA.

Searle, J. (1980), "Minds, Brains and Programs", in, *The Behavioural and Brain Sciences*, in, *The Behavioural and Brain Sciences*, 3, 417–457.

Searle, J. (2004), *Mind. A Brief Introduction*, Oxford University Press, Oxford.

Sen, A. (1988), "Rights and Agency", in Scheffler, S. (ed.), *Consequentialism and its Critics*, Oxford University Press, Oxford, 187–223.

Sen, A. (2004), "Elements of a Theory of Human Rights", in *Philosophy and Public Affairs*, 32, Blackwell Publishing, Oxford, 315–356.

Shue, H. (1980), *Basic Rights. Subsistence, Affluence, and U.S. Foreign Policy*, Princeton University Press, Princeton NJ.

Shute, S. and Hurley, S. (eds.), (1993), *On Human Rights. The Oxford Amnesty Lectures 1993*, Basic Books, New York NY.

Siegel, H. (1987), *Relativism Refuted: A Critique of Contemporary Epistemological Relativism*, Reidel Publishing Company, Dordrecht.

Siep, L. (1979), *Anerkennung alz Prinzip der praktische Philosophie: Untersuchungen zu Hegels Jenaer Philosophie des Geistes*, Verlag, Freiburg.

Stamenov, M.I. (ed.), (1997), *Language Structure, Discourse and Access to Consciousness*, Benjamins, Amsterdam.

Steiner, H.J. (1998), 'Working Rights', in Kramer, M.H., Simmonds, N.E., Steiner, H. (eds.), *A Debate Over Rights. Philosophical Enquiries*, Clarendon Press, Oxford, 235–302.

Steiner, H.J. and Alston, P. (1996), *International Human Rights in Context. Law, Politics, Morals. Text and Materials*, Clarendon Press, Oxford.

Strauss, L. (1957), *Diritto naturale e storia*, Neri Pozza editore, Venezia.

Summers R.S. (1984), *Lon L. Fuller*, Edward Arnold, London.

Sun Tzu ([IV BC] 1963), *The Art of War*, in, Griffith, S.B. (ed.), *Sun Tzu. The Art of War*, Oxford University Press, Oxford.

Svorou, S. (1994), *The Grammar of Space*, Benjamins, Amsterdam.

Sweetser, E. (1987), "Metaphorical Models of Thought and Speech: a Comparison of Historical Directions and Metaphorical Mappings in the Two Domains", in, *Proceedings of the Fourteenth*

Annual Meeting of the Berkeley Linguistics Society, University of California Press, Berkeley CA, 389–405.

Sweetser, E. (1990), *From Etymology to Pragmatics*, Cambridge University Press, Cambridge MA.

Talmy, L. (1988), "Force Dynamics in Language and Cognition", in, *Cognitive Science*, 12, 49–100.

Teubner, G. (1992) "The two faces of Janus: rethinking legal pluralism", in, *Cardozo Law Review*, 13, 1443–62.

Teubner, G. (1998), "Legal Irritants: Good Faith in British Law or How Unifying Law Ends up in New Divergences", in, *Modern Law Review*, 61, 11–32.

Tuck, R. (1979), *Natural Rights Theories. Their Origin and Development*, Cambridge University Press, Cambridge MA.

Turner, M. (1990), "Aspects of the Invariance Hypothesis", in, *Cognitive Linguistics*, 1, 247–255.

Tversky, A. (1977), "Features of Similarity", in, *Psychological Review*, 84, 327–352.

Wagner Decew, J. (1990), "Moral Conflicts and Ethical Relativism", in, *Ethics*, 101, 27–41.

Waldron, J. (1984), *Theories of Rights*, Oxford University Press, Oxford.

Waldron, J. (ed.), (1987), *'Nonsense upon Stilts'. Bentham, Burke and Marx on the Rights of Man*, Methuen, London.

Waldron, J. (1993), *Liberal Rights. Collected Papers 1981–1991*, Cambridge University Press, Cambridge MA.

Waldron, J. (1999), *Law and Disagreement*, Clarendon Press, Oxford.

Waldron, J. (2005), "Torture and Positive Law: Jurisprudence for the White House", in, *Columbia Law Review*, 105, 1681–1750.

Walzer, M. (1994), *Thick and Thin: Moral Argument at Home and Abroad*, University of Notre Dame Press, Notre Dame.

Washburn, M.F. (1916), *Movement and Mental Imagery*, Haughton Mifflin, Boston MA.

Wassertrom, R. (1964), "Rights, Human Rights, and Racial Discrimination", in *The Journal of Philosophy*, 61, 628–641.

Watson, Alan (1977), *Society and Legal Change*, Scottish Academic Press, Edinburgh.

Watson, Alan (1988), *Failures of the Legal Imagination*, Scottish Academic Press, Edinburgh.

Watson, Alan (1993), *Legal transplants: an approach to comparative law*, University of Georgia Press, Athens Ga.

Weber, M. (1978 [1922]), *Economy and Society*, 1 and 2, University of California Press, Berkeley CA.

Wellman, C. (1995), *Real Rights*, Oxford University Press, Oxford.

Werner, H. and Kaplan, E. (1952), *The Acquisition of Word Meanings: A Developmental Study*, Child Development Publications, Evanston IL.

Wierzbicka, A. (1988), *The Semantics of Grammar*, Benjamins, Amsterdam.

Wildt, A. (1982), *Autonomie und Anerkennung. Hegels Moralitätskritik im Lichte seiner Fichte-Rezeption*, Klett-Cotta, Stuttgart, 312–365.

Williams, R. (1997), *Hegel's Ethics of Recognition*, University of California Press, Berkeley CA.

Wittgenstein, L. (1953), *Philosophical Investigations*, Anscombe, G. E. M. (trans.), Macmillan, New York NY.

Wong, D. B. (1995), "Relativism", in Singer P. (ed.), *A Companion to Ethics*, Blackwell, Oxford, 442–449.

Wong, D.B. (1986), *Moral Relativity*, California University Press, Berkeley CA.

Wong, D.B. (2006), *Natural Moralities. A Defence of Pluralistic Relativism*, Oxford University Press, Oxford.

Yoshioka, T., Dow, B.M. and Vautin, R.G. (1996), "Neuronal Mechanisms of Color Categorization in Areas V1, V2, and V4 of Macaque Monkey Cortex", in, *Behavioural Brain Research*, 76, 51–70.

Zekoll, J. (1996), "Kant and Comparative Law: reflections on a reform effort", in *Tulane Law Review*, 2747–2771.

Zolo, D. (2002), *Cosmopolis. La Prospettiva del Governo Mondiale*, Feltrinelli, Milano, 2002.

Author Index

A
Abel, R., 139
Adorno, T. W., 94 n14
Allison, H. E., 101 n 26, 103 n 31
Aquinas, T., 113, 125–126
Archibugi, D., 150, 151 n 25
Aristotle, 113–115
Austin, J. L., 113, 115–116, 116 n 3
Avineri, S., 64, 67

B
Beitz, C. R., 144
Benhabib, S., xiii, 107
Bentham, J., 106, 115
Bernstein, R. J., 47
Bix, B., 116, 121 n 7
Blackstone, W., 116
Bohman, J., 109 n 40
Brandt, R., 40, 42 n 3
Buchanan, N., 130

C
Cederman, L. E., 152 n 28
Chan, S., 45 n 23
Cicero, 113, 125
Clark, H. H., 12 n 11
Coleman, J. L. and Leiter, B., 118 n 5

D
Daniels, N., 41, 43
Davidson, D., xi, 4, 6–8, 10 n 7–8, 38–39, 93
Derrida, J., 107
Dershowitz, A., 90, 90 n 8
Dewey, J., 32
Doyle, M., 145, 151
Dworkin, R. M., 93 n 11, 118, 119 n 6

E
Eriksen, E. O. and Weigård, J., 90 n 7

F
Ferrara, A., xvi, 44 n 4, 82
Fichte, G., 66, 66 n 19
Finnis, J., 113, 124
Foot, P., 59
Foucault, M., 48
Fraser, N., xv, 98 n 20, 98 n 22
Freeman, M., 92 n 9
Fuller, L., 113, 117 n 4, 121–124

G
Garroni, E., 101 n 27
Gewirth, A., xiii, 73, 75–77, 80–83, 81 n 4, 100 n 23, 134
Glock, H. J., 15
Graham, G., 45
Gray, J. N., 92 n 9
Griffin, J., 97 n 19

H
Habermas, J., xii–xiii, 3, 29–30, 46, 48–49, 48 n 5, 63 n 12, 68, 73, 75, 82–89, 85 n 6, 93–94, 94 n 13, 102 n 29, 108 n 39, 152
Hacker, P. M. S., 15
Harman, G., xii, 35, 37, 49–53
Harré, R. and Krausz, M., 5 n 1, 10 n 9, 140
Hart, H. L. A., 111, 113, 116–119, 117 n 4, 124, 132
Hegel, G. W. F., 47, 62–68, 64 n 13–14, 65 n 15–18, 74, 94 n 14, 95, 96 n 17, 152
Herskovits, A., 5
Hohfeld, W. N., 111, 131
Hollis, M., 12
Holmes, S., 107, 107 n 37
Honneth, A., 31–32, 63 n 12, 94 n 15, 97 n 20, 97 n 22

I
Ignatieff, M., 90–92

J

Johnson, M., 12 n 10, 21, 23 n 19, 24 n 20, 32
   n 27–28, 33 n 29

K

Kant, I., 17, 20 n 15, 21, 28–31, 48–49, 52, 56,
   63, 69, 96, 100, 100 n 24–25, 101, 103, 103
   n 32, 104 n 33, 145–146, 148, 150–152
Kramer, M. H., 133 n 14, 135 n 16
Kuhn, T. S., 5, 5 n 1

L

Lakoff, G., 9 n 4, 12 n 10, 19, 19 n 13, 20 n 14,
   23 n 19, 25 n 23, 26 n 25, 33 n 29
Leibniz, G. W., ix
Levi, P., ix
Locke, J., 14, 113, 125–127, 128 n 10
Lyotard, J. F., 5

M

Mac Callum, G. C., 96, 96 n 18
McCloskey, H. J., 133 n 15
Mac Cormick, N., 117 n 4
McGinn, M., 16
MacIntyre, A., 5, 16–18
Malinowski, B., 5
Maoz, Z. & Russet, B. Z., 145, 147
Marsilius, 113, 114
Mill, J. S., 45
Moesteller, T., 13
Moody-Adams, M., 38, 38 n 1
Morgenthau, H., 143 n 22
Murphy, M. C., 124 n 9, 125

N

Nagel, T., xii, 36, 47, 53–58, 53 n 6, 57 n 7,
   58 n 8
Newton-Smith, W., 13 n 12
Nickel, J. W., 45–46, 120
Nussbaum, M., 59, 92 n 9

O

Oakeshott, M., 63 n 11

P

Przeworski, A., 108 n 38
Putnam, H., 5, 9, 9 n 5, 14, 18–19, 27, 63 n 11

Q

Quine, W. V. O., 11–12

R

Rawls, J., xii, 4, 41–44, 59, 62, 73, 77–79, 78 n
   3, 82–83, 90, 98 n 22, 150, 152, 152 n 26
Raz, J., x, 80, 113
Reidy (Nickel and), D., 45
Rorty, R., 5, 18
Rousseau, J. J., 106

S

Scanlon, T. M., 59
Searle, J., xv, 9 n 6, 24, 87
Sen, A., 82, 104 n 34, 136 n 20
Shue, H., 82, 131 n 13, 135 n 19
Siegel, H., 13
Spinoza, B., 64
Strauss, L., 115, 129
Strawson, P. F., 12
Sun Tzu, 147

T

Teubner, G., 140–142
Thucydides, 143

W

Waldron, J., 93 n 10, 106 n 35, 135 n 18
Walzer, M., 38
Wassertrom, R., 130 n 12
Watson, A., 138–140, 142
Whorf, B. C., 5
Wittgenstein, L., x, 5, 5 n 1, 13–16
Wong, D. B., xii, 36–37, 59–62, 60 n 9–10

Z

Zekoll, J., 139
Zolo, D., 5 n 2

Subject Index

A

Agent-neutral,
  morality, 57
  reasons, 54–56, 58
Agent-relative,
  reasons, 54–55, 57
Agents-community, 55
Anti-schematism, xi
Autonomy, 30, 54, 63 n 11, 85, 99 n 22,
    101 n 26, 138, 140
  abstract, 96
  as achievement, 80
  as capability, 80
  intersubjective, 98
  of law, 140
  of legal change, 138
  mediated, 96–97
  of the moral imperative, 52
  political, 99
  private, 86
  to self determination, xv

B

Basic rights, 85, 104, 132
  to basic well-being, 131
  as enabling conditions, 93
  as system, 86
Body-mind, 48

C

Capability, 80, 92, 92 n 9,
    98, 136
Cognitive relativism, 6, 8
Commensurability,
  absolute, xi
  on balance, xiv
  interlinguistic-, xi
  legal partial, 141
  linguistic, 27

moral, 39
partial, x, xi, xv, 5–6, 25, 39, 48, 92, 137
total, 7
Communicative action, xii–xiii, 48, 66, 68,
    73–74, 75, 84–89, 92–94, 98, 99, 141
  meta-condition of, 95
  presuppositions, xiii
Communicative agency, xi
Conceptual bridgeheads, xi, 27
  rational, 12
Conceptual schemes, x, xi–xii, 6–8
  competing, 19, 28
Consequentialism, 77 n 2
Context, x, xiv, 3–4, 10 n 9, 11, 13, 13 n 12,
    16–18, 19 n 13, 26–29, 33, 48, 58 n 8,
    62–63, 68, 88–90, 100, 102–103, 103 n
    31, 106, 108, 115, 140–141, 152
  cultural context, 37
  democratic, 145
  -dependent, 37
  of disagreement, 147
  -free, 140
  interaction, 62
  legal, 138–139
  political, 142
  requirement, 97 n 19
  social, 78
  variation, 46, 79
Conventionality, 49, 114–116
Correlates of War (COW), 146
Correlativity, 132
  principle of, 132
  of rights, 135
Counterfactuality, 95, 95 n 16
  counterfactual anticipation, 18, 29

D

Deliberation, 32, 55, 57, 84, 106–107, 106 n
    36, 109 n 39, 110, 114–115, 142

conditions of, xii, xiv, 40, 46
    idealized, 77
    moral, 55
    principle (D), 84
    process of, 85
    public, xiii, 67
    rational, 78, 85, 129
    valid, 4
Democracy, xv, 83–85, 145–149
    wars for, 112
Descriptive relativism, 37–39, 38 n 1, 44
Dialectic(al), 47
    components, 63
    discursive, 68, 95, 119
    mediation, 99, 106–109
    moment, 96
    movement, 36, 74
    negativity, 66
    process, 63, 68, 98 n 21, 99
    recognition, 67–68, 79
    unification, 96 n 17
Dialogue, 68
    constitutional, xv
    court dialogue, 152

E

Epistemic accessibility, x, 8, 28–29, 93
Epistemic relativism, x, 3, 12–19, 28–31
Ethical life, 35, 62–65, 66–67, 66 n 15, 81, 95
Evil, 51, 54, 90–92, 116 n 3, 126
Exclusive legal positivism, 113
Exemplarity, 5, 18, 31, 46, 52, 62, 80, 137
Exemplar judgment, 69
Exemplar universality, x, xiv, 28, 62,
    95–96, 102
Experience, x, xii, 5 n 2, 8 n 4, 10 n 9, 11–12,
    16–18, 19–32, 48, 52, 54–55, 60,
    63 n 11, 65–66, 94 n 14, 97 n 20,
    103–105, 126
    of the evil, 90–91, 90 n 8
    exemplar, 92
    judgement of, 101

F

Finality of rights, xiii, 62, 102 n 30, 102–105
Freedom, 58 n 8, 66 n 20, 75–82, 85–86, 92,
    95–100, 106, 107 n 37, 130, 131, 132,
    137, 137 n 21
    abstract, 65
    equal, 142
    moral, 63
    negative, 134
    principles of, xiii
    public, xiii–xiv

right to, 74
    system of, xii
Fundamental rights, xi, 63, 74 n 1, 79, 86, 99,
    104, 131–132, 134, 136, 137, 141, 145,
    146
    respect of, 147–148, 151
    system of, 106, 106 n 35, 108

H

Holism, 105
Human rights, xi–xiv, xv, 45, 74, 75, 80–83,
    90, 93, 99, 106–108, 119, 137, 148,
    149, 151
    and agency, 80
    conflict, xiv
    exemplar force of, 137
    exemplar universality of, 28
    formal categories, 142, 152
    internal tensions of, 120
    judgements, xi, 47–49, 73–74, 101, 120
    justification of, 83–86, 90
    language of, 91
    legal dimension of, 111, 120
    legal provisions, 100, 142
    legal status of, 137
    legal terms of, 115
    liberal *ethos pro*, 150
    moral principles of, 4
    non relativist justification of, 35
    policy, 92
    a posteriori status of, 102
    post-metaphysical conception of, xv, 112
    precommittment to, 107
    principles of, 45–46, 82, 104, 109, 120, 137
    protection of, 105
    reflective judgements, 141
    as socio-political conditions, 83
    system of, 69, 102–103, 130, 134, 137,
        138, 141
    theory of, xi, xiii, 74 n 1, 105,
        132–134, 141
    transplantability, 111, 138, 142
    universality of, 46, 75, 82, 92
    validation of, 119
    validity of, xi–xii, 3, 62, 73, 105
    violation of, 130–131, 135

I

Illocutive function, 87, 89
Illocutive speech acts, 73–74, 83,
    89–90, 94, 99
Image schemas, xi, 8 n 4, 12 n 10, 20–21, 20 n
    15, 21 n 16, 25 n 23, 27
Imperfect duties, 132

Inclusive legal positivism, 112, 130
Incommensurability, xi, 3–4, 5 n 1, 5 n 2, 6–8,
    28, 35, 37–39, 48, 80, 93
Inner-judgment(s), 49
Interest theory, 134 n 16
Intersubjective, 10 n 8, 17, 30, 63–65, 66 n 20,
    90, 96, 132–133
    for action(ing), 118 n 5, 129
    claim of recognition, 94–96, 99, 100
    conditions of purposive agency, 98
    dialectic, 68
    dimension of validity, 95
    duty, 93
    experiential, 9
    form of autonomy, 96, 98
    impersonal, 36, 57
    internal, 46, 51–57
    intersubjective, 136
    moral, 45, 118
    motivating, 124
    neutral, 58
    objective, 53, 57
    prudential, 116–118
    public, xiv
    rationality, 68
    reasons, 3, 13, 28, 31, 54–55, 76, 87–89,
        95, 112 n 1, 113, 117, 118, 120, 130 n
        11, 135, 137, 148–149
    variety of, 133

J
Judgment of knowledge, 104
Justice, 32, 51, 63, 115, 123, 125, 126, 127,
    129, 130, 143, 144
    conception of, 79, 98 n 22
    as fairness, 78–79
    international, 150
    natural justice, 114
    political justice, 79, 114, 114 n 2
    principles of, 67, 77–78
    theory of, xi, 41, 51, 77–78, 79, 91
    transitional, 4

L
Legal irritants, 142
Legal positivism, 112–113, 115, 119, 130
Legal transplant(s), 138–141
Liberty-rights, xiv, 95, 99, 106, 111,
    130–131, 137

M
Metaethical relativism, xii, 37, 40–45,
    49–50, 59
Metaphor(s), 21–22, 23 n 19, 107 n 37

Metaphoric (al), 33 n 29
    concepts, 8 n 4, 25 n 23
    projections, 20
    status of thought, xi, 12 n 10
    structure, 23 n 19
Methodological individualism, 100
Mixed positions, 59, 61
Moral relativism, xi–xii, 28, 35–38, 44–47, 49,
    50, 53

N
Natural law, 82, 84, 95, 113–121, 124–129,
    143–144
Negative duties, 121, 133
Negative rights, 134
Neutrality, 5, 13, 54
    no-neutrality hypothesis, 16–18
Normative relativism, 36–37, 40, 40 n 2
Normativists, 144–145

O
Objectivism, xi–xii, 22–23, 35, 46–47, 59,
    73, 128
Objectivity, 10 n 8, 24 n 20, 29–30, 45, 46, 53
    conventional, 97 n 19
    moral, 53, 59
Ontological relativism, 11

P
Peace theory, 142–146, 146 n 24, 147, 150–151
Perlocutory function, xiii, 87
Pluralism, 36, 60, 62, 67, 73, 79–80, 82, 90,
    106–108, 152
Pluralistic universalism, 36, 46–47, 59, 61–62,
    75, 106, 141, 143
Positive duties, 92, 111, 131, 134
Positive rights, 130, 133–134
Pragmatic-transcendental conditions, 30, 48,
    52, 68
Primary goods, 42, 62, 73, 77–80
Principle of charity or The charity principle,
    7, 39
Private language, x, 14–16, 35
Propositional content, 87
Public reason, xiv, 4–5, 73, 109, 142
Purposive agency, xi, xiii–xiv, 36, 39,
    48, 52, 61–62, 73, 75–76, 80–83,
    87, 91–93, 96–100, 97 n 20, 102,
    105, 108–109, 109 n 40, 119–120,
    130, 132–133

Q
Quasi-absolutism, 49–50

R

Realism, 30, 53, 128
Realists, 143–145
Reasonable pluralism, xi, 79
Recognition, 79–81, 85–86, 89–90, 94–96, 98,
        98 n 21, 100, 109, 123, 127, 130, 130 n
        11, 151
    dialectically mediated form of, 106
    of individual rights, 100
    mis-, 109
    of otherness, 94, 99, 139
    process of, 90
    rule of, 113, 117–118, 117 n 4, 118 n 5,
        119–120
    as a social practice, 111
    theory of, 96 n 17
Reflective equilibrium, 41–44, 77
Reflective judgment, 18, 49, 69, 103, 119–120

S

Secondary rules, 117, 117 n 4
Sensus communis, 31, 48, 62, 103, 120
Solipsism, 5, 13–14
Strong metaethical relativism, 45, 59

T

Transcendental conditions, 30, 106
    procedural, 82
Transplantability,
    human rights, 111–112, 137–138, 141–142
Truth, xii, 10 n 8, 11, 13, 14, 19, 30, 35, 50, 60,
        73, 122, 128, 140
    -claims, xi, 13, 14, 29–31, 90
    cognitive, 4
    concept of, 38
    condition of, 87
    -conditions, 11, 13, 23, 28, 29–30, 50,
        59–61
    as correspondence, 22 n 18
    counterfactual anticipation of, 18
    epistemic, 5, 73
    experiential, 29
    historical, 4
    intersubjective, 10 n 8
    judgmental, 33
    moral, 37, 40
    objective, 10 n 8, 45
    -paradox, 140
    propositional, xii, 13, 53

    relativist, 14
    standard of, 47
    transcendental anticipation of, 18
    transcultural notion of, 17
    -validity, xiii, 31, 36, 40–41, 59–61, 94
    -values, 23

U

Untranslatability, 7
Utilitarianism, 77, 77 n 2

V

Validity, 17–18, 37, 44, 45–48, 50, 57, 84, 102,
        124, 134, 140
    claims, xiv, 68, 83, 87–90
    conditions of, x, 29, 82, 87
    contextual, 18, 94
    counterfactual, 94
    epistemic, 4
    ethical, 4
    exemplar, xiii, 46, 74, 100, 103, 141
    of experience, 10 n 9
    experiential, 53
    of human rights, xi–xii, 3, 46, 73, 105
    of judgments, 31–32, 48–49
    of law, 111–119, 130
    meaning, 9
    moral, 35, 40, 44, 47, 53, 59–61
    normative, 28, 44, 46, 86, 94
    objective, 50
    of practical reason, 47
    propositional validity, xii, 14
    public, 66, 106, 109 n 40
    situated, 53
    of speech-acts, xiii, 74, 94, 98–99
    standard of, 5, 18, 29, 31, 40, 62
    of a system of freedoms, 99
    truth-, xiii, 29–31, 36, 40–41, 59–61, 94
    of truth-claims, 29

W

War, xi, xv, 112, 128 n 10, 145–150,
        146 n 24, 151
Weak metaethical relativism, 41, 43–44, 59
Weak naturalist thesis, 120
Well-being, xiii–xiv, 56, 75–77, 80–81, 97, 97
        n 19, 106, 131, 142
Will theory, 134 n 16

Breinigsville, PA USA
09 April 2010
235803BV00003B/48/P